AMERICAN DECLARATIONS

Harold K. Bush, Jr.

AMERICAN

DECLARATIONS

Rebellion and Repentance in

American Cultural History

University of Illinois Press

Urbana and Chicago

I 2 3 4 5 C P 5 4 3 2 I

This book is printed on acid-free paper.

Library of Congress Cataloging-in-Publication Data
Bush, Harold K. (Harold Karl), 1956–
American declarations : rebellion and repentance in American cultural history / Harold K. Bush Jr.
p.   cm.
Includes bibliographical references (p.) and index.
ISBN 0-252-02428-1
ISBN 0-252-06735-5 (pbk.)
1. American literature—History and criticism. 2. Christianity
and literature—United States—History. 3. National characteristics, American, in literature. 4. Literature and history—
United States—History. 5. Puritan movements in literature.
6. Culture conflict in literature. 7. United States—Civilization. 8. Repentance in literature. 9. Myth in literature. I. Title.
PS166.B87   1999
810.9'3823—ddc21
98-9009
CIP

For Hiroko

Ye must be born again.
—Jesus Christ

The country needs to be born again.
—Margaret Fuller

This nation, under God, shall have a new birth
of freedom.
—Abraham Lincoln

To-day, ahead, though dimly yet, we see, in vistas,
a copious, sane, gigantic offspring.
—Walt Whitman

Give birth again
To the dream. . . . Here on the pulse of this new day.
—Maya Angelou

Contents

Acknowledgments

The compilation of acknowledgments has become a standard practice in works of this sort—and rightfully so. These statements show a profound awareness of the communal aspect of an author's intellectual endeavors and also attest to a deeply personal thankfulness for help, support, and friendship over lengthy periods. Many authors have concluded that their creations, and, to some degree, their lives, are spliced together in a manner that Mark Twain labeled "unconscious plagiarism"—and more often than not, I feel the same.

I dedicate this book to an ideal audience: Hiroko Hara Bush. Not only is she a brilliant and wonderfully giving person who has been a constant source of companionship and care, but she has also stuck by me, worked with extreme diligence and undaunted talent to help provide for our worldly needs, and been the person I most wanted to please. Somehow, we have together managed to maintain our vows, overcome huge professional and personal disappointments, and still have good fun and great friends.

Special thanks must also go to our parents: Mary Lyon, Harold and Ione Bush, and the Haras in Kyushu, Japan. I also thank all of our siblings for support and good cheer over the years, as well as our extended families sprinkled over two continents.

My list of professional co-conspirators is lengthy, and, like Twain, I am profoundly aware of the extent to which little of what I say is original with me. I thank all those who have contributed—directly or indirectly—to the development and maturation of the thoughts and ideas in this book. Foremost of these is my mentor and now good friend David Nordloh, whose technical brilliance and unwavering faith in this project have been legendary. Not only did he read and re-read several parts of the manuscript and collaborate in shaping the major arguments as we sat over endless styrofoam cups of lukewarm coffee in Indiana University's Ballantine Hall, but he also remained my greatest advocate throughout the writing process. I was also fortunate enough to come under the influence of a number of wonderful and wise professors: Jim Justus, Cynthia Dominik, and Jim Andrews; Lew Miller, whose seminar on Robert Frost was a watershed in my development; John Eakin, whose seminar on autobiography eventually led to my chapter on Twain; and Murray Sperber and Michael Shelden, who encouraged me to look beyond the ivory tower and write for the general public. I also thank Don Gray, Chris Lohman, Ken Johnston, Pat Brantlinger, Steve Watts, Terence Martin, Kathy Smith, Ray Hedin, Bob Gross, Jonathan Elmer, Carey Wolfe, Stuart Sperry, Bob Gross, the late Cynthia Jordan, Purnima Bose, Kathryn Flannery, JoAnn Campbell, David Hertz, and Sumie Jones.

The following people have read all or parts of the manuscript for this volume, and their comments and questions greatly improved my work. In particular, I thank Richard Wentworth of the University of Illinois Press and the two outside readers: John McWilliams and David S. Reynolds. The lengthy and challenging critiques by Professors Reynolds and McWilliams were scrutinous, timely, and above the call of duty. A number of other outstanding scholars also provided excellent feedback: Christopher Felker, Greg Garvey, Arthur Versluis, Susan Belasco Smith, Elizabeth Ammons, Gary Scharnhorst, Bob Fleming, and Earl Wilcox.

I also thank the Department of American Thought and Language at Michigan State University, including Doug Noverr and Etta Abrahams but especially my lecturer colleagues. I also need to thank my colleagues and friends in the reading group at Liberty Christian Church of Lansing, who supplied the encouragement that saw me through some tough times. At Butler University I also encountered personal and professional friendship that was a great encouragement, especially from Marshall Gregory, William Watts, and Carol Reeves. And, for their support, I extend my thanks to my new colleagues at St. Louis University, especially Thomas Moisan and Ray Benoit.

During the 1996–97 academic year I was asked by Michigan State and the University of Illinois to serve as director of an overseas program at Konan University in Kobe, Japan, and it was there that I completed much of the final work on this book, with the extravagant support and encouragement of the wonderful people at the university. My appreciation goes to Jack Williams of Michigan State and Edward Sullivan of the University of Illinois at Urbana-Champaign for selecting me to lead the program.

I also thank the board chair and the president of Konan University, Oga-wa-sensei and Nakanishi-sensei, for outstanding support and friendship; Uemura Kuniko, director of the Konan International Exchange Center and professor of French; Professors Omori, Kugo, and Ueno, associate direc-tors; and David Rycroft, who "sang" with me in moments of duress. The superb office staff led by Imai Keiko helped me greatly during the hec-tic, hot, and humid summer months in 1997, and Yokoyama Manami was outstanding through it all, as were Mima Keiko, Okumura-san, and Ya-mada-kun.

The Book of James tells us that "every good gift comes down from above, from the Father of Lights, the Giver of all." My thanks would be incomplete without mentioning my awareness of the profound givenness of my life—especially of all the fine people listed above.

AMERICAN DECLARATIONS

Introduction

Metanoia, Declarations of In/Dependence, and America's Regnant Myth of Concern

To note that various aspects of the Christian worldview have a striking affinity with the perspectives of newness and regeneration evident throughout much early American literature is virtually a commonplace. From its beginning, American literary culture has fostered a view of the country as having a special purpose among nations. The Puritan founders viewed themselves as carrying the true light of life to the heathen nations and considered North America a "city set upon a hill," invoking the words of Christ. The "newness" of the civilization implied that it was also innocent and therefore capable of achieving the harmony and brotherhood of all humanity. A special destiny, its locus squarely in the New World, pervaded virtually all of Puritan literature beginning with John Winthrop's *Model of Christian Charity*, which was composed aboard the *Arbella* as it led the way to the new Promised Land.[1]

The resulting ideology of an "American incarnation" invested the nation's teleology with a strong sense of entelechy: "a perfect and complete potentiality moving of itself to its realization," it includes a "potential, not for this or that achievement, but for achievement as such—for potential as such."[2] Such endless potentiality culminating in perfection and fullness has much in common with the millennial hopes expressed in the Christian religion, and numerous eighteenth-century writers were intrigued by the mystical entelechy of the American incarnation.[3] Michael Wigglesworth's long poem "God's Controversy with New England" describes the New World as the place where "the King of Kings set up his throne / To rule amongst the nations." Jonathan Edwards revealed his prejudice in a sermon title, "The Latter-Day Glory Is Probably to Begin in America": "what is now seen in America, and especially New England, may prove the dawn of that glorious day." Philip Freneau wrote of "The Rising Glory of America," and in "Greenfield Hill" Timothy Dwight also waxed eloquent about the potential of America, which he considered "by heaven designed / Th' example bright, to renovate mankind."[4]

According to these and other early writers, the nation was founded on the "perfect and complete potentiality" of its initiating ideals.[5] The confusion and misdirection following the American Revolution, however, threatened America's mythic potential. Many feared that the newly formed country might easily slip into the "despair, cynicism, and anger that [had] destroyed other post-revolutionary societies," and to alleviate that danger "[early national] writers like Dwight and Freneau approached literature with a sense of religious mission and strove to give America a vision of herself as a promised, New World utopia."[6] Thus, as a result of the political and religious agendas of many of the country's early writers, the tropes of newness and regeneration became mythical elements that even by the outbreak of the Civil War had achieved wide resonance.

The most important sources of the regenerative theme central to antebellum America's regnant myths were the Bible and the Christian religion. As the young nation's preeminent and pervasive religious tradition, the Christian mythos constitutes the logical starting point for an analysis of American myth.[7] Both Christian and the American myths are best exemplified by the words of John the Baptist: "Repent ye: for the kingdom of heaven is at hand" (Matthew 3:2).[8] That message began with a simple call to action followed by a declaration of faith. Likewise, Jesus's message shortly thereafter consistently included, and often began with, an identical imperative: "The time is fulfilled, and the Kingdom of God is at hand: repent ye, and believe the gospel" (Mark 1:15), and "Repent: for the kingdom of heaven is at hand" (Matthew 4:17).

Literally a combination of two Greek words—*meta* (with or after) and *nous* (the mind or the seat of reflective consciousness)—*metanoeo*, the verb translated "repent" in all these cases, is a term brimming with entelechy. From it comes the noun *metanoia*, which suggests "an afterthought, change of mind, repentance."[9] The Hebrew word for repent, which served as the Old Testament precursor, is a dance term that means "a turning on the heel," indicating a total change of heart or what now might be called a paradigm shift.

Thus, John invited listeners to be utterly changed as a result of hearing his message and join him in declaring an allegiance to a kingdom different from the earthly one. A new dispensation was imminent and included a vision of world history that would radically alter any reasonable listener's conception of life and how to live it. In addition, the term *Kingdom of Heaven* conflates the civil realm of political power with the religious realm of supernatural power. According to such a formulation, governmental principles derive from a transcendental source.

Besides the primary task of introducing the Lamb of God to the awaiting society, John's message, like much of Puritan literature that grew from it, was "designed to join social criticism to spiritual renewal," making it a classic jeremiad.[10] As Perry Miller has cogently described it, that mode developed into a fine art during the second generation of Puritan leaders in New England: "The most polished, thoughtful, and impressive creations of these decades . . . are lamentations over the 'declension' of New England and tirades against its lengthening list of sins." Like John the Baptist's similar wailings, these rhetorical creations were meant to be delivered publicly "on the great occasions of communal life, when the body politic met in solemn conclave to consider the state of society, the one kind of sermon it attended . . . was a jeremiad in which the sins of New England were tabulated over and over again."[11] The principal burden of jeremiadic speech, in the seventeenth century as well as in the contemporary public arena, is to foster repentance among listeners, largely by cataloguing a steady deterioration of society and then hearkening back to an earlier time of pristine innocence and greater moral uprightness.

Americanists interested in locating central premises of the nation's commonly held myths can usefully consider the jeremiadic root of John's (and subsequently Jesus's) teaching: the simple imperative "repent" (metanoeo) and "repentance" (metanoia), the noun derived from it. That act fixes a moment which ensures that those who are enlightened will never be, or think, the same. Even popular contemporary evangelical writers have hearkened to the Greek roots of the term. One, for example, notes that repentance is "commonly thought of as simply an acknowledgement and confession of sin. . . . But the repentance of God is not just contrition over particular sins; it is also a daily attitude, a perspective."[12]

Despite prevalent notions (often negative in contemporary culture) concerning its meaning, repentance should be understood as a daily process of personal reevaluation and contemplation. Metanoia is the "essential manifestation of regeneration that sets us straight in our relationship to God and so radically alters our perspective that we begin to see the world through God's eyes . . . [it is] the ultimate surrender of self."[13] For many Christians, both contemporary and in the nation's past, the exact moment of regeneration can be fixed to a specific time, date, and place. A 1983 study showed that "among contemporary American Evangelicals interviewed, 94.2 percent reported having had a conversion experience at an identifiable point. . . . the soteriological emphasis within Evangelicalism is on a specific turning point in a person's biography."[14]

Moreover, the paradoxical nature of the mythos that John the Baptist presented juxtaposes the relationship of a radically changed attitude (newness) with the rituals of generations of Jews, including the Hebrew Bible and the conception of omnipotent God (oldness). A vision of a millennial future is firmly founded on the prophetic and timeless visions of the past. Similarly, John's words foreground a contrast between the "ultimate surrender of self" by the single, penitent sinner (individualism) and the effect of such a commitment, resulting in the culmination of a human consensus and a caring brotherhood (community).

At the heart of Christian religion is a consensus based on an agreement among numerous agents of change to rebel against the demonized ruling authorities, the old ways of doing things, and the darkness of iniquity. It is, in Sacvan Bercovitch's often-quoted formulation, a consensus through dissensus. Such a paradoxical mythos also characterizes the underlying myth of America. The "ultimate surrender of self" for both the Christian and American myths begins with a verbalized declaration of departure from an old, oppressive kingdom (Satan's domain of darkness) and allegiance to a new kingdom (the Kingdom of God): "If thou shalt confess with thy mouth the Lord Jesus, and shalt believe in thine heart that God hath raised Him from the dead, thou shalt be saved" (Romans 10:9). Adherents of both kingdoms are called slaves in the New Testament (translated "servants" in the KJV): "Ye were the servants of sin, but ye have obeyed from the heart that form of doctrine which was delivered you. Being then made free from sin, ye became the servants of righteousness" (Romans 6:17–18).

The paradox of declaring independence from Satan's realm lies in the fact that in order to do so one must fully depend on God's infinite grace and mercy, as well as his prescribed law and prophecies of the past, in order to move into an ordained, millennial future. Thus, metanoia is simultaneously a declaration of independence from Satan, his devices, and the power of sin and a declaration of dependence on God and his word and plan. Thus, as a tribute to this paradoxical doubleness, Christian conversion might be termed a "declaration of in/dependence" asserted by every genuine Christian. True Christians declare independence from slavery and oppression (Satan's kingdom) while simultaneously declaring dependence on timeless moral standards, millennial vision, and community (God's kingdom).

Such a religious conversion illustrates the strong desire of humans "to attach [themselves] to, or live in or among, a specific kind of community." As Northrop Frye often argued, belief "is essentially a form of attachment to a community: in other words, belief is also primarily social in reference."[15] Attachment to the American community has involved in the not-so-distant past (and perhaps still does for some) a doctrinal confession most easily associated with the dogmatics of a religious organization. A powerful rhetorical feature of America's mythic religion is its consistent employment of a jeremiadic listing of sins and insistent reliance upon the Christian construct of metanoia. That reliance has dramatically inspired the way Americans have envisioned their own and others' achievement of "Americanness."[16] In a manner similar to the born-again experience of Evangelicals, exemplary Americans have often been depicted as entering fully into the nation's convenant at a specific moment and subsequently giving public testimony of such an experience. Thus, American belief is grounded on a declaration of in/dependence that bears a striking family resemblance to its older sibling, the Christian act of metanoia.

As Leo Marx, one of the foremost cold war critics, has admitted, an "awareness of the culture's multilayered, fragmented character has made problematic the very existence of anything like a single, coherent, unified national culture."[17] Accordingly, this volume will not involve a vexed attempt to locate categorical coherence and unity—unless such coherence, problematic as it surely is, might be found lurking just below the surface of ongoing national debates. Instead, I will focus on the rhetorical and social aspect of myth and argue that critics, through a close analysis of mythical constructs, can discover contributions to what Kenneth Burke has described as the "unending conversation" about a society's culture, ideologies, and myths.[18]

Stephen Mailloux slightly alters Burke's original term to emphasize its social nature when he studies the "cultural conversation" regarding various myths of America. Such conversation fosters, revises, and negotiates the meanings and contents of mythic figures and public events. By considering an array of cultural sources, including the rhetorical and mythic content of the key literary texts, especially speeches, the resulting public reception of these works, and the texts' relationships to other literary works published previously or concurrently, I seek to provide a history of how particularly influential features of America's mythic discourses have evolved. Doing so locates the "shared strategies of interpretation as made up of historical sets of topics, arguments, tropes, ideologies [and myth] which determine how texts are established as meaningful through rhetorical exchanges." As Mailloux's method of "rhetorical hermeneutics" suggests, valuable cultural information can be gained by "listening in" on such conversations as they developed during critical periods of public involvement over the meaning, relevance, and rhetorical value of the American idea.[19]

Approaching myths as vital components in a society's gigantic and everchanging "cultural conversation" is prominent in Northrop Frye's analyses, and I will employ two of his key terms regularly throughout this study. Frye envisioned American myth (and social myth in general) as a site for carrying out the unending negotiations between two "parties," conservative and radical in essence, both of which participate vigorously in determining a society's reigning beliefs. These parties, which Frye called "concern" and "freedom," are forever pushing and pulling at each other in a constant dialectical revision of what a society should mean and believe. The so-called myth of concern is fully developed and encyclopedic and exists to hold society together. It is most intent on maintaining traditions, rituals, and continuity, and thus Frye associates it with the conservative ideology of a society. In America, that myth has incorporated both Christian repentance and individual declarations of in/dependence.

Furthermore, and central to my argument, the myth of concern sometimes comes "very close to anxiety, especially when threatened." When the general myth of concern is attacked or denigrated publicly, the "voices of doubt or dissent are to be muted . . . and silenced altogether if there is a real danger, as in a war."[20] Frye terms the voice of dissent the "myth of freedom," a category that includes such attitudes as tolerance, suspension of judgment, and respect for the individual, thus linking this party with the liberal ideology of a society. Upon reflection, however, it becomes evident that freedom also manifests aspects of Christian repentance and depends upon jeremiadic speech modes. Often the radical element challenges corrupt authority, lists and identifies social injustices (or sins), and calls for renewed commitment to age-old American values and ideals, frequently those elaborated in the Declaration.

Thus it appears that the most boisterously radical spokespersons of mythic freedom in U.S. culture are swallowed up by the traditional modes of the hegemonic myth of concern. Furthermore, mythic freedom characteristically becomes symbolic in later generations of that concern. One example is the steady cooptation of the radical young Ralph Waldo Emerson, who many later radicals later transformed into a conservative lack-ey. Of course such a critique of the mythologized radicalism of Emerson is not unwarranted. After all, he "lived out his time like Dr. Holmes (whom he admired), secure in his provincial superiority, voting Whig and Republican, associating the idea of the Democratic Party with vulgarity, with General Jackson and tobacco-chewing."[21] It is for good reason that the sins of the fathers (and mothers) are typically attacked and rebuked by ostensibly even more radical sons and daughters. It appears that sons have ineluctably needed fathers in American cultural history; in that way the myth of freedom is always a segment of the overall myth of concern. It must be embraced, by definition, as a welcome, valuable aspect of any social hegemony. The myths of concern and freedom cohabit in an in-terdependent symbiotic relationship that is effective for a society. With-out concern, as Frye observes, *Brave New World* results; without free-dom, *1984*.[22]

In arguing that a healthy and fruitful public discourse depends on full participation by both the agents of concern and the champions of free-dom, Frye identifies cultural forces described in more detail by some of today's more compelling cultural critics. James Davison Hunter, for ex-ample, has recently espoused a model that defines cultural conflict as "political and social hostility rooted in different systems of moral under-standing" and asserts that contemporary cultural disagreements can all be "traced ultimately and finally to the matter of moral authority." Hunt-er identifies the two vying parties by asserting that "the cleavages at the heart of the contemporary culture war are created by what I would like to call the impulse toward orthodoxy and the impulse toward progres-sivism." Hunter's "cleavages" are similar to Nathaniel Hawthorne's analysis of the schism underlying New England in the 1830s, and Haw-thorne's stories depicting the genesis of America, "Endicott and the Red Cross" and "The May-Pole of Merry Mount," illustrate that "a myriad of self-contained cultural disputes actually amounts to a fairly compre-hensive and momentous struggle to define the meaning of America."[23]

The processes by which these two fundamental parties, concern and freedom, interact and redefine each other can be investigated by closely studying significant cultural moments, especially public acts and speech-es that resulted in considerable public reaction. Such cultural moments often reflect, capture, and foster in an unusually concentrated way the tensions and negotiations present in the general society.[24] Thus we might usefully begin here by recalling the preeminent and archetypal represen-tative anecdote in American history, one that clearly turns on the con-cept of Christian repentance: the Declaration of Independence of 1776, written primarily by Thomas Jefferson.[25] Jefferson himself admitted that his famous document exemplified something unique to American culture; his aim in writing the Declaration was to "justify ourselves in the independent stand we are compelled to take . . . it was intended to be an expression of the American mind."[26]

In his attempt to locate a central "expression of the American mind," Jefferson deployed the defining feature of the American metanoia as I have described it: the urge to defend and justify the stand against the tyrannies of the world and declare independence. That rhetorical move has often been repeated throughout American public history; in particular, it illustrates a constant dissent of freedom against concern. Paradoxically, it should also be understood as a manifestation of concern. To be independent is to depend on certain ideals (the inalienable rights and truths of the Declaration) and depend on other good folk making the same decision so a community of believers might be formed to usher in a millennial future. Each signer of the Declaration, as is well-known, risked everything. What is little considered is how each depended on the others, and on all like-minded Americans, for shared independence. Such a paradox typifies both the Christian religion and the Puritan hegemony as it asserted its rights from England.

From the perspective of Jefferson's text as an evangelical document dominated by the metaphor of slavery, the dramatic myth underlying the Declaration depends on perceiving the colonists as slaves: "When in the course of human events, it becomes necessary for one people to dissolve the political bands which have connected them with another, and to assume among the powers of the earth, the separate and equal station to which the Laws of Nature and of Nature's God entitle them . . . they should declare the causes which impel them to the separation."[27] "Political bands" must be extinguished, and the right to do so comes from nature and God, the right to stand "separate but equal." Following that opening, the document leads directly into the well-known passage expressing the self-evident truths upon which the American metanoia would be based: that "all men are created equal" and given "inalienable rights" of "Life, Liberty, and the pursuit of Happiness." These claimed, inherent rights constitute an antithesis to notions of slavery and political oppression. Further, governments are formed to protect such rights. The government of the king, however, as indicated throughout the document, does the opposite. The king's performance is associated with such words as "destructive," "absolute Despotism," "abuses," "usurpations," and "repeated injuries." The direct objective of the king, according to the Declaration, is to institute "absolute Tyranny" over the "patient sufferance" of the Colonies. Each in the long list of grievances that follows begins with the pronoun "He," meaning that the enemy is personified by the king himself. Such a rhetorical move reifies the king as an absolute power of darkness, in the manner of Satan. The verbs following each "He" tend to be negative in that they illustrate how the king has disallowed the free rights of the colonies: "He has refused," "He has forbidden," "He has dissolved," "He has obstructed," "He has plundered," and "He has constrained." In short, the Declaration depicts the king as a "Prince, whose character is thus marked by every act which may define a Tyrant . . . [and who] is unfit to be the ruler of a free people." Moreover, the document's form owes a great deal to the public speeches of the Puritans: "The jeremiad, which in origin had been an engine of Jehovah, thus became temporarily a service department of the Continental Army."[28]

Much has been written concerning the rhetoric of the Declaration.[29] The story of "America's 'declaring independence' has hitherto emphasized the drama of the second term at the expense of the drama of the first," however. That is, a full appreciation of the cultural work accomplished by the Declaration as representative anecdote would need to consider the performative function of the act of declaring as much as the text itself. To understand the document fully, one must consider the act of "'declaring' as performance": "'independence' [is] something that is rhetorically performed."[30] That insight is relevant to countless other public speech acts. The performative acts of individuals "declaring independence," in numerous forms and settings and from various tyrannies and masters, constitute a pervasive American motif and a central tenet of the national myth of concern, beginning in the myriad conversion testimonies (or "relations") proffered by the Puritans.[31] As one critic has put it, "The American conception of the self has stressed the roles of choice and volition to an unprecedented degree. In [Perry] Miller's memorable phrase, 'being an American is not something inherited but something to be achieved.' . . . [All true Americans] are 'protestants' who place the claims of conscience and innovation ahead of established practices or beliefs. . . . To be a 'protestant' in this sense is to believe in the virtue of a defiant stand against corrupt authority."[32]

A central thesis of this book will be that American literature and culture are shot through with similar "protestant" efforts. America's primary mythic forms, shaped especially by the motif of declaring independence through protest (and endlessly transforming the Christian and Jeffersonian models), have continued to inspire and intrigue Americans from a multitude of cultural perspectives. By fostering discussion and often heated disagreement, the evolution of these myths has helped define the country's myriad meanings and agendas. Both Christian and American myth are characterized by an inherent paradox that pits the old against the new and the individual against the community. Furthermore, these oppositions constitute the heart of both myths, forming a revolutionary quality upon which they are built and by which they retain considerable cultural power and persuasion. As Northrop Frye observed, "It is hard to overstate the importance for today of the fact that the Western myth of concern is in its origin a revolutionary myth."[33] By emphasizing the engagement of fundamentally oppositional participants in what constitutes a Burkean "unending conversation," I will identify how myths of concern and freedom have continually been represented and negotiated in American cultural history, and thus have evolved. My focus is also on how public events and personae have become entangled in the construction of these social myths.

The two sections of this book correspond broadly with what I take to be two primary aspects of American public discourse: an insistent effort at cohesion and defense of a central myth against the agents of freedom and a powerful inclination to lash out against the myth of concern in idealist and jeremiadic form. The sections comport with the two poles of the inherent paradox that inform American culture and yet are not an opposition as much as a dynamic synergy.

The first five chapters are a discussion of some of the ongoing cultural conversations that contributed to the building of a nearly impervious American myth of concern in the antebellum American North, as well as a chronological analysis of this unfolding evolution of the revival of the Declaration. Of particular interest is the development of the idea of the American metanoia and the importance of declarations of in/dependence in the public acts and their literary depictions in the writing of Nathaniel Hawthorne, David Walker, Nat Turner, Frederick Douglass, the Grimké sisters, Elizabeth Cady Stanton, Maria Stewart, Jarena Lee, Sojourner Truth, and Harriet Beecher Stowe. My study of the rising hegemonic status of the Declaration culminates with the eloquence of Abraham Lincoln, who, as Garry Wills has noted, ostensibly and single-handedly reinvented the Declaration as a fundamental aspect of the perpetual American myth.[34] Wills's emphasis on the agency of Lincoln, however, strikingly discounts the steady revival of interest in the Declaration demonstrated by the writers listed previously as well as many other authors who drew heavily upon its founding idealism.[35] In fact, the powerful ideological resonance of Jefferson's document was exploited with great success by virtually every disenfranchised group attempting to gain a foothold in antebellum America, including abolitionists, former slaves, feminists, labor leaders, radical Christian reformers, and Native Americans. Specifically, African Americans such as Stewart, Lee, Truth, Walker, Turner, and Douglass proclaimed independence from tyranny in a manner that bespoke their dependence on mythic tropes suggested by Christian and Jeffersonian ideals. My analysis of these cultural conventions suggests how male and female impulses are brought together comprehensively in Stowe's masterwork, *Uncle Tom's Cabin*, a novel whose insistence on "doing the Word" exemplifies the American metanoia.[36] Although I do pay my respects to Lincoln's very great tributes to the Declaration, it is far better to end the first section with him and to document some of the rhetors who laid the groundwork for Lincoln's reconstruction of what actually happened "four score and seven years ago."

PART I

Building the Myth

1 Reinventing the Puritans

George Bancroft, Nathaniel Hawthorne, and the Birth of Endicott's Ghost

In the early decades of the nineteenth century, largely in an attempt to establish a historical basis for the development of a national consensus, political and cultural spokespersons frequently envisioned the Puritans as mythic forbears of the American nation. Conservative and liberal factions alike participated vigorously in an attempt to co-opt the Puritans as symbolic ancestors of their own contemporary moral and political agendas, and all participants accepted a common premise—that Puritans, however defined, were central players in America's emergent version of what Northrop Frye has labeled a regnant "myth of concern." Whosoever could most convincingly define the Puritans would be strengthened in the attempt to become more politically influential. According to Frye, "In every structured society the ascendent class attempts to take over the myth of concern and make it, or an essential part of it, a rationalization of its ascendency."[1] Linking a particular political agenda with the fundamental features of an established social myth introduces the agenda into the mainstream of consensus and enhances its claim to ascendancy.

It is by now nearly a commonplace that Nathaniel Hawthorne published his many tales of the Puritans within the context of the cultural debate regarding the nature and meaning of New England's forebears.[2] Marion Kesselring's exhaustive account of Hawthorne's reading, based upon the surviving records of his borrowings from the Salem Athenaeum, indicates that Hawthorne was an earnest student of the region's traditions and social history.³ Hawthorne was fully aware of the contemporary attempts by Daniel Webster, Rufus Choate, George Bancroft, and a host of others to establish historical views of the Puritans. His depictions constitute direct participation in the political controversy. As Michael Colacurcio has stated, "I have merely been emboldened by . . . modern commentary to notice that the texts Hawthorne read really do have the most fascinating social and psychological implications, and that it is not at all absurd, therefore, to imagine Hawthorne as entering into significant dialogue with them."⁴

Hawthorne's tales of the Puritan past served as a way of engaging in "significant dialogue" with romantic historians of the period, such as George Bancroft, his friend and later supervisor at the Salem Custom House. In such tales as "Endicott and the Red Cross" and "The May-Pole of Merry Mount" he challenged and corrected the pervasive constructions of Puritanism.⁵ His description of the public sphere in these tales anticipated much later models of cultural conflict, such as those posited by Frye and James Davison Hunter.

As a group, Hawthorne, Frye, and Hunter all articulate remarkably similar structural oppositions as the fundamental parties engaged in cultural debate, all warn against any unilateral domination of the public sphere, and all seek to foster an openly democratic form of public discourse that might ultimately ensure the preservation of a civilized order. Hunter's insights into the "cleavages at the heart" of the contemporary cultural milieu, for instance, are similar to Hawthorne's analysis of the "cleavages" underlying colonial America as well as New England of the 1830s. A number of Hawthorne's stories, including "Endicott and the Red Cross" and "The May-Pole of Merry Mount," illustrate Hunter's assertion that "a myriad of self-contained cultural disputes actually amounts to a fairly comprehensive and momentous struggle to define the meaning of America."⁶ Both stories also demonstrate his preoccupation with the two fundamental parties vying for cultural power, parties that anticipate Frye's and Hunter's conceptions. To understand Hawthorne's entrance into such a struggle it is necessary to identify the views of Puritanism—and in turn of the genesis of the American idea—that he challenged, views that culminated in the works of George Bancroft.

⁓

The most influential historical work in the early national debate concerning the true interpretation of the Puritan legacy was Thomas Hutchinson's *The History of Massachusetts Bay*, a critical and primarily unfriendly Tory account published before the Revolutionary War. Hutchinson's largely

Loyalist motives, betraying as they do a deeply conservative allegiance to the Crown and a highly unsympathetic view of what he termed the "inferior people" of the mob, typified the widespread Tory conservatism of the years before American independence.[7] In the years following independence, however, the cultural debate over how to reenvision the Puritans' seminal contribution to American republicanism included writers and speakers from a variety of political perspectives. In one manner or another, most implicitly challenged Hutchinson's critical depiction.[8]

An early example of the conservative Unionist depiction of the Puritans was what one commentator has called "Daniel Webster's Myth of the Pilgrims."[9] Webster and any number of other prominent Americans of the early national period, including Washington Irving and Hawthorne, held a deeply conservative fear that democracy posed a threat to the American Union and that King Mob might degenerate finally into an anarchical system threatening its continuation.[10] Among the best known of Webster's speeches concerning the Puritans was his address to the Pilgrim Society of Plymouth, delivered in December 1820 on the occasion of the bicentennial of the Pilgrims' landing. Entitled "The First Settlement of New England," it established the Pilgrims as political forebears of the American ideal and the Union as final result of a providential scheme begun through their agency. Webster characterized the Pilgrim-Puritan vision in the following terms:

> [We are] but links in the great chain of being, which begins with the origin of our race, runs onward through its successive generations, binding together the past, the present, and the future, and terminating at last, with the consummation of all things earthly, at the throne of God. . . . If God prosper us, we shall here begin a new work which shall last for ages; we shall plant here a new society, in the principles of the fullest liberty and the purest religion; we shall subdue this wilderness which is before us. . . . From our sincere, but houseless worship, there shall spring splendid temples to record God's goodness; from the simplicity of our social union, there shall arise wise and politic constitutions of government, full of the liberty which we ourselves bring and breathe.[11]

Webster felt that the "spirit of innovation threatened the government and the country," and his chief political aim was to "[call] on his listeners to preserve and transmit—and not to change or invent—civil and social institutions."[12] In working toward such aims he presented the Puritan past as a set of poetic tales resembling myths by which he hoped not only to enforce a strong sectional identity for New England but also to recreate a history that might aid in saving the Union. Webster and other conservatives deemed such renderings necessary in a time when "the alliance between the magistracy, the clergy, property and culture, was collapsing. . . . The eclipse of the Federalists . . . robbed it of one of its strongest supporters. The influence of the clergy, which had been one of the main props of the Federalists, was being thrust out of lay society."[13] Webster's depiction of the Puritans as orderly, obedient, and loyal to an agreed-upon covenant with both God and each other provided one version of a national past upon which to build his own contemporary political vision.

Webster was among the most prominent Americans of the early national period to depict the Puritans as "America's venerable ideological grandfathers," but he would not be the last.[14] By the 1820s it became common for local governments to invoke the Puritans in local festivities. As Michael Kammen notes, "the landing of the Pilgrim Fathers . . . became a powerful legend for New Englanders, commemorated annually on Forefathers' Day (December 21)."[15] The town of Salem, for example, celebrated the bicentennial anniversary of the Puritan leader John Endicott's landing not once but twice, first in 1825 and again three years later.[16]

Numerous spokespersons, according to political need, invoked the Puritans during the 1820s and 1830s. Rufus Choate, one of the most skilled trial lawyers of the time and, like Webster, a deeply conservative advocate of traditional New England culture, advocated historical accounts of America's past that would enhance social cohesion. In "The Importance of Illustrating New England History by a Series of Romances like the Waverly Novels," an oration given at Salem in 1833, Choate called for a "series of romantic compositions . . . the incidents and characters of which should be selected from the records and traditions of [the Puritans], our heroic age." He recognized that "amply written" conventional histories already existed for the "lawyers, politicians, and for most purposes of mere utility, business, and intellect." That new kind of history, for Choate, would serve an explicit purpose: to create "a form in which [history] should speak directly to the heart and affections and imagination of the whole people."[17]

Much to the chagrin of conservatives such as Choate, more liberal spokespersons led the way in answering his call for heroic histories of America's past. Romantic historians of the Puritans, as exemplified by George Bancroft and his highly influential *History of the United States* (the first volume of which appeared in 1834), published their work amid the renewed historical interest in the Puritan forebears and the desire to foster a nationalistic revival. Bancroft used a form of biblical typology enlisting historical figures and events as foreshadowings of future events; in the actions of characters such as John Winthrop, John Endicott, and

John Cotton he envisioned prophetic types containing the seeds of what would later become the American Revolution.[18]

In framing the Puritans as typological forebears of America's destined greatness, Bancroft depicted early colonial leaders as epic figures personifying courage, faith, vision, and moral strength. Taken together, they were "kindred spirits, men of religious fervor, uniting the emotions of enthusiasm with unbending perseverance in action." John Endicott, for example, is described as a "man of dauntless courage, and that cheerfulness which accompanies courage; benevolent, though austere; firm, though choleric; of a rugged nature, which his stern principles of nonconformity had not served to mellow—[and] was selected as a 'fit instrument to begin this wilderness work.'"[19] New England reverence for such leaders is apparent in hagiographical descriptions that portray a man to whom the Lord in mercy had revealed himself and who "was selected as a 'fit instrument.'"

The association of faith and republicanism as central tenets of the Puritans and compatible and necessary ingredients of national political life was an essential feature of Bancroft's historical project. He thought that the Republic owed a profound debt to the Puritans, the oldest tradition providing the philosophical seed linking religious and political reform. The fruit of the Puritan seed, according to Bancroft, included fundamentals such as popular sovereignty and liberty of conscience:

> [The] church existed independent of its pastor, who owed his office to its free choice; the will of the majority was its law; and each one of the brethren possessed equal rights with the elders. The right, exercised by each congregation, of electing its own ministers was in itself a moral revolution; religion was now with the people, not over the people. Puritanism exalted the laity. . . .
>
> Puritanism constituted not the Christian clergy, but the Christian people, the interpreter of the divine will. The voice of the majority was the voice of God; and the issue of Puritanism was popular sovereignty. . . .
>
> Puritanism was a life-giving spirit. . . . The people did not attempt to convert others, but to protect themselves; they never punished opinion as such; they never attempted to torture or terrify men into orthodoxy.[20]

Thanks to Puritanism, religion was no longer "over the people," the "voice of the majority" was holy and sacrosanct, and dissent was "never punished." In contrast to more conservative depictions, Bancroft focused on individual rights and the high value of free choice. He also moved toward a fuller separation of church and state insofar as moral authority rests much more prominently with the individual and the joint population rather than with the religious establishment. The people as a whole, rather than forming a threatening and anarchistic mob, as feared by conservatives such as Webster, constituted the "voice of the majority." Further, the citizenry provided "the voice of God." Bancroft emphasized a more democratic and privileged exaltation of what Hutchinson had brazenly termed the "inferior people."[21]

Bancroft accepted the premise of the developing debate: The Puritans, however conceived, were central to contemporary American ideals. Puritanism was the primary historical agent responsible for initiating the movement toward the millennial fulfillment of these lofty ideals. By framing the Puritans in such liberalized terms, Bancroft and others, such as Theodore Parker, fostered a transcendental view of American history in which the new nation sought to realize a universal law of the spirit. That law, according to both Bancroft and Parker (and, later, Abraham Lincoln), was most powerfully depicted in the opening paragraphs of the Declaration of Independence. It was a direct result of the Puritan legacy of New England working through the agency of providence.[22]

As Jan Dawson has observed, Bancroft should be viewed as the leading voice in "the early nineteenth-century contest" to define America's historical mission and meaning, primarily by reframing Puritanism as necessary for all things good and bright. He was "representative of his generation's search for an American historical identity that would both confirm and inspire the faith that linked republicanism and Christianity." In trying to achieve the prominent critical authority needed to confirm such a faith, Bancroft moved to "claim inheritance of the prestigious legacy of Puritan leadership in New England."[23] To a great extent he succeeded. His account of the Puritans held historical authority that was "virtually unchallenged for over fifty years, primarily because [it] was able to enunciate—with conviction, elegance, and learning—what nearly everyone already believed."[24]

~

Nathaniel Hawthorne was one of the historians who frankly reckoned with and sometimes explicitly challenged Bancroft's nearly impervious account. He was widely read in the history of New England and well aware of the conflict regarding the revisionary renderings of the Puritans and founders of the American republic. He was also familiar with Hutchinson's *The History of Massachusetts Bay* and read voraciously among the Salem Athenaeum's dusty volumes of New England history: John Winthrop's *Journal*, Cotton Mather's *Magnalia Christi Americana*, Edward Johnson's *Wonder-Working Providence of Sion's Savior*, Nathaniel Ward's *New England's Memorial* (which included William Bradford's "Of

Plymouth Plantation"), William Hubbard's *Narrative of the Troubles with the Indians of New England*, Willem Sewel's *History of the Quakers*, and Thomas Morton's *New English Canaan*.[25] According to the records of the Athenaeum, Hawthorne had charged out the first volume of Bancroft's *History* from April 3 to May 6, 1837, just months before he composed "Endicott and the Red Cross."[26] Michael Colacurcio also asserts that Hawthorne "clearly read" Bancroft's "monumental" *History* as soon as the first volumes began to appear in 1834.[27]

Hawthorne, like Webster, Bancroft, and the political exponents they typified, agreed that the Puritans should be understood as seminal characters in America's past, and his tales can be read as contributions to the ongoing creation of that past. His vision plainly engaged, for example, Bancroft's liberal assertions concerning Puritanism's social and civil practices. He was also ambivalent about a much more conservative view of the Puritans, such as Webster's, that championed a solid cohesion of civil and religious elements. That ambivalence is obvious in "Endicott and the Red Cross" and "The May-Pole of Merry Mount." The stories critique both perspectives in an attempt to create a balanced historical view of Puritanism that privileges the full participation of all parties in an open public sphere that might provide the best of both worlds.

The action of "Endicott and the Red Cross" (first published in 1837 in the 1838 edition of *The Token*) covers an event in the life of the Puritan leader. One day in the fall of 1634, John Endicott calls his soldiers into the main square of Salem for military exercises. The mood is uneasy because Charles I and Archbishop Laud of Canterbury seem determined to rule Plymouth and Massachusetts tyrannically. Prominent in the scene are a church meetinghouse fronted by a whipping post, a pillory, and stocks. On the meetinghouse steps stand a man labeled "WANTON GOS-PELLER" (434) and a woman wearing a "cleft stick on her tongue" (435). Both are being disciplined openly at noonday for speaking against civil authorities. As the troops begin to drill, Roger Williams approaches and gives Endicott a sealed letter from Governor Winthrop of Boston. Endicott reads the letter and becomes furious. The "papistical" Charles I and "idolatrous" Laud intend to send a governor to deliver New England to the pope. Endicott draws his sword before the mustered militia and defaces the English flag by removing its red cross, and the tale abruptly ends with a short comment by the narrator: "We look back through the mist of ages, and recognize, in the rending of the Red Cross from New England's banner, the first omen of that deliverance which our fathers consummated, after the bones of the stern Puritans had lain more than a century in the dust" (441).

With that brief closing commentary Hawthorne appears to frame the story in familiar romantic terms as the initial act of defiance against England, making Endicott the typological precursor of America's move toward independence. But such an initial reading is unsatisfactory. A close investigation of the setting of Endicott's drama demonstrates Hawthorne's resistance to a merely patriotic and flattering version of the Puritan leader.

The opening pages of "Endicott and the Red Cross" feature a number of military images: a "martial exercise" for practicing "the handling of their weapons of war" in view of imminent "dissensions," "dangers," and "struggle," as well as the "polished breastplate of John Endicott," leader of the military exercises (433–34). Extended description of the breastplate is supplied: it is "highly polished," made of "glittering steel," and the "central object" reflected upon it is the "house of prayer." That description clearly places an image of the religious upon and coexistent with an image of the civil or military authority.

Hawthorne's reliance on allegory throughout much of his fiction occasions a symbolic reading of the image of the breastplate, which covers the very heart of Endicott. Given the prominence of that image in the opening passages of the story, the breastplate would also appear to suggest the "heart" of Puritan thought. It represents the orthodoxy of the regnant myth of concern in Puritan New England. For Sacvan Bercovitch, it is the "dominant symbol" of the story and would have been highly suggestive of rich biblical echoes for Hawthorne's scripture-reading antebellum audience.[28] Indeed, in scripture the "breastplate of righteousness" is discussed as an essential part of the garb of every true believer (Isaiah 59:17; Ephesians 6:14), a military metaphor stressing the believer's engagement in the cosmic struggle of good against evil. In Ephesians, chapter 6, for example, the "breastplate of righteousness" is used in conjunction with the "shield of faith," so the saint's actions are directly related to the saint's beliefs. Similarly, the narrator proclaims that "many other characteristics of the times and manners of the Puritans" were "vividly . . . reflected in the polished breastplate of John Endicott" (434).

Such characteristics and manners indicate the prevalent hegemony of the newborn Puritan myth of concern: Action emanates naturally from the covenant of consensus designed and enforced by the Puritan leaders. In fact, according to the narrator, the "whole surrounding scene had its image in the glittering steel" of Endicott's breastplate (434), so that every facet of society is a reflection of the Puritan ideological covenant. The covenant, as later critics have characterized it, would become the single most powerful tool for advancing the mission of America. It would result in a mythical construct that has been described as a "nearly impervious ideological vehicle assuring a powerful consensus within the confines of middle-class American political hegemony."[29] In its embodiment of "the fusion of the roles of high priest and governor," the breastplate is no less than an "emblem of theocracy."[30]

After the description of the breastplate Hawthorne focuses on "that important engine of Puritanic authority, the whipping post" (434). Immediately, the image appears to "convey the suppression, rather than the assertion, of liberty in America."[31] Hawthorne's point identifies what he considers, in contrast to Bancroft's romantic notions, an important factor in Puritan social belief: Religious freedom was not, in any recognizable sense, a central objective. For example, the Rev. Richard Mather, patriarch of New England's first dynasty, stated, "If the discipline which we practice be (as we are persuaded of it) the same which Christ hath appointed and therefore unalterable, we see not how another can be lawful." Likewise, his son Increase deplored the "hideous clamors for liberty of conscience."[32]

In contrast to Bancroft's claim that the Puritans initiated the social institution of liberty of conscience, Hawthorne's imagery of discipline and punishment suggests that the Puritan divines' efforts can best be characterized as a "giant effort at cohesion and control" that fundamentally opposed true religious freedom.[33] The tale's opening passages, then, even well before Endicott's flourishes, depict a civil-religious authority that is omnipotent, authoritarian, and well armed.

At the scene's opening, Hawthorne provides a telling and alarming symbol of the futile attempt to subvert such authority: As a token of the "perils of the wilderness," a "grim head of a wolf . . . was nailed on the porch of the meetinghouse," its blood "still plashing on the door-step" (434). In terms of biblical imagery, the wolf echoes Jesus's warning to the flock against the incursions of the "wolves in sheep's clothing." In the context of the tale, the image warns against the wild beasts of the forest as well as the wily voices of dissension among other citizens of Salem. Hawthorne hints at the certain demise of any intruders into the flock: They will be beheaded and their heads nailed to the church meeting place. Frederick Newberry suggests that the bloody image also foreshadows the demise of Charles II at the hands of Cromwell and the Puritans.[34]

In effect, Hawthorne's opening passages repudiate Bancroft's happy claims of the Puritans' democratic freedoms of religion and conscience. His rendition of the Puritan public sphere, described by Bancroft as equating the "voice of the majority" with "the voice of God" and championing "popular sovereignty" through a benevolent "life-giving spirit," focuses on the certain fate of those sympathetic to any emerging party of freedom. One such observer of the unfolding events, standing with a woman on the steps of the meetinghouse, is representative of the various "blasphemers" and "evil-doers": "The man was a tall, lean, haggard personification of fanaticism, bearing on his breast this label,—A WANTON GOSPELLER,—which betokened that he had dared to give interpretation of Holy Writ, unsanctioned by the infallible judgment of the civil and religious rulers" (434–35).

That passage articulates the Puritan view of such dissenters. The word *wanton*, for example, suggests the waywardness and even perversity of the man's beliefs in contrast to the Puritan Way. He is further accused of "fanaticism," of which he surely was guilty in the eyes of the prevailing orthodoxy. In contrast to Bancroft's claims regarding the Puritan focus on the sanctity and value of individual liberty of conscience, Hawthorne foregrounds the distressing fact that the offender is singled out for daring "to give interpretation of Holy Writ, unsanctioned by the infallible judgment of the civil and religious rulers." Puritanical discipline is severe. In front of the Gospeller is the "head of an Episcopalian and suspected Catholic . . . grotesquely encased" in the pillory, and a "fellow-criminal" is "confined by the legs" in the stocks (434).

In the context of such atrocities, it is important that Hawthorne also conflates the leadership of New England to include both "civil and religious rulers." As Sacvan Bercovitch has noted, the Puritans wedded theology to politics most commonly in the form known as the "political sermon," a mode grounding America's mission in both religious and civil realms.[35] A key feature of that mode, identified by Bercovitch as the "jeremiad," is the creation of a myth that "imaginatively conflates religious and political issues."[36] Such a move to conflate the religion of the Puritans with democratic politics, a central premise of Bancroft's writings, becomes problematized by Hawthorne's ironic depiction of a man bound because of an attempt to speak out against the ruling elites.

In this oppressive setting Endicott speaks openly and brazenly of liberty. It is both typical and highly ironic that he delivers the jeremiad in an attempt to advance a political agenda. In one passage, he appeals to the ostensible reason for migration to the new continent: "Fellow-soldiers,—fellow-exiles . . . wherefore did ye leave your native country? . . . Wherefore have we come hither to set up our own tombstones in a wilderness? A howling wilderness it is! . . . The wolf and the bear meet us within hallo of our dwellings. . . . The savage lieth in wait for us in the dismal shadow of the woods. Wherefore, I say again, have we sought this country of a rugged soil and wintry sky? Was it not for the enjoyment of our civil rights? Was it not for the liberty to worship God according to our conscience?" (438–39).

Many of the marks of American myth that would be delineated more than a century later by historians and literary critics are depicted in this passage, and they lend credence to Michael Colacurcio's description of Hawthorne as a cagy cultural critic. Biblical tropes are included ("fellow-exiles," the "howling wilderness," and the Abrahamic "[leaving of] your native country"), and the landscape is conjured in images of both beauty and fear. It is a "country of a rugged soil and wintry sky" populated by the "wolf and the bear." The wolf recalls the earlier image invoking the gory demise of dissenters. Native Americans are "savages" and thus sub-human, frightful apparitions that hover just beyond the fringes of the encampment in the "dismal shadow of the woods." None of these images is surprising considering the real and persistent dangers that early settlers faced. Richard Slotkin argues that "on this level of concern, myth and ideology form a consensus. They agree on the terms in which the problem of existence and social survival will be stated."[37] To a certain extent, the survival of the infant colony depended on the cohesion of public philosophy and ideology as exemplified in such social myths. Endicott later summarizes the key motivation of the Puritans by rehearsing the mythic version of America's founding: "We have sacrificed all things, and have come to a land whereof the old world hath scarcely heard, that we might make a new world unto ourselves, and patiently seek a path from hence to Heaven" (439).

But Hawthorne has preceded Endicott's pious invocation of myth-ic liberty with a catalog of Puritanical punishments. Directly opposing Bancroft's claim that the Puritans "never attempted to torture or terri-fy men into orthodoxy," Hawthorne provides a strikingly different ver-sion of Puritanical persecution.[38] The tale's opening pages are replete with an array of images that invoke slavery, bondage, and perverse dem-onstrations of public torture and humiliation. Many follow the initial description of the "WANTON GOSPELLER": tongues with "cleft sticks," "cropt ears," "branded cheeks," "slit and seared nostrils," "halters," "ropes," "stocks," "pillories," and, finally, the well-known reference to a "young woman . . . whose doom it was to wear the letter A" (434–35).

Simultaneously, Endicott's speech encompasses a myth of colonists breaking free from severe bondage. The Crown's enslavement of the Colonies, as depicted by Endicott, justifies rebellion, after which a re-bonding would produce a "shared independence": "Charles of England, and Laud, our bitterest persecutor, arch-priest of Canterbury, are resolute to pursue us even hither . . . so that, when Laud shall kiss the Pope's toe, as cardinal of Rome, he may deliver New England, bound hand in foot, into the power of the master! . . . Who shall enslave us here?" (440). Endicott justifies his act of rebellion by claiming oppressive enslavement by Charles and Archbishop Laud, whose plan is no less than to "deliver New England, bound hand in foot." Thus Endicott's focus, as in the Declaration of Independence, is on the enslavement of the colonists. Such epithets as "bitterest persecutor" and "arch-priest" associate the British leaders with the wiles of Satan. Ironically, however, those statements come only after the singular brand of Puritan punishment and "slavery" have been described fully, including torture and the demeaning silencing of all civil and religious opponents. In that way the narrator simultaneously defines Endicott as oppressor and oppressed, slave and master. That depiction warns against the inevitable move away from the more moderate stance evinced by earlier Puritan leaders such as John Winthrop. As Frederick Newberry explains, "Their powers of conciliation . . . recede in New England history as the intolerant side of Puritanism, represented especially by John Endicott, increasingly dominates the first century of settlement and becomes *the* Puritan tradition."[39]

The next event in Hawthorne's story is an overt clash between the competing agents of concern and freedom. It is foregrounded by a significant interruption that diverts Endicott's energies in the midst of his mythic jeremiad, just as he invokes the sacred concept of liberty of conscience: "'Wherefore, I say again, have we sought this country . . . ? Was it not for the liberty to worship God according to our conscience?'" Suddenly, Endicott is challenged: "'Call you this liberty of conscience?' interrupted a voice on the steps of the meetinghouse."

The challenger is the Wanton Gospeller. A "sad and quiet smile" crosses the face of Roger Williams, but Endicott, in the excitement of the moment, shakes his sword wrathfully at the culprit—an ominous gesture. "'What hast thou to do with conscience, thou knave?' cried he. 'I said liberty to worship God, not license to profane and ridicule him. Break not in upon my speech; or I will lay thee neck and heels till this time tomorrow!'" (439). The open challenge to the Puritan divine comes from the Wanton Gospeller, but the more telling detail of the scene is the presence of Roger Williams.

Bell has claimed that Hawthorne's "use of Williams is one of the more curious features of 'Endicott and the Red Cross'" and suggests that a full understanding of the story entails dealing with Williams's presence.[40] Colacurcio not only attends to the meaning and purpose of Williams's presence in great detail but also pins the meaning of the tale on an awareness of Hawthorne's idiosyncratic use of Williams: "[No] historical evidence places Williams . . . at the scene of Endicott's famous cross-cutting. . . . But we are not sufficiently instructed until we can fairly surmise what Hawthorne may have meant by his outrageous fusion of elements that are, historically, disparate. . . . Hawthorne has chosen (once more) to manipulate the historical record for the purpose of his tale." What, then, is the purpose of Hawthorne's subtle manipulations? He invokes Williams to make more explicit his conception of cultural conflict as the central feature of America's evolving myth of concern. As Colacurcio points out, "It was Roger Williams who first awakened the separatist consciousness in John Endicott; and . . . Endicott was merely enacting one of Williams's own revolutionary theories when he cut the Red Cross out of the banner."[41] The historical fact of Williams's direct encouragement of Endicott's dissenting attitude directly contradicts the tone and sense of Hawthorne's tale.

For Endicott, the purpose of separation was clearly to establish a civil religion in alliance with a dominant cultural structure that might lead to millennial splendor. He embodies two key features that form the "rock-foundation" of the nation's prevailing myth of concern: an insistent effort at cohesion and a powerful inclination to lash out and defend the myth against the subversive interventions of agents of freedom. Taken together, the two features make up "Endicott's ghost," the residual presence of which still marks American mythic discourse. In contrast to Endicott's military presence, Williams resembles a shepherd when he enters the tale. He carries a staff, and his shoes are "bemired" from his constant treks "on foot through the swamps of the wilderness" (436), both images suggesting Williams's concept of himself as "seeker after the true church of the apostles."[42] As he stoops to drink from a fountain upon his approach to Endicott's company, Williams first "turned his face heavenward in thankfulness," an act emphasizing his piety. In contrast to the garb of the militarists, Williams wears a "black cloak and band, and a high-crowned hat, beneath which was a velvet skull-cap" and has a "mild visage" (436, 439). He is also presented as "a pilgrim, heightened also by an apostolic dignity" (436–37), a view conforming to the historical Williams's sense of the individual as "seeker" or moral agent on a spiritual journey. According to Mark A. Noll, Williams denied government the power to force people not confessing Christ to embrace a social covenant, a view Endicott radically opposed. Historically, Williams argued that true Christian commitment emanates from the heart of regenerated believers rather than from the statutes of the state apparatus, and he saw no future for a Christianity compromised by vain attempts to rule the world.[43] Williams, unlike Endicott, viewed any notion of a "civil religion" as fundamentally vexed. For him, religion and government were to be forever separated.

For Colacurcio, the "sad and quiet smile" that "flitted across the visage of Roger Williams" indicates his understanding that these two very different ideologies are "utterly distinct and unreconciled . . . they are competing; and that the far more conservative sort is about to win out."[44] According to Hawthorne's version of the interruption from the bound Wanton Gospeller, Endicott "shook his sword wrathfully at the culprit,— an ominous gesture from a man like him." It is especially ominous because it suggests Williams's own troubled future. He would eventually also be labeled a culprit and banished from the Puritan community. Thus Roger Williams functions typologically in Hawthorne's story as a prophetic spokesperson for freedom and conscience who contrasts with the oppressive powers led by Endicott. Hawthorne recognized the dangers of the development of a hegemonic discourse that would overrule the agents of an opposing competing vision such as Williams's.

Hawthorne's acute sense of two competing visions of America is also demonstrated in other tales of the Puritans, notably "The May-Pole of Merry Mount," which dramatizes the public conflict between two strongly opposed visions of the nation's meaning and purpose. The "Merry Mount" colony is a stark contrast to the nearby Plymouth Colony and Endicott's new Bay Colony. The revels, gaiety, and merriment that Merry Mount esteems, symbolized by the decorated maypole, come to a crashing halt when Endicott appears during the May Day celebration and violently strikes the maypole to the ground with a single blow of his sword. The tension in this tale and in numerous others by Hawthorne is clear: grisly saints versus gay sinners and sunshine and flowers versus clouded visages and hard toil. Merry Mount is described as a place "where jest and delusion, trick and fantasy, kept up a continued carnival." In Merry Mount, where it was considered "high treason to be sad," people came to enact "a wild philosophy of pleasure" and "[dance] by the blaze all night." Such a life-style, however, from the perspective of the Puritans, was comparable to "the masques" of "those devils and ruined souls, with whom their superstition peopled the black wilderness" (62). Merry-Mounters, in the eyes of the Puritan divines, were demonic heathens similar to the Indian tribes, lost and misled by superstitious deviltry. As Thomas Pribek has noted, the high places of Baal in ancient Israel often included maypole-like idols, making Hawthorne's Merry-Mounters symbolically linked with the backslidden Israelites.[45] Such an association also links Endicott with the prophetic champions of God's law, such as Jeremiah and Elijah, a linkage made more explicit when Endicott accuses Blackstone of being a "priest of Baal" (63).

As the young couple Edgar and Edith, representatives of Merry Mount, are converted and restored to the true way of the Puritans at the tale's end, the narrator laments: "It was a deed of prophecy. As the moral gloom of the world overpowers all systematic gaiety, even so was their home of wild mirth made desolate amid the sad forest. [Edgar and Edith] went heavenward, supporting each other along the difficult path which it was their lot to tread, and never wasted one regretful thought on the vanities of Merry Mount" (65). The mirth and merriment of youth's freedom and vigor become absorbed into the cultural juggernaut fashioned by the likes of Endicott. The ending leaves the reader wondering about the accuracy of the narrator's comments. Did they "never" think back on their mirth at Merry Mount? Why must we accept the tale's ending as "their lot"? And of what future event is the tale a "prophecy"?

Bell and Newberry associate the gaiety and flamboyance of the Merry-Mounters with the Old World of England: "The 'scarlet' side of Hester cannot survive in New England."[46] But the Merry-Mounters' joy surely includes more than that, suggesting as it does the freedom and progressivism opposed to consensus and hegemony. Yet Hawthorne's privileging of the progressivism of the Merry-Mounters over the Puritans is also ironic, a point clarified in numerous later fictions such as "The Celestial Railroad" and *The Blithedale Romance*. Colacurcio is correct in claiming that the "moral choice offered—Puritan or Reveller, Gloom or Jollity . . .—is entirely spurious," because each faction is at various points both venerated and ridiculed.[47] Rather than favoring one party over the other in "The May-Pole of Merry Mount," Hawthorne suggests that both are needed for a healthy public construction of concern.

In typical allegorical fashion Hawthorne refrains from specifics, but the conflict in "The May-Pole of Merry Mount," as in "Endicott and the Red Cross," conforms to the general tension between myths of concern and myths of freedom. Thus, it is possible to read the two stories (and a good deal of Hawthorne's other fiction) as depicting a public transaction of myth and ideology. Hawthorne illustrates how cultural conflicts deeply rooted in a society are openly dramatized in such highly public moments as the rending of the cross or the destruction of the maypole. Furthermore, his model was to be applied not just to the historical past of the Puritans but, as the word *prophecy* suggests, to his contemporary cultural scene. In describing the feud that "The May-Pole of Merry Mount" narrates, for example, Hawthorne offers an important aside: "The future complexion of New England was involved in this important quarrel. Should the grisly saints establish their jurisdiction over the gay sinners, then would their spirits darken all the clime, and make it a land of clouded visages, of hard toil, of sermon and psalm, forever. But should the banner-staff of Merry Mount be fortunate, sunshine would break upon the hills, and flowers would beautify the forest, and the late posterity do homage to the May-Pole!" (62). Consequently, "The May-Pole of Merry Mount" should be read as a depiction and critique of Hawthorne's milieu. That is, characters such as Endicott and the Merry-Mounters are to be regarded as typological forebears, and their essential quarrel is also a type for the "complexion" of the emerging New England way—and in effect of all American ideological expression.

Given Hawthorne's representation of a quintessentially American type of cultural conflict, Williams's suggestive presence, especially its mythic nature, becomes even more telling within "Endicott and the Red Cross." The hegemonic dominance of the public sphere associated with Endicott is to be considered as truly "ominous," according to Hawthorne, if full participation of the important myth of freedom is permanently disenfranchised from the American public sphere. The foreboding nature of Endicott's ghost derives from its insidious attempt to carry out just such a disenfranchisement. In depicting the dangerous consequence of the hegemonic oppression Endicott exercises, Hawthorne suggests that both concern and freedom, vital factors in America's ongoing process of cultural dialogue, should be not just tolerated but perhaps even cherished and embraced. Contrary to the rosy pictures of the Puritans presented by romantic historians such as Bancroft, Hawthorne's version of New England's seventeenth-century privileging of concern over freedom shows how political oppression and civil corruption were created. That revelation greatly aids in explaining the mystery of Roger Williams's "sad and quiet smile."

In arguing that a healthy and fruitful public discourse depends on full participation by the likes of both Endicott and Williams, or by both Endicott and the Merry-Mounters, Hawthorne identifies cultural forces described much later by the models of conflict that Frye and Hunter advanced. All three critics suggest that a full contribution from both parties (concern and freedom; orthodoxy and progressivism) is the truest type of public discourse upon which to enact an idealistic social experiment. Bell describes "Endicott and the Red Cross" as the "symbolic birth of the American character," with Endicott representing the "archetypal American."[48] That claim is only partially true, however, for it discounts Roger Williams's archetypically American activity, which is equal and yet opposite to Endicott's. In addition, in pitting concern against freedom

Hawthorne's Endicott tales also represent an archetypically American conflict. Both "Endicott and the Red Cross" and "The May-Pole of Merry Mount" depict a typological conflict so seminal that the "future complexion of New England was involved in this important quarrel" (62).

Endicott, as archetypal predecessor and central agent in that conflict, is one of Hawthorne's major symbolic figures. On the one hand, he embodies at his best the American myth of concern, which Hawthorne appears to venerate at different times in the tales: Endicott "laid the rock foundation of New England," a striking biblical echo suggesting Jesus Christ as the "cornerstone" of the Christian church. On the other hand, however, Endicott at his worst violates the ideal American mode of public discourse by denying the agents of freedom a sphere in which to exercise their liberties of conscience. In his unswerving and relentless dedication to building consensus and cohesion, Endicott inexorably defends America's evolving myth of concern against the subversive interventions of the Wanton Gospeller, the Merry-Mounters, and finally even Roger Williams. John McWilliams is right to conclude that "Hawthorne is willing to slight neither the strength of Puritan self-reliance nor the narrow cruelty that is its consequence . . . the heroic will to independence and the hidden evil of intolerance were not only equally real, but interdependent qualities forming an American character."[49]

As Hawthorne's tales so chillingly suggest, Americans must beware of the continuing appearances of Endicott's ghost. In the place of such a remorseless milieu Hawthorne proposes a utopic version of the American public sphere that encourages openness and discourages untoward manifestations of the ghost. Such a public sphere may be America's only chance for maintaining any semblance of meaningful and enlightened cultural dialogue as would be befitting of the social experiment of democracy. In the end, America's hope of achieving such a public sphere is only possible by facing the facts of history, as Hawthorne tried to do, rather than romanticizing them for political ends in the manner of George Bancroft, Rufus Choate, Daniel Webster, and countless other American historiographers, both then and now.

Finally, Hawthorne's fictive recreation of John Endicott broaches the mythologizing process by which the Declaration of Independence of the 1830s was rapidly attaining a scriptural status central to an emerging American civil religious consensus.[50] Hawthorne's subtle analysis of Endicott's foreshadowing of the act of declaring independence in "Endicott and the Red Cross" is a reminder that by the late 1830s it had become commonplace for political spokespersons to draw upon the power of the Declaration and the American metanoia and invoke their origins in the Puritans. Hawthorne's depiction of Endicott and his Protestant efforts highlights the Puritan leader's courage and reveals his inherent self-contradictions. In doing so, Hawthorne participates in the creation of a largely impervious myth of concern that centers on earnest acts of religious and civil rebellion/repentance, even as he strongly disclaims it. Like Roger Williams, Hawthorne is somewhat caught in the middle. Williams's "sad and quiet smile" prophetically becomes Hawthorne's own, an ironic signal of an American citizen disquieted by the hegemony being birthed in the image of Endicott's ghost.

2 Revolutionary Enactment

Frederick Douglass, the African American Metanoia, and the Cultural Work of the Declaration of Independence

> May [the Fourth of July] be to the world, what I believe it
> will be, . . . the signal of arousing men to burst the chains
> under which monkish ignorance and superstition had
> persuaded them to bind themselves.
> —Thomas Jefferson (*Writings*, 1517)

> A long time ago, but not too long ago, a man said:
>   ALL MEN ARE CREATED EQUAL . . .
> His name was Jefferson. There were slaves then,
> But in their hearts the slaves believed him, too,
> And silently took for granted
> That what he said was also meant for them.
>
> Who said those things? Americans!
> Who owns those words? Americans!
> —Langston Hughes ("Freedom's Plow")

After the War of 1812, especially throughout the 1820s and
1830s, the cultural and ideological stature of the Declaration of Independence slowly increased until the document was established as the fundamental creed of the American metanoia. Of course, an array of cultural and religious spokespersons had long associated the civic idealism of
republicanism with the Christian idealism of "God's New Israel," but a
sustained focus on the founding document of 1776 did not come until well

after the Revolution.[1] Not until the Jacksonian period were the promised ideals announced in the Declaration's preamble glorified again and again by American Jeremiahs seeking their fulfillment in practical reality. The document's idealistic message of equality took on a life of its own in the hands of a wide range of social reformers. Slaves, too, as Langston Hughes would write, began to realize that those most hallowed of American words were "also meant for them."[2]

In what became ritualistic invocations of the Declaration's most important philosophical ideals, antebellum visionaries converted the document into what Thomas Gustafson has called America's "representative words" by continuously calling for their redemption through action.[3] That call occurred most prominently in Fourth of July community celebrations, which featured public readings of the document followed by extensive and highly laudatory orations evoking its patriotic and moral weight as the founding American creed. As Rush Welter has put it, these annual performances constituted "religious observance[s], in which the Declaration of Independence (customarily read at the start of the day's festivities) served in lieu of a religious text, and the oration in lieu of the sermon."[4]

The revival of attention paid to the nature and meaning of the Declaration throughout the antebellum era by such diverse agents as slaves, former slaves, abolitionists, woman's rights activists, Indian spokespersons, preachers, labor leaders, historians, and utopian visionaries reinvented the document for subsequent generations. The word *revival* may seem an overstatement, but there is good reason to use it to describe the increasing interest in and reliance upon the Declaration throughout this period. The Second Great Awakening, running roughly from 1800 to 1830 and culminating in the work of Charles Grandison Finney, consisted of an "organizing process" that combined emotional and religious fervor with a search for unifying symbols, values, beliefs, and myths.[5] William G. McLoughlin has defined an awakening as a "period during which old symbols are clothed with new meaning." At the forefront of such a movement will always be a revivalist, whose role is "to sustain the reality of the culture myths, to reinterpret them to meet the needs of social change, and to clothe them with an aura of reality that grows from his own conviction that he is a messenger from God."[6]

To accept McLoughlin's definition of an awakening as a time when "old symbols are clothed with new meaning" leads to the observation that America, whose vigorous cultural conversations are always evolving, is constantly in a state of awakening. The definition expands previous conceptions of the Second Great Awakening beyond the year 1830 to include manifestations of Finney's New Light theological innovations in any number of commentators of the 1820s, 1830s, and 1840s, culminating in the oratory of Abraham Lincoln before and during the Civil War. Further, one of antebellum America's preeminent symbols that established "powerful, pervasive, and long-lasting moods and motivations" among a variety of spokespersons and auditors is surely the Declaration as transcendent moral code and its attendant connotation urging "practical action."[7]

Spokespersons such as George Bancroft, Theodore Parker, and others (including, on a notably ambivalent level, Nathaniel Hawthorne) fostered a transcendental view of American history in which the nation was depicted as the sublime realization of an immutable and universal law of the spirit. That spiritual law, according to both Bancroft and Parker (and, later, Abraham Lincoln), was most powerfully depicted in the opening paragraphs of the Declaration of Independence and was a direct result of the Puritan legacy of New England, which worked through the agency of providence.[8] Simultaneously, the original Declaration became inscribed as a central doctrine of the American myth of concern because it invited individuals to participate directly by enacting personal declarations. Complete deliverance from the tyrannies of this world, according to that model, is first and foremost founded on the performative function of the act of an individual declaring. Thus, a full appreciation of the cultural work accomplished by the Declaration as "representative anecdote" would need to consider the performative function of the act of declaring and the manner in which individuals modeled personal declarations on the revolutionary moment symbolized by the events of 1776.

Historians and critics have often ignored "the fact that the Declaration was written to be read aloud," but, as Jay Fliegelman's study demonstrates, readers must envision the act of "'declaring' as performance" to understand the cultural weight of the document.[9] The Declaration was ritualistically performed again and again for the first hundred years of America's history, particularly as part of Fourth of July oratory but also more generally in the lives of myriad "true Americans" who individually stood against whatever tyrannies tried to revoke their liberties.[10] Traditionally, however, the contributions of Anglo-Americans to such emergent egalitarian writing have received the majority of scholarly and popular attention. Wendell Phillips, William Lloyd Garrison, Henry Seward, and Gerritt Smith certainly played major roles in constructing the rhetoric, but to focus on them is to neglect other worthy social voices. As John Lucaites and Celeste Michelle Condit have argued, these white abolitionists should not even be mistaken as "*the* primary source of antebellum egalitarian discourse. The generative force of abolitionist discourse was not solely the product of white sympathizers, but emerged in equally large measure from the public rhetorical efforts of African Americans."[11] Most obvious in this context would be the practical actions taken by slaves to free themselves and assert their humanity—runaways who, in the words of Frederick Douglass, "acted out the Declaration of Independence."[12]

Between 1827 and 1831 a cultural shift took place, and many localized African American voices began to merge into a nationalized public voice.[13] In 1827 the first black newspaper, *Freedom's Journal,* began publication by announcing its desire to articulate a national black political viewpoint, and in 1830 the National Negro Conventions were organized to foster a unified African American vision. Perhaps most significant, such men as David Walker (whose *Appeal* was published in September 1829) and Nat Turner (who led a slave uprising in August 1831) began to propound a revolutionary impulse among African Americans that drew significantly upon America's regnant myth of concern. Increasing African American emphasis on revolutionary discourse and at times armed resistance to tyranny emerged during a period of unprecedented mob violence and rioting in many of America's major cities. For a variety of reasons Boston, New Haven, Detroit, Newark, Camden, and Buffalo all were scenes of rioting between 1826 and 1834. Riots related to issues of race and judged as major also occurred in Providence, Philadelphia, New York, and Cincinnati.[14]

The growth of mob violence was attributed to a number of sources, including a rise in abolitionism and the cursedness of the slave system. Whatever its causes, many observers noted the explosive growth of violence. A committee of the New York Assembly, for example, remarked that a "spirit of anarchy and insubordination has been waked in our land," and the attorney general of Massachusetts lamented that a "wicked and furious spirit" was at work in the American citizenry.[15] The bloody riots of Philadelphia in August 1842 caused Robert Purvis to associate the "wantonness, brutality and murderous spirit" of the mob with the African American citizenry's "utter and complete nothingness in public estimation."[16]

David Walker's political vision must be considered in light of the shocking growth in mob violence and the emergent African American revolutionary voice. Walker was never a slave but his father was, and Walker had traveled enough in the south to know what the slave system entailed. The publication of *Appeal, in Four Articles; Together with a Preamble, to the Colored Citizens of the World, but in Particular, and Very Expressly, to Those of the United States of America* in 1829 marked a milestone in a new era of revolutionary African American writing. The fiery Walker appealed fervently and directly to the enslaved blacks of the South, and his powerful sense of Christian mission and God's ordained call on his life deeply informed the project. He argued for the full humanity of blacks and thus for their inclusion into the precepts of the Declaration. Jefferson's claim that the Fourth of July (or the Declaration celebrated on that day) would be to the world "the signal of arousing men to burst the chains" enslaving them is a prediction echoed and expanded in the heart of Walker's message: "I appeal to Heaven for my motive in writing—who knows that my object is, if possible, to awaken in the breasts of my afflicted, degraded and slumbering brethren, a spirit of inquiry and investigation respecting our miseries and wretchedness in this *Republican Land of Liberty!!!!!*" Walker frankly urged readers to enact their own form of independence by violent resistance, a striking appeal in 1829: "The man who would not fight under our Lord and Master Jesus Christ, in the glorious and heavenly cause of freedom and of God . . . ought to be kept with all of his children and family, in slavery, or in chains, to be butchered by his *cruel enemies.*"[17] That directive openly links the cause of the slaves with the Kingdom of Christ, providing heavenly sanction for armed resistance.

Walker's continuing refrain was to act against "tyrants" and "tyranny," a direct echo of the language of the Declaration. At times he ironically questioned that document's author: "Here let me ask Mr. Jefferson, (but he is gone to answer at the bar of God, for the deeds done in his body while living,) I therefore ask the whole American people, had I not rather die, or be put to death, than to be a slave to any tyrant, who takes not only my own, but my wife and children's lives by the inches? . . . Hayti, the glory of the blacks and terror of tyrants, is enough to convince the most avaricious and stupid of wretches."[18] In large part because of domestic slave uprisings such as that led by Denmark Vesey in 1822, Haiti and all it signified for antebellum whites—what Eric Sundquist has called "the trope of San Domingo"—had become by 1829 "the fearful precursor of black rebellion throughout the New World. . . . a prophetic simulacrum of events feared to lie on the horizon of American slavery."[19] Thus, the reference to the bloody uprising in Haiti, which began in 1791, invoked the most resonant model for black revolutionary acts that antebellum audiences could imagine. In the *Appeal*, the uprising in Haiti was not murderous sin but rather the "glory of the blacks," a successful type for American slaves as envisioned and fully encouraged by Walker.

Walker died on June 28, 1830, before the Nat Turner insurrection of August 1831, an event many observers linked directly to the *Appeal*.

Turner's major achievement lay in his assertion that slaves, like the founding colonists, inherently held a "right of revolution." Consequently, he called for the commission of mayhem and bloodshed in a way that ingeniously implemented and fully enacted the central American myth of open hostility against corrupt tyranny: "In his rhetorical crusade against slavery . . . or even in his millenarian uprising against it . . . the slave rebel, one could say, became most American." As Eric Sundquist has noted, the brilliance of Turner's momentous rebellion was that it fully "embodied the spirit of the Age of Revolution."[20] To justify his violent acts, Turner, who deployed "the accents of the Declaration of Independence and the Rights of Man," openly appealed to the reigning ideologies of the American Revolution.[21]

Like Walker before him, Turner continually claimed that he was motivated by a spirit, or "enthusiasm," emanating from God: "The Lord had shewn me things that had happened before my birth. . . . I was intended for some great purpose. . . . my superior judgment . . . was perfected by Divine inspiration. . . . Having soon discovered to be great, I must appear so, and therefore studiously avoided mixing in society, and wrapped myself in mystery, devoting my time to prayer and fasting."[22] Turner viewed himself as the prophet of God's judgment announcing in visionary language the coming of a cosmic battle through which a newly ordered America would emerge, free and victorious: "There were lights in the sky to which the children of darkness gave other names than what they really were—for they were the lights of the Saviour's hands, stretched forth from east to west, even as they were extended on the cross on Calvary for the redemption of sinners." His mission, ordained by God, had been announced via recent astronomical phenomena, especially "the eclipse of the sun last February." Heavenly signs of God's impending judgment are in keeping with numerous biblical passages, notably those in the apocalyptic book of Joel. Moreover, God's planning is significant because the commencement of judgment was, according to Turner, "to have begun the work of death on the 4th July last." By conjoining the visionary apocalypse of God's wrath against the Demon Slavery with the annual celebration of the Declaration, Turner greatly expanded the trope of San Domingo to include the civil and religious in a classic reformulation of the American jeremiad.[23]

Frederick Douglass's reliance on the Declaration's preamble, and his insistence on the need of each individual to enact independence from oppressive ruling tyrants, was indebted to these earlier proponents of the African American metanoia. Douglass, along with numerous earlier African Americans such as Walker and Turner, was a revivalist contributing to an ongoing attempt to construct an inclusive body of writing and define a vision of the American idea that drew upon the longstanding symbols and tropes of a national identity. He provided a powerful and prophetic voice that sought consensual embrace of America's transcendental myth of concern, a growing element of which was the recently sacralized egalitarianism of the Declaration. Beginning with Walker and Turner between 1829 and 1831, fostered by William Whipper, James Forten, Henry Highland Garnet, and Charles Lenox Remond during the 1830s and 1840s, and stretching into the 1850s to include the culminating African American voice of Douglass, important statements and acts coincided with unprecedented social upheaval and dissent. In the midst of that hostile social climate, Douglass and the others carried out the work of jeremiadic revivalists by calling for a return to the vision and "representative words" of the Revolutionary Founders and railing against subversive elements they deemed threatening to the American vision.

That *My Bondage and My Freedom* (1855) exemplifies Douglass's affinities with the Declaration of Independence as trope is illustrated most powerfully in the confrontation with Edward Covey, "the Negro Breaker," especially insofar as Douglass's depiction of that event evolved over a decade. His growing emphasis on that episode is clarified in light of the changes he made in recounting it between the initial *Narrative* (1845) and the second autobiography published ten years later. *My Bondage* demonstrates that Douglass can be understood as a revivalist bent on fostering a consensual version of the American myth of concern by which the Union might cohere and be sustained.[24]

According to William Andrews, the genre of the slave narrative is pervaded by a desire to declare through a human act by which an individual is able "to tell a free story." That person at once declares and inscribes personhood. For Andrews, doing so constitutes a deeply felt need to "be recognized as someone to be reckoned with," a necessary step along the road to the promised land of "freedom from physical bondage and the enlightenment that literacy can offer." Further, an important means of being recognized is "the appropriating of empowering myths and models of the self from any available resource." An important resource for Douglass was a personal revolutionary model based on the Declaration of Independence.[25]

For Andrews, Douglass's second autobiography is superior to his first and advances his standing as an artist and philosophical thinker. *My Bondage* constitutes a "greater testimony of freedom" than the earlier version, primarily because Douglass gained a greater liberty from enslavements other than the slave system: "So long as Garrison and all he symbolized remained an unquestionable standard for the ex-slave, he would not be able to pen a truly free story, for he would not feel himself at liberty to declare himself independent of the claims of Garrisonianism on his loyalties." Andrews invokes the cultural power of the original Declaration in foregrounding Douglass's inherent desire to "feel himself at liberty to declare himself independent." The second volume, far from being merely an "updating second installment" to the original *Narrative,* demonstrates through its "tone, dominant metaphors, and structure" that it constitutes a "quiet but thorough revision of the significance of the life of Frederick Douglass."[26] Douglass's attachment to American ideals also allows Andrews to rank him as one of the great transcendental artists of American Romanticism and a visionary, prophetic champion of the nation's prevailing myth of concern.

In contrast to such stirring commendations, however, Andrews appears to claim elsewhere that Douglass became "marginal to, if not alienated from, many of the authorities and ideals" of America; and, in another essay, that "Douglass did not feel free to express fully his sense of alienation from the American ideals."[27] Other critics are willing to go even further by suggesting that Douglass is best understood as a helpless soul caught in a web of authoritarian codes, resulting in a person overcome by alienation. In such a reading, Douglass's use of American ideals and myths is a desperate and perhaps disingenuous appropriation of language put to use as an "instrument for extracting meaning from nothingness."[28]

That view seems strained, however, and more in tune with postmodern concepts of language than the antebellum perspectives of his milieu. If such a critique were reliable, for example, then Douglass becomes guilty of the same moral hypocrisy he laments throughout both versions of his story. Rather than foregrounding his alienation from American ideals, as Andrews only implicitly suggests at times and as others do more explicitly, Douglass should be understood as a powerful voice seeking consensual embrace of the American ideologies of self-reliance, the self-made man, and fundamental equality as self-evident natural right. As Waldo Martin has asserted, Douglass's "Negro idealism" far "outspanned the depth of his alienation" suggested by Houston Baker and others. Further, Martin finds little reason to doubt the authenticity of Douglass's characteristic religiosity, prominent in *My Bondage,* or his espousal of a "thoroughgoing Americanism."[29] Douglass, in embracing versions of America's prevailing myth, lamenting the sad fall from grace of American society in a characteristically jeremiadic mode, and defending the national myth of concern against subversive interventionists (most prominently symbolized in the slave-breaker Covey), casts himself as a revivalist of those myths.

Numerous commentators have noted a central moment in both autobiographies and a point at which Douglass is "at liberty to declare himself independent": the encounter with Covey in 1834. After much rebellious behavior toward his master Thomas Auld, Douglass was sent to Covey on New Year's Day of that year to be broken of his insubordination. The episode grew in importance for him over the ten years between the two books. In the *Narrative,* the tale occupies nearly thirteen pages of chapter 10; in *My Bondage,* however, it begins in chapter 15 and works its way through nearly twenty-six pages of chapters 15 through 17—roughly twice the space given to the incident in the *Narrative.*[30]

The growing value of the incident can be explained by considering Douglass's conviction that his rebellion against Covey constituted a transcendent moment in history in which he was converted and baptized fully and irreversibly into the American metanoia. For Douglass, the moment becomes his declaration of in/dependence, by which he moved from mere speechifying to practical action. The central importance of the episode cannot be exaggerated. As Donald B. Gibson argues, "The literal conflict between them, in Douglass's eyes, is a microcosmic conflict between all true religions and false ones, all slavery and freedom, all fathers and sons, all black and white, all authority and liberty, all truth and error."[31] Thus, Douglass's depiction of the scene can be directly related to the twin themes of the "power of enactment" and the importance of each individual's declaration of in/dependence.

In the shorter, starker original version given in the *Narrative,* Douglass is sent to Covey to be disciplined and broken (101). He receives a first, severe whipping (102). Covey, a master of deception who always makes slaves feel his presence, is immoral, a reprobate, and altogether detestable, so much so that Douglass sometimes considers murdering him and committing suicide (103–6). Douglass dreams of freedom as he longingly watches the majestic sailboats dart by on Chesapeake Bay (106–7). One hot August day he faints from exhaustion, leading Covey to attack him almost to the point of death (107–9). Douglass runs off to complain to his owner Auld, who disparages the complaints but allows him to spend the night (109–10). He returns, is chased away again by Covey, and spends the night with Sandy, an older slave who gives him a magical "root" to carry that would save him from being whipped (110–11). When Douglass returns, Covey acts genially (he is on his way to church), but the next morning he tricks Douglass, and a violent fight of nearly two hours ensues (111–13). Following that narration, the final section of which is dramatically lumped into one long, unbroken paragraph (108–13), comes the central epiphany of the autobiography wherein Douglass comments on the incident:

This battle with Mr. Covey was the turning-point in my career as a slave. It rekindled the few expiring embers of freedom, and revived within me a sense of my own manhood. It recalled the departed self-confidence, and inspired me again with a determination to be free. . . . He can only understand the deep satisfaction which I experienced, who has himself repelled by force the bloody arm of slavery. I felt as I never felt before. It was a glorious resurrection, from the tomb of slavery, to the heaven of freedom. My long-crushed spirit rose, cowardice departed, bold defiance took its place; and I now resolved that, however long I might remain a slave in form, the day had passed forever when I could be a slave in fact. (113)

Douglass's analysis of his salvation is strikingly similar to the model of religious conversion that typified, by midcentury, the mythical struggle that all true citizens must undertake to experience a personal declaration of in/dependence. Like the Declaration, the confrontation invokes the concept of "equality": man against man, one on one. That decisive moment marks Douglass's transition from "a state of existential inferiority . . . to a vital consciousness of equality with his slave master."[32] Moreover, it is critically important that the language he uses is largely religious, specifically Christian: "It was a glorious resurrection, from the tomb of slavery, to the heaven of freedom." As Douglass makes plain through the heavy use here of the prefix *re*, true admission into the family Americana involves a return to previously held ideals, a reaffirmation of age-old traditions that had lain dormant and abused. The dramatic public encounter is said variously to have "rekindled," "revived," "recalled," and brought about a "resurrection" and "resolved" tenacity; it "inspired me again" (that is, it reinspired); and it constituted a "turning-point." It is the moment of his entrance into a uniquely American metanoia. He has been born again through his employment of practical action. In a manner similar to that found in the works analyzed in R. W. B. Lewis's *American Adam*, Douglass portrays his younger self mythically as "an individual standing alone, self-reliant and self-propelling . . . in his very newness he was fundamentally innocent."[33]

Over the following ten years, however, the story became much more complicated, to the point, as Andrews has claimed, that it should be reevaluated as a "quiet but thorough revision."[34] Close consideration of the two texts shows that Douglass made significant changes during the span of a decade. The opening story about being sent to get the wood, resulting in the first beating by Covey, increases in size dramatically in *My Bondage* (from fewer than two pages to almost six), with added attention paid to the fact that the cruel treatment is thoroughly unjust. Douglass supplies a much more complete and detailed analysis of the tactics of deception

Covey uses to make slaves "feel that he was always present" (*My Bondage* 133). The general tone of *My Bondage*, not surprisingly, is more sophisticated than the *Narrative*, and the account laden with deeply ironic embellishments. Early in the book, for example, Douglass refers to "Mr. Covey (my brother in the Methodist church)" (129), and later he remarks that "few men could seem more devotional than he, when he had nothing else to do" (134). Such asides are rarely found in the *Narrative* and attest to Douglass's growing conception of equality in referring to himself as a true "brother" of white folk and his increasing readiness to critique a white man.

Several other significant features mark Douglass's alterations in the second volume. He is keenly interested in developing a fuller picture of Covey as representative of a certain class of persons who demonstrate all that is foul and degraded about the slave power. Douglass and his friend Bill always refer to Covey as "the snake," and similar metaphors surface two other times ("his snakish habits" and his "peculiar snake-like way"), a comparison never articulated in the *Narrative* (134, 144, 149). Douglass also makes clear that ideals with no practical action tied to them are worse than no ideals at all: "His religion was a thing altogether apart from his worldly concerns. He knew nothing of it as a holy principle, directing and controlling his daily life, making the latter conform to the requirements of the gospel" (*My Bondage* 135). Considerably more time is spent in *My Bondage* describing Covey's hypocrisy in ignoring Douglass the runaway slave upon his return. Ironically, Douglass happens to return to the farm on the Sabbath as Covey and his wife are leaving for church, "smiling as angels" and "dressed in their Sunday best" (148). For Douglass, a "holy principle" only has weight insofar as it is actively "directing and controlling" an individual life. Covey exemplifies the divorce of holy principles from daily living.

In illustrating Covey's failure to enact his ostensibly holy principle, Douglass elaborates several other incidents that found their way into the original *Narrative* but were muted in their power. In *My Bondage*, however, he gives fuller vent to a gathering hatred of all that Covey, reified as archetype of the slave-holding devil, stands for. In the original account of Covey's purchase of the slave woman Caroline as a "breeder," for example, Douglass's language is reserved: After the purchase, Covey hired a married slave and habitually "used to fasten [him] up with her every night" (*Narrative* 105). That simple statement, encompassing only a part of a single sentence, is nevertheless a highly suggestive judgment delivered in the *Narrative*'s characteristically sparse manner. In *My Bondage*, however, the detail expands, allowing Douglass to harangue the reprobate Covey with a stirring jeremiad:

Mr. Covey had himself locked up the two together every night, thus inviting the result.

But I will pursue this revolting subject no further. No better illustration of the unchaste and demoralizing character of slavery can be found than is furnished in the fact that this professedly christian slaveholder, amidst all his prayers and hymns, was shamelessly and boastfully encouraging, and actually compelling, in his own house, undisguised and unmitigated fornication, as a means of increasing his human stock. (135)

Again, Douglass was careful to note, in the midst of the criticism, that Covey was "professedly christian," a fact that made the act even more heinous for those who believe in the American myth of concern and privilege practical action over pious platitudes. In essence, Covey, the master of deception, has "deceived himself into the solemn belief, that he was a sincere believer of the most high God." That observation in the first story appears to produce in Douglass a sense of compassion and mercy for his gruesome master, so much so that he wrote, "Poor man!" (*Narrative* 104). In the same spot in the second version (*My Bondage* 134–35), however, any sense of mercy for the likes of Covey had vanished, as had the exclamatory remark.

Another important change in *My Bondage* concerns the increased emphasis Douglass gives to the communal support other slaves accorded him throughout the stay with Covey. The encounter with Sandy, for instance, is only briefly related in the original: "I went home with him, and talked this whole matter over, and got his advice as to what course was best for me to pursue. I found Sandy an old adviser" (111). That, along with the mention of Sandy's advice to carry the magical root, is all that appears in the *Narrative*. But the same episode takes on greater significance in *My Bondage*. Douglass recounts in some detail the dinner, the topics of discussion, and the possible reason why Sandy is so interested in him and his problems: Douglass's knowledge, especially his ability to read, had become "the pride of my slave brothers" (*My Bondage* 146). Thus, he has become a leader of the slave brotherhood, one who might stand for them and represent them, and thus someone worthy of their allegiance and support. Special and loving attention is given to the presence of Sandy's wife and her careful preparation of the meal, which echoes the Last Supper before Jesus's passion and persecution. Douglass brims over with enthusiastic praise and thankfulness for the couple, who are taking a chance by harboring a runaway slave, especially in light of their power of enactment: "My supper . . . with Sandy, was the meal, of all my life, most sweet to my taste, and now most vivid in my memory" (146). It is even more than that, because Douglass later memorializes Sandy by claiming that he "had been to me the good Samaritan, and had, almost providentially, found me, and helped me when I could not help myself; how did I know but that the hand of the Lord was not in it?" (147).

The incident with Sandy suggests a providential God, and the agency of those like Sandy and his wife is worthy of comparison with the actions that characterize one of Jesus's most moving accounts of the power of enactment: the parable of the Good Samaritan (Luke 10). Moreover, that parable, in which the racially segregated and victimized Samaritan is shown to be virtuous in helping an injured man (compared with the hypocritical religious leaders who cross the street and avoid his needs), highlights Douglass's call to redeem America's civil and religious ideals through direct actions.

Douglass is also determined to show that his revolt against Covey could not have been successful through his agency alone. It requires the help of fellow slaves and a providential God all joined together communally. During his physical struggle with Covey, for example, two other slaves, Bill and Caroline, are important contributors to Douglass's ultimate victory. Both were commanded by Covey during the struggle to come to his aid, but both, in different ways, resist doing so. They are the man and woman previously exploited as breeders, and their open rebellion, as in the original Declaration, has already been revealed as justified in the eyes of a "candid world." Bill is mentioned in the *Narrative*, but there Douglass seems to imply that the reason he resists Covey's orders is simply because "his master hired him out to work, and not to help to whip [Douglass]" (113). The scene takes on a different significance in *My Bondage*, however. Douglass states that it "had something comic about it," because Bill, who "knew precisely what Covey wished him to do, affected ignorance, and pretended he did not know what to do" (150). The mocking tone of *My Bondage* is completely missing from the account in the *Narrative*, and several more lines of humorous dialogue show Bill's attempts to deceive his master, a scene reminiscent of the episodes in *Uncle Tom's Cabin* in which Sam and Andy work together in affecting ignorance to thwart the slavetrader Haley in his attempt to capture Eliza.

More important, Caroline's resistance to Covey's direct orders during the battle, unmentioned in the *Narrative*, strengthens Douglass's emphasis of his victory as a communal project. Caroline "was a slave of Covey, and he could do what he pleased with her" (151), an ominous statement suggesting that she resists Covey with a full understanding of the painful consequences. "It was not so with Bill, and Bill knew it," because he, a hired slave but under orders from his owner not to be whipped, risks no physical brutalization. Douglass makes it clear that as a result of her disobedience she "did not escape the dire effects of her refusal. He gave her several sharp blows. . . . We were all in open rebellion, that morning" (151). Unlike the *Narrative,* in which the struggle is framed as a cosmic battle involving only the two titans, in *My Bondage* Douglass goes to some lengths to show that his final victory depends fully on the practical actions of Sandy the day before and Bill and Caroline on the day of the fight. Thus he foregrounds his conviction that a truly American declaration involves not only independence but also, and simultaneously, dependence.

In light of the important changes in the depiction of the action leading up to the all-important declaration, it is not surprising to find subtle yet informative alterations in the description of the central moment. First, in the passage leading up to it in *My Bondage,* Douglass establishes a much easier familiarity with the reader than at any time in the *Narrative.* At the end of chapter 16 of *My Bondage,* for instance, he sets the stage for the unfolding of his mythic resurrection: "My kind readers shall have, in the next chapter—what they were led, perhaps, to expect to find in this—namely: an account of my partial disenthrallment from the tyranny of Covey" (143).

In mentioning "kind readers" and forecasting the fulfillment that "perhaps" any reader might "expect to find in this," Douglass indicates ready acceptance of, and alignment with, the reigning American myth of concern as well as concern for his audience. Similarly, the key paragraph begins, "Well, my dear reader" (151). In softening his tone and including readers through such nuances, Douglass frames himself as a voice seeking consensus and communion in a manner typical of Stowe's sentimental novel. A comparison of the passages is useful:

> This battle with Mr. Covey was the turning-point in my career as a slave. It rekindled the few expiring embers of freedom, and revived within me a sense of my own manhood. It recalled the departed self-confidence, and inspired me again with a determination to be free. . . . He can only understand the deep satisfaction which I experienced, who has himself repelled by force the bloody arm of slavery. I felt as I never felt before. It was a glorious resurrection, from the tomb of slavery, to the heaven of freedom. My long-crushed spirit rose, cowardice departed, bold defiance took its place; and I now resolved that, however long I might remain a slave in form, the day had passed forever when I could be a slave in fact. (*Narrative* 113)

> Well, my dear reader, this battle with Mr. Covey,—undignified as it was, and as I fear my narration of it is—was the turning-point in my *"life as a slave."* It rekindled in my breast the smouldering embers of liberty; it brought up my Baltimore dreams, and revived a sense of my own man-

hood. I was a changed being after that fight. I was *nothing* before; I WAS A MAN NOW. It recalled to life my crushed self-respect and my self-confidence, and inspired me with a renewed determination to be A FREEMAN. A man, without force, is without the essential dignity of humanity. Human nature is so constituted, that it cannot *honor* a helpless man, although it can *pity* him; and even this it cannot do long, if the signs of power do not arise.

He only can understand the effect of this combat on my spirit, who has himself incurred something, hazarded something, in repelling the unjust and cruel aggressions of a tyrant. Covey was a tyrant. . . . It was a resurrection from the dark and pestiferous tomb of slavery, to the heaven of comparative freedom. . . . my long-cowed spirit was roused to an attitude of manly independence. (*My Bondage* 151–52)

The excerpts are similar in format but different in critical details. The turning point in "my career as a slave" becomes "my *'life as a slave,'*" with quotation marks and italics as double emphases of irony, because it could hardly be described as a real human life and certainly not a career. The "few expiring embers of freedom" become "smouldering embers of liberty." They cannot ever expire, but instead continually "smoulder" and are resolutely "in my breast." Furthermore, the word *liberty* is more suggestive of the words of the original Declaration. In fact, the entire first section becomes longer. Douglass invokes his "Baltimore dreams," the time in his life when he was treated humanely and learned to read. Through capitalized letters he emphatically declares that "I WAS A MAN NOW" and that he had become "A FREEMAN," so that his inherent humanity, a social and philosophical issue of prime importance in light of the most famous passage in the original Declaration, is sharply proclaimed. In the passage from the *Narrative* he claims that the only readers who might truly understand what he has experienced are those who have "repelled by force the bloody arm of slavery." Yet in the passage from *My Bondage*, Douglass's epiphany can be comprehended by any person "who has himself incurred something, hazarded something, in repelling the unjust and cruel aggressions of a tyrant." That change from the representation of a fight against slavery to that of a struggle against a more generalized "tyranny" recalls the argument of the Declaration. Moreover, the passage describes the young slave as having an "attitude of manly independence" and solicits empathy from readers who identify with the motives that underpinned the Declaration. From "whence came the daring spirit to grapple" with Covey? Douglass wonders as the fight begins in the *Narrative*. But at the moment of rebellion in *My Bondage*, he states, "We stood as equals before the law" (149). The spirit that has imbued the young slave should be associated with the Spirit of '76, and the immoral and corrupt authority of the slaveholder, in concert with memories of the Declaration, fans the smoldering embers of liberty.

Douglass's dependence on the American myth of concern, specifically the Declaration, was not limited to *My Bondage*. It was a central feature of much of his published writings in the early 1850s that foreshadow revisions in *My Bondage*. In speeches and editorials during the years leading up to publication of the second autobiography, for example, Douglass placed growing emphasis on America's mythic ideals, specifically as sanctioned by God:

> The mission of the political abolitionists of this country is to abolish slavery. . . . The end sought is sanctioned by God and all his holy angels, by every principle of justice, by every pulsation of humanity, and by all the hopes of the republic. (*Frederick Douglass's Paper*, Nov. 19, 1852)
>
> Aliens are we in our native land. The fundamental principles of the republic, to which the humblest white man . . . may appeal with confidence . . . are held to be inapplicable to us. The glorious doctrines of your revolutionary fathers, and the more glorious teachings of the Son of God, are construed and applied against us. . . . We plead for our rights, in the name of the immortal Declaration of Independence. . . . The outspread wing of American Christianity . . . refuses to cover us. (speech, May 1853)
>
> We point to your principles, your wisdom, your great example. . . . That "all men are created equal": that "life, liberty, and the pursuit of happiness" are the rights of all . . . that resistance to tyrants is obedience to God—are American principles and maxims. . . . We are Americans, and as Americans, we would speak to Americans. (speech, July 1853)[35]

Publicly, Douglass held dearly to the governing ideals and myths then prominent in American discourse. His increased zeal for the American myth of concern can in part be explained by the political conversion he underwent after breaking from the Garrisonians and his subsequent embrace of the Constitution as primarily an anti-slavery instrument.[36] As David Blight has put it, "Douglass's increasing political consciousness led him inexorably to a radical antislavery view of the Constitution, and by July, 1851, his conversion was complete. . . . Douglass always garnered hope from America's founding creeds. . . . Without this promise and foundation, Douglass's vision of a future for blacks in America would have crumbled."[37] Such a political shift allowed greater influence to be placed on the founding documents, the most prominent of which is the Declaration, and brought about the perspective that allowed Douglass to write his most famous public address, "What to a Slave Is the Fourth of July?" (1852).

That speech contains specific instances of alienation, and one of Douglass's primary aims was to distance himself and his black brothers and sisters from the hypocrisy of American society as it was currently constituted. He emphasizes his marginalized, nonparticipatory status as alien:

> What have I, or those I represent, to do with your national independence? Are the great principles of political freedom and of natural justice, embodied in that Declaration of Independence, extended to us? . . . I say it with a sad sense of the disparity between us. I am not included within the pale of this glorious anniversary.
>
> Your high independence only reveals the immeasurable distance between us. . . . This Fourth of July is yours, not mine. You may rejoice, I must mourn . . . your celebration is a sham; your boasted liberty, an unholy license; your denunciation of tyrants, brass fronted impudence.[38]

Douglass's efforts as revivalist are exemplified in his Fourth of July speech, in which he employs the second person, as in "your revolutionary fathers" or "your principles, your wisdom, your great example." His overt desire to distance himself from the Fourth of July and the Declaration ironically signifies an earnest desire to embrace the true, radical sense of that document. Douglass's references to the Declaration came at a time of growing cultural emphasis on the document as the debate raged over the Constitution's stance toward slavery. For Garrison and his followers, the Constitution could be written off completely as a pro-slavery instrument. For Douglass, if America should hope to remain true to its founding vision, a serious reappraisal of the originating documents was necessary. In true jeremiad form transcending race and gender, Douglass called for a return to the original vision upon which the nation was ostensibly founded. In framing his appeal as he did, he became a revivalist calling for the reapplication of that old time religion—the American metanoia.

Thus, rather than dwell on the heroic efforts of the past, as he did for considerable time in the first section of the speech in what amounts to a tribute to prevailing national myths, Douglass argued that the true "eternal principles" the Founders "seized upon" must be reapplied to the contemporary American scene.[39]

> My business, if I have any here to-day, is with the present. The accepted time with God and His cause is the ever-living now.
>
>> "Trust no future, however pleasant,
>> Let the dead past bury its dead;
>> Act, act in the living present,
>> Heart within, and God overhead."[40]

Invoking Henry Wadsworth Longfellow's "A Psalm of Life," one of the century's most beloved poems, Douglass explained his focus, which was comparable to that of numerous black women commentators as well as to Stowe's *Uncle Tom's Cabin.* To honor the venerable and useful ideals that formed the backbone of the American enterprise in its infancy, true patriots must apply them to the existing social scene through the power of enactment. Douglass was emphatically not alienated from America's central creeds. He yearned instead for true demonstrations of the practical action inherent in them: Americans must not just talk a certain talk but should always be "up and doing," as Longfellow put it. Through his use of the poem he hoped to valorize the Founders, the work they accomplished, and the centrality of the Declaration as gem of the revolution and guiding doctrine of the present and future Union.

Although it can be argued, as Andrews and others have, that Douglass did resist paternalistic forms and felt alienated by the "authorities and ideals" of America, the conservative aspect of his ideological agenda has not been fully explored.[41] The need for heroic and intellectual leadership to deliver a mythic vision of consensus and inclusion must not be overlooked in considering the unbelievably dire straits antebellum slaves faced. John Louis Lucaites is correct in his judgment that they "possessed no sense of a common culture, let alone a collective or national identity," a salient fact that drove Douglass's project.[42] The burden to supply such an identity can be detected in the benediction in the final passage of *My Bondage:*

> I have felt it to be a part of my mission—under a gracious Providence— to impress my sable brothers in this country with the conviction that, notwithstanding the ten thousand discouragements and the powerful hindrances, which beset their existence in this country . . . progress is yet possible, and bright skies shall yet shine upon their pathway; and that "Ethiopia shall yet reach forth her hand unto God."[43]
>
> Believing that one of the best means of emancipating the slaves of the south is to improve and elevate the character of the free colored man of the north I shall labor in the future, as I have labored in the past, to promote the moral, social, religious, and intellectual elevation of the free colored people; never forgetting my own humble origin, nor refusing, while Heaven lends me ability, to use my voice, my pen, or my vote, to advocate the great and primary work of the universal and unconditional emancipation of my entire race. (247–48)

Douglass's closing words are filled with America's mythic elements. He describes himself as on a "mission" endorsed and supplied by "a gracious Providence" and "Heaven" and quotes the Bible as legitimation. Douglass's vision for his "entire race" is steeped in the images of the secularized view of progress exemplified by Longfellow's poem: "progress is yet possible, and bright skies shall yet shine upon their pathway." He would help to "improve and elevate the character" and "promote the moral, social, religious, and intellectual elevation of the free colored people." That passage endorses fully and unequivocally a version of the American myth of concern, of which Douglass viewed himself a central prophetic revivalist.

Moreover, Douglass, like Walker and Turner, embraced the mission of prophetic revivalism to such an extent that all of these men, despite their obvious disdain for hypocrisy and the corruption of the original "representative words," can still be understood as powerful voices seeking consensual embrace of America's founding vision and principles, which had yet to be fulfilled or fully understood. First, the writers championed individual declarations of in/dependence, resulting in the American metanoia, and thus became heirs of Endicott's ghost. In addition, through the practical actions of former slaves such as Douglass in "repelling the unjust and cruel aggressions of a tyrant," the power of enactment lends vastly more weight to their admonishments that all true citizens, black or white, north or south, return to the founding principles and defend the American vision against the corrupting influence of godless agents of the slave power, represented by the likes of Covey. Clearly, those founding principles were in the midst of the most daring reinscription in American history, primarily because of the exploits of these and other African American leaders. Douglass, Walker, Turner, and others like them, different as they surely were on issues of Christian doctrine, African colonization, or violent rebellion on the part of slaves, were united in their work as revivalists. They all fervently tried "to sustain the reality of the culture myths."

Insofar as they all worked passionately to "reinterpret [the myths] to meet the needs of social change" and consciously moved to reclothe central symbols, particularly the Declaration, in their common mission to save the Union, they embody the profoundly conservative impulse as well as the radically revolutionary impulse upon which the nation was founded.[44] In that way they all became "most American" and were at the forefront of a growing number of cultural spokespersons who called for an immediate and irrepressible enactment of a truly American metanoia.[45]

3 Holiness and the Sanctification Gap

Sojourner Truth, African American Women, and the Cultural Work of Doing the Word

> I believe that man can be elevated; man can become more and more endowed with divinity; and as he does he becomes more God-like in his character and capable of governing himself. Let us go on elevating our people, perfecting our institutions, until democracy shall reach such a point of perfection that we can acclaim with truth that the voice of the people is the voice of God.
>
> —Andrew Jackson

The deeply religious tone of these words, spoken by Andrew Jackson on the occasion of his inauguration in 1829, should not surprise anyone familiar with the social milieu of that moment in America. Indeed, the quotation epitomizes what had become, by 1829, the prevalent religious mood not only among many of the nation's cultural elites but also among the middle and lower classes, as attested by the rhetoric at revival camp meetings throughout the states. "Man" should aim to be "elevated," "endowed with divinity," moving toward a "point of perfection" that would culminate in the "truth that the voice of the people is the voice of God." Thus, from the pulpit of the newly inaugurated president came a brief version of the Puritan political sermon uniting civil and religious initiatives.

Jackson's speech also indicates that by 1828 the "transformation of American theology in the first quarter of the nineteenth century [had] released the very forces of romantic perfectionism that conservatives most feared. . . . As it spread, perfectionism swept across denominational barriers and penetrated even secular thought."[1] Timothy L. Smith has articulated this phenomenon cogently: "A religious and political ideology described most accurately as perfectionist became pervasive in Jacksonian America and remained normative to the end of the century; . . . widespread reading of the Bible and growing reverence for its authority was a principal factor in shaping that ideology; and . . . the combination of the millennial with the American dream was a prime catalyst, and not simply one of its fruits, of the quest for personal and social holiness."[2]

This perfectionism, founded on the strong movement toward arminianism and against standard Calvinism, is chiefly associated in America with Timothy Dwight, Lyman Beecher, Nathaniel Taylor, and perhaps most significantly Charles Grandison Finney. Finney's evangelical approach focused on the role of freedom of will in determining individual relationships with God. He demanded that people "make up their minds then and there to give themselves to God. Their destiny lay in their own hands, no matter what the Calvinists told them." In reality, staid New England divines were much more shocked to hear that "the will is free and . . . sin and holiness are voluntary acts of the mind" than they were to listen to Emerson's more famous Divinity School Address of 1837.[3]

Earlier Calvinism had insisted that individuals must be well down the road to living a holy life before they could dare claim conversion. In the 1700s John Wesley, by way of contrast, led the movement dubbed Methodism against what he took to be the extreme Calvinism that had dominated England throughout the seventeenth century. Wesley placed great emphasis on the religious experience of conversion, the daily growth toward perfection, and the universal access to salvation. Moreover, he identified two phases of Christian experience. First there was conversion, or justification, through which individuals are "born anew" and embraced by God. Second, newly converted Christians must seek "Christian perfection," or sanctification, the Wesleyan concept that would result in some of the most sweeping changes in Christian churches for the next two centuries.

Attaining the so-called Wesleyan second blessing was, for Methodists, a possibly lifelong quest that might be concluded either sooner or later. As Wesley described sanctification, "Entire sanctification or Christian perfection is neither more nor less than pure love; love expelling sin, and governing both the heart and life of a child of God. The Refiner's fire purges out all that is contrary to love."[4]

Those who struggle to accept the realism of highly sentimentalized characters—Little Eva, for example, in *Uncle Tom's Cabin*—would do

well to consider Wesley's influence upon writers such as Harriet Beecher Stowe. Out of the Wesleyan emphasis on Christian love and perfection came some of the most historically sustained developments in
American church history, among them the Holiness movement of the
nineteenth century and ultimately the Pentecostal and Charismatic
movements of the twentieth century. Each initiative keenly emphasized
the individual experience of the believer, the growth in personal grace and
holiness, and the need to demonstrate faith through works of humani-
tarianism and good will.

A renewed emphasis on holiness became the major burden of the
Methodist General Conferences in 1824 and 1832. In 1839 the first religious publication devoted exclusively to the brash and influential new
doctrine appeared. *The Guide to Christian Holiness,* founded in Boston
by Timothy Merritt, featured the writings of the woman who would become the most influential leader of the movement, Phoebe Parker. As
Vinson Synan has observed, "by 1840 perfectionism was becoming one
of the central themes of American social, intellectual, and political life."[5]

Beecher, Finney, and others followed indirectly the footsteps of Wesley by strongly dissenting against the impossibly high standards of doctri-
naire Calvinism simply to enter into conversion; rather, they claimed that
individuals could instantaneously commit to God and receive redemption.
Their reinscription of the Wesleyan distinction between justification (the
conversion experience) and sanctification (salvation through holy living
and discipleship) and their insistent emphasis on immediate justification
were emphasized in debates among church leaders and believers during
the 1820s and 1830s, to a large extent because of the controversial results
of the teachings of Methodist (or Methodist-like) preachers such as Finney.
Despite their indefatigable attempts to preach sanctification, the "Wesleyan synthesis was not always present in America. . . . the roughness of frontier life and the richness of urban life militated against the doctrine."
Methodist circuit riders found it difficult to convince the "hard-living,
hard-drinking, and hard-fighting pioneers to go on to perfection."[6]

As Richard Lovelace has asserted, Finney and his followers "discon-
nected sanctification from conversion and made it easy for men to enter
the kingdom. . . . Having unloaded conversion, however, they failed to
reinsert sanctification in its proper place in the development of Christian life." The result of this change, according to Lovelace, was a large-
scale "sanctification gap." Multitudes asserted their Christian faith and
yet did not commit to the lifelong quest toward holiness and Christian
perfection in the Wesleyan tradition.[7] Finney himself recognized this
problem in the mid-1830s and began to preach perfection to a much greater extent than he had previously.[8] Yet the sanctification gap had already

been created, a phenomenon to which numerous critics and observers made constant reference.

After 1835 the closing of the gap became the informing burden of not only Finney but also countless other Christian leaders and writers. The burden was manifested also within the social realm of reform as dozens of societies and associations sprang from the groundswell of perfectionism to assert the values they held dear, whether woman's rights, temperance, literacy, anti-Masonry, or, perhaps most spectacularly, abolition. Longfellow's secularized poem "A Psalm of Life," perhaps the most famous verse of the century, memorably articulated the pragmatic call to active participation in life's cosmic struggle toward some vaguely utopian future. Like Longfellow, Finney, other religious revivalists, and social reformers all worked to move people to action, progress, evolution, and millennial perfection:

> Not enjoyment, and not sorrow,
> Is our destin'd end or way;
> But to act, that each to-morrow
>   Find us farther than today . . .
>
> Life is real—Life is earnest— . . .
> Let us then be up and doing, . . .
> Still achieving, still pursuing![9]

The emphatic urge to always be "up and doing" was a primary feature of many African American commentators of the antebellum period, including Frederick Douglass, who quoted from Longfellow's poem in his most famous speech. Public acts of doing, including making speeches, provided personal versions of the Declaration of Independence. These defiant acts by former slaves such as Douglass and, even more startling, by women like the Quaker Angelina Grimké and a host of African Americans, including Maria Stewart, Jarena Lee, and Sojourner Truth, embodied unequivocal stands against received codes of behavioral tyranny that had culturally oppressed the speakers and their society. Such public shows of dissent through doing foreshadowed far more violent acts of later years, such as those of John Brown.

According to Karlyn Kohrs Campbell, such public moves in which "the speaker incarnates the argument" constitute a distinct rhetorical form called "enactment."[10] Those who make public comments on issues lend vast power to their arguments when they are willing not only to voice them but also enact them—to "incarnate" them. Campbell's formulation alludes to the announcements of Jesus of his status as incarnation of the transcendent: "I am the Bread of Life. . . . I am the resurrection and the life. . . . before Abraham was, I AM" (John 6:35, 11:25, 8:58).

Just as Jesus implored his followers to manifest the truth of his gospel, all true-blooded American Jeremiahs were to challenge listeners to incarnate the Declaration and the precepts of the American civil religion. Speakers must be willing "to act, that each to-morrow / Find us farther than today." True Americans not only talk but must also be constantly "up and doing." That is how the exhortation to invest rhetorical speech with practical action became a central feature of the American idea and the prevailing myth of concern. For the myriad church-related societies of the early nineteenth century, the key "objective was to 'do good': to assist the poor, convert the heathen, and lift up the fallen."[11] What Carla Peterson has shown to be the burden of numerous African American women can be expanded to include much of middle-class antebellum culture: All Protestant churches echoed the overpowering desire to become not only hearers but also "doers of the Word." And, as Peterson argues, "for these and other activists . . . speaking and writing constituted a form of doing."[12]

As Peterson suggests, the call to do the Word was aimed not merely at the religious but at American citizens in general. What had begun as a Christian principle of sanctification had subtly transformed into a patriotic national initiative by which the Union might become a better place for all. The call to close the sanctification gap by living in fuller holiness was duplicated by a similar yet more secular call among believers in the American metanoia to close that same gap. Religious critics disdained the "easy conversion" that had manifested among Christian believers; similarly, other cultural critics castigated the "easy conversion" by which so-called Americans claimed to have repented but in fact had continued to live the sorts of lives that indicated a betrayal of fundamental national creeds and values.

As a result of this perceived sanctification gap among both Christians and American citizens, others, including members of marginalized populations such as slaves and former slaves, began to speak of a heightened sense of repentance. Many drew on revolutionary and biblical models to enact endless new manifestations of the American metanoia, and through countless declarations of in/dependence the Declaration began to take on a new life. The construction of the core of American ideology during the antebellum period was not limited to participation of male speakers and writers, however. A vast growth in women's participation in the public construction of myth and ideology indicates the spirit of the dissenting myth of freedom that marked so much of American culture of the period.

Jean Fagan Yellin has declared that "the discourse of the antislavery feminists has been lost," and clearly the profound impact of antebellum feminist rhetoric has somehow been misplaced.[13] My focus will be on how matriarchal discourse appealed to, incorporated, and fostered the same mythical constructs as did that of the patriarchy.[14] As revivalists, these women not only fostered conceptions of important symbolic constructs such as the Declaration but also contributed profoundly to the interpretive act of "reclothing" them publicly.

The spiritual writings of Maria Stewart and Jarena Lee, for example, represented the establishment of a new women's rhetoric of doing, and its concomitant practice, in antebellum America. Stewart and Lee were important in the establishment of the Declaration as a central American creed and the act of declaring as mythic practice. They were precursors of the later rhetorical achievements of Sojourner Truth as enacted in her "real" historical life and Harriet Beecher Stowe in *Uncle Tom's Cabin.* All four women conformed to the definition of revivalist as advanced by McLoughlin and worked to sustain cultural myths of America, reinterpret these myths in various manners, and clothe them with an aura of divine sanction. In addition, they championed "doing the Word" and reflected the general religious concern that resulted in the highly influential Holiness revival: the need to close the sanctification gap among the faithful.

In addition, each woman was involved in the grounding of the American mythic creed in the Declaration of Independence. Women were among the first to champion the concept of equality as espoused in the Declaration and applied not only to slaves but also to women. The watershed moment of woman's rights rhetoric in antebellum America was conceived in Waterloo, New York, during the early part of July 1848. Significant meetings were held there among a group of women who, just a few days earlier, had published a notice in the *Seneca County Courier* announcing a meeting to be held for women in Seneca Falls, New York, on July 19 and 20. Among those in Waterloo were Elizabeth Cady Stanton, Lucretia Mott, and their Quaker friends Jane Hunt, Mary McClintock, and Martha C. Wright, Mott's sister. Their agenda was to draft a "Declaration of Principles and Resolutions." When they encountered difficulties in doing so, however, Stanton rescued the day by picking up a copy of the Declaration of Independence and reading it aloud dramatically, a move that convinced the others that the original Declaration should become the model for their subsequent endeavors.[15]

The speech they produced became the most celebrated aspect of the Seneca Falls Convention, and its wording closely follows Jefferson's original: "We hold these truths to be self-evident, that all men *and women* are created equal." Stanton's devotion to the "sacred" Declaration was genuine and exemplifies that of less well-known figures: "By every principle of our republic, logically considered, woman's emancipation is a foregone conclusion. The great 'declarations' by the fathers, regarding individual rights and the true foundations of government, should not be glittering generalities for demagogues to quote and ridicule, but eternal laws of justice, as fixed in the world of morals as are the laws of attraction and gravitation in the material universe."[16] Thus, while espousing a version of mythic concern, Stanton simultaneously foregrounded the tension between what should be and what is, between what demagogues (Endicotts?) say and what they do.[17]

While symbolic formulations such as America as redeemer nation and a close association of the nation with the Christian church and the American metanoia abounded throughout these women's works, they agreed that the central religious symbol in the prevailing national myth of concern is the Declaration as fundamental and sacred moral creed. As Garry Wills has argued, Lincoln may be the figure most responsible for the shaping of an American mythical ideology that still resonates for many Americans. Wills terms Lincoln a "great artist of America's Romantic period" who was able, virtually singlehandedly, to accomplish the "recontracting of our society on the basis of the Declaration as our fundamental charter."[18] That description accords with McLoughlin's definition of awakening as a time when "old symbols are clothed with new meaning" but greatly underplays the significance of Lincoln's predecessors, including former slaves and women revivalists.

The women were not simply prophets of the feminine, but prophets of the American idea and important cultural forebears of Lincoln's culminating achievement. What they had in common was a strong attachment to the emerging American myth of concern. Each passionately defended a vision of America in which the precept of equality as depicted in the Declaration would reign in the real world of civil and moral rights. They all presented personal prophetic versions of an American metanoia, asserting that the nation must turn once again to the valued traditions upon which it was ostensibly founded and, in accordance with those ideals, be "up and doing." Each also spoke sharply against any agents attempting to mask or undermine the underlying precepts dictated by the Declaration. Thus, each manifested, in various manners and to varying degrees, the jeremiad mode and tactics of Endicott's ghost.

⁓

Angelina and Sarah Grimké are rightly considered to be chief forerunners of feminine enactment in antebellum public speech. Yellin argues that the Quaker sisters can be distinguished by their individual focuses. Angelina was concerned with secular themes, whereas Sarah was more concerned with the theological and moral issues of womanhood.[19] But they shared a philosophy that would mark the work of women throughout the antebellum years. The Grimkés, Angelina in particular, associated the bondage white women experienced with the bound condition of slaves, all the while drawing upon the Declaration's central ideal of equality.

> The denial of our duty to act, is a bold denial of our right to act; and if we have no right to act, then may we well be termed "the white slaves of the North"—for, like our brethren in bonds, we must seal our lips in silence and despair.
>
> [Women's present condition is] *a violation of human rights, a rank usurpation of power,* a violent seizure and confiscation of what is sacredly and inalienably hers.[20]

The word *inalienably* hearkens to the rights of "all men" as spelled out in the Declaration, and the charge of a "usurpation of power" also echoes the Declaration. But what may be most remarkable about these statements are their early dates (1837–38). Well before Lincoln's interpretive work on the Declaration and near the beginning of the Holiness movement some women were attempting to "reclothe" the document. The words are imbued with a call to action: It is "our duty to act." Overall, appeals to the inarguable tenets of the American faith, as contained in the Declaration, are a prominent feature of the writings of the Grimkés:

> We must come back to the good old doctrine of our forefathers who declared to the world, "this self-evident truth that *all* men are created equal, and that they have certain *inalienable* rights among which are life, *liberty,* and the pursuit of happiness."
>
> Slavery is contrary to the declaration of our independence . . . [and] it is contrary to the first charter of human rights given to Adam, and renewed to Noah. . . . [America's] books and papers are mostly commentaries on the Bible, and the Declaration.[21]

The excerpts are typical in two important ways. The act of returning ("come back to the good old doctrine") invokes the sense of repentance, and the two key creeds of the nation ("the Bible, and the Declaration") are the central authorizing texts of the project. By claiming that all of America's "books and papers" are mere "commentaries" on the central creeds, Angelina Grimké simultaneously raised the Declaration to the level of sacred literature and maintained it as the transcendental goal toward which all American public documents point.

As Barbara Bardes and Suzanne Gossett have argued, debate in the nineteenth century over women's political power centered on three themes: the private versus the public role of women, the power of the female voice, and the fear of women's sexuality.[22] In the context of these disputes, Sarah Grimké's call to women in *Letters on the Equality of the Sexes* (1838) was a bold one. They were to "arise in all the majesty of moral power, in all the dignity of immortal beings, and plant themselves side by side on the platform of human rights, with man." The religious element of the inalienable rights of women is evident, and the prophetic, ministerial function of Quaker women, equal to that of men, emphasized. It is a call for an American metanoia. The nation was to repent and turn back to the original ideal of the Declaration, and women were to declare independence from the constraints of assigned roles and authorities. Sarah Grimké's statement also foregrounded a key symbolic feature of the sisters' rhetoric, a point Yellin makes abundantly clear in a thorough investigation of the iconography of the kneeling slave (i.e., woman). It was a call for females to stand and incarnate their status, erect and elevated. It was also a call to "arise" and "plant [themselves] side by side on the platform of human rights, with man."[23]

Speaking openly in the America of 1837 was a courageous act for Angelina Grimké, considering that her public speeches were constantly met with ridicule, slanderous rumors about her alleged sexual misconduct, and even biblical epithets. When a woman voiced her opinion on public issues, she simultaneously rebelled against the severe limits placed on her by strict cultural codes, identified herself as "unladylike" and "masculine," and risked being chastised as sexually deviant and promiscuous. Angelina Grimké, for example, came to be dubbed "Devilina" and characterized as a "loose woman" in the press. She and numerous other women like her were treated as sexual deviants, as demonic incarnations of Jezebel from the Old Testament and the Whore of Babylon from the New. Similarly, when Elizabeth Cady Stanton began appearing in public wearing the "Bloomer costume" in 1851, severe criticism and ridicule followed her actions, which other feminists soon copied. Preachers denounced the apparel based on Deuteronomy 22:5: "A woman shall not wear that which pertaineth unto a man."[24]

For Grimké, the culmination of such ugly manifestations of the unseemly side of Endicott's ghost undoubtedly occurred when an angry mob attacked and burned to the ground the new Pennsylvania Hall in Philadelphia before her speaking engagement there.[25] Yellin surmises that the violent eruption was exacerbated by the fact that the scheduled speech was to occur just three days after Grimké's marriage to Theodore Weld. As bad as it was to speak openly as a single woman, to do so when married was considered to be even more serious. In the face of such social myopia and antagonism, the fact that the Grimkés and others spoke publicly made their acts profoundly rhetorical: "Appearances of the antislavery women on the platform were praised as angelic and excoriated as diabolical, but in and through their public presence they dramatized the possibility of female freedom on a human level."[26]

The courageous public acts of the Grimkés paved the way for further exploits by other white women. Yet their African American peers were both the wrong sex and the wrong race to speak in public. The exploits of early black women commentators predated those of the Grimkés and Stanton by several years, however. As Sue E. Houchins has noted, when Maria W. Stewart and Jarena Lee published spiritual autobiographies in 1835 and 1836 they simultaneously "seized authority," "laid claim to their rights as citizens," and as evangels hoped to "produce both a comparable spiritual and a political metanoia" among readers.[27]

The *Productions of Mrs. Maria W. Stewart* (1835) asserts the fixed moment of conversion as the occasion when the author was struck by a powerful urge not only to do the Word but also to see that others would do it: "From the moment I experienced the change, I felt a strong desire, with the help and assistance of God, to devote the remainder of my days to piety and virtue" (4). Moreover, Stewart's religious conversion is elided with a more political conversion: "[I] now possess that spirit of independence, that, were I called upon, I would willingly sacrifice my life" (4), and, "Do you ask the disposition I would have you possess? Possess the spirit of independence. The Americans do, and why should not you?" (17). The willingness to die a martyr's death verifies the fullness of the American metanoia: "I would willingly sacrifice my life for the cause of God and my brethren" (4); "if there is no other way for me to escape, [God] is able to take me to himself, as he did the most noble, fearless, and undaunted David Walker" (5); and "religion is pure; it is ever new; it is beautiful; it is all that is worth living for; it is worth dying for" (9). The invocation of Walker is noteworthy. Stewart's adoption of the mode of the jeremiad in shaping a public persona can be attributed largely to her close relationship with Walker, who influenced her through his early insistence on the "inclusion of African Americans into a reformed American nationhood."[28]

Stewart eloquently called for African Americans to work toward the "uplift" of themselves and their brothers and sisters: "[My] prayer to god is, that there might come a thorough reformation among us. . . . [let us] walk before the Lord our God with a perfect heart, all the days of our lives. . . . the day on which we unite, heart and soul, and turn our attention to knowledge and improvement, that day the hissing and reproach among the nations of the earth against us will cease. . . . let us make a mighty effort, and arise" (14–15). Throughout these and many other passages Stewart demonstrated fervent devotion to closing the sanctification gap, which she believed hindered the African American community from rising as a group in social status. She viewed the task of living a holy life and walking with God in "perfect love" (one of the defining idioms of Wesleyan theology) as co-equal with being a devoted and virtuous citizen. Altogether, Stewart's passionate memoir should be viewed as a pure and early instance of civil religion, declaring in jeremiadic form that Christians (and American citizens) need to return to the radical nature of their commitment to the Christian (and American) cause. They were to seek with greater diligence to close the sanctification gap between their alleged beliefs and their daily lives.

The memoir, entitled *Religious Experience and Journal of Mrs. Jarena Lee, Giving an Account of Her Call to Preach the Gospel* (1836), differs from Stewart's book in form and content, but it similarly aimed at moving readers toward doing the Word and thus closing the sanctification gap. The story begins almost immediately with Lee's dramatic retelling of her miraculous moment of conversion:

> That instant, it appeared to me as if a garment, which had entirely enveloped my whole person, even to my fingers' ends, split at the crown of my head, and was stripped away from me, passing like a shadow from my sight—when the glory of God seemed to cover me in its stead.
>
> That moment, though hundreds were present, I did leap to my feet and declare that God, for Christ's sake, had pardoned the sins of my soul. (5)

Lee marked the momentous "confession unto salvation" that this event encompassed as the day of her salvation, the genesis of her journey as God's child; it thus bore the marks of Wesleyan conversion as well as the American metanoia. Throughout the narrative Lee's public testimony is regularly described as a declaration. Her claim of spiritual authority, proof of which was her assertion of being covered with God's glory, was made in the presence of the Rev. Richard Allen, a prominent preacher and leader in the African Methodist movement, thus providing an additional argument for sexual coequality. Later, as Lee struggled to come to terms with her belief that God had called her to preach, she submitted the call to the prophetic judgment of Allen. Such a submission would have been the recognized form of "testing the Word," and her awareness of and submission to the orderliness of church government indicated a humility and earnestness that is much to be honored. She was neither out of order nor given over to antinomianism or witchcraft; instead, she initially tried to live according to biblical orderliness and aspired to be recognized by ordained church authority.

Allen told her, however, that his movement "did not call for women preachers" (11). At first, Lee was relieved, but as time passed she could not deny the call and thus began to construct arguments against a male-dominated pulpit.

> Why should it be thought impossible, heterodox, or improper for a woman to preach? seeing the Saviour died for the woman as well as the man.
>
> If the man may preach, because the Saviour died for him, why not the woman? . . . Is he not a whole Saviour, instead of half a one? as those who hold it wrong for a woman to preach, would seem to make it appear.
>
> Did not Mary first preach the risen Saviour, and is not the doctrine of the resurrection the very climax of Christianity—hangs not all our hope on this, as argued by St. Paul? Then did not Mary, a woman, preach the gospel? for she preached the resurrection of the crucified son of God. (11)

It is apparent that early in the nineteenth century women such as Lee thought deeply to uncover biblical means of supporting their public efforts on behalf of the gospel. By noting that Mary was the original preacher of the most sacrosanct doctrine of the New Testament, Lee suggested that women are not only equal but also perhaps superior to men as originators of the gospel message. "Judge a tree by its fruit," Jesus said, and Lee described the "fruit" of her evangelical efforts:

> In my wanderings up and down among men, preaching according to my ability, I have frequently found families who told me that they had not for several years been to a meeting, and yet, while listening to hear what God would say to this poor female instrument, have believed with trembling—tears rolling down their cheeks, the signs of contrition and repentance toward God. I firmly believe that I have sown seed, in the name of the Lord, which shall appear with its increase at the great day of accounts, when Christ shall come to make up his jewels. (12)

Her self-description of being a "poor female instrument" was somewhat ironic, but she was also sincere in an unwavering faith in the true source of her power and the belief that strength and grace are one and the same. That awareness of empowerment became a major motif in her narrative: "The Lord was pleased to give me light and liberty among the people" (19); "I had life and liberty, and the Lord was in the camp with a shout" (21); and, "Though weak in body, the good Master filled my mouth and gave me liberty among strangers" (26). Such passages illustrate the motifs of God's sovereignty and the joining of God's presence with liberty, a rhetorical strategy that moves religious emphasis into the realm of the political. The term *liberty* suggests not merely the true liberty of a Christian believer but also the lines of the Declaration that guarantee all citizens "life, liberty, and the pursuit of happiness." As the spirit comes, argued Lee, liberty increases. At other times, however, she claimed to have "but little liberty," although she steadfastly "[labored] on in the best manner" she could (19).

Finally, Lee detailed several supernatural events of such awesome magnitude that they could only be regarded as signs from Heaven sanctioning her earthly ministry. Her first came from the sound of "a voice which I thought I distinctly heard" saying "Go preach the gospel!" (10). On the occasion of her second blessing, Lee felt strongly "impressed" to go to her prayer closet and "carry [her] case once more to the Lord." There, she witnessed a vision of a "form of fire," followed by a "man robed in a white garment" (12). At another time God spoke to Lee in a dream (13), and still later she had a vision of "the Saviour in full stature, nailed to the cross" (16). Often throughout the narrative her actions seem articulated by the Spirit, an echo of the Acts of the Apostles: "I got about three miles on foot, when an apparent voice said 'If thou goest home thou wilt die.' I paused for a moment. . . . Again I was startled by something like a tapping on my shoulder, but, on turning around, I found myself alone" (33). Similar miraculous cues abound throughout the story and suggest an everyday awareness by which a sojourner on the road to preach can be sensitive to and guided by the spoken word of God. Such a relationship exemplifies Lee's *Religious Experience,* and the effect at which she aimed seems clear enough. She believed that each Christian, male or female, slave or free, could know and experience God's spirit, and the American spirit of liberty, as she knew them. Women, like men, thus are given the responsibility and call to receive and enact individual versions of love and liberty.

∼

Numerous early-nineteenth-century women drew upon and fostered the tradition of the Declaration as highly public act, enacting by themselves declarations that drew upon America's myth of concern and aided women in the drive to gain full citizenship and independence. Through such acts, women made public moves that argued for co-equality and by which "the speaker incarnates the argument."[29] Although speaking out publicly in the manner of the Grimkés, Stanton, Stewart, and Lee constituted enactments of their claims of independence, perhaps the female public figure who most powerfully enacted her argument in antebellum America was Sojourner Truth.[30] By claiming women's superiority, not equality, to men, she made the next logical step and then backed that claim rhetorically with numerous striking enactments. As *Narrative of Sojourner Truth* recounts:

It was at a crowded public meeting in Faneuil Hall, where Frederick Douglas was one of the chief speakers. Douglas had been describing the wrongs of the black race, and as he proceeded, he grew more and more excited, and finally ended by saying that they had no hope of justice from the whites, no possible hope except in their own arms. It must come to blood; they must fight for themselves and redeem themselves, or it would never be done.

Sojourner was sitting, tall and dark, on the very front seat, facing the platform; and in the hush of deep feeling, after Douglas sat down, she spoke out in her deep, peculiar voice, heard all over the house,

"Frederick, *is God dead?*"

The effect was perfectly electrical, and thrilled through the whole house, changing as by a flash the whole feeling of the audience. Not another word she said or needed to say; it was enough.[31]

The episode itself was related to Harriet Beecher Stowe by Wendell Phillips and originally appeared in a memoir by Stowe.[32] In contrast to Douglass's masculine call to violent arms, Truth interjected a feminized response focussing on God's omnipotence and providence, thus emphasizing feminine versus masculine tension. Fittingly, her public declaration was set in Faneuil Hall in Boston, site of important historical events along America's long road to independence. A woman needed boldness to speak out in such a "deep, peculiar voice, heard all over the house" in disagreement with Douglass—the rhetorical act of a declaration of co-equality and moral superiority in relation to the famous male speaker.

Claiming sexual superiority was a major burden of Truth's public career and in her transcribed autobiography. While moves to bring about a more feminized culture held sway during the 1850s, Truth showed that women were capable of taking on certain so-called masculine characteristics. In the *Narrative,* she describes her early years as a slave in New York, her escape from her lying master the year before emancipation under state law in 1827, and the subsequent trials and tests of her attempt to gain a sense of self-identity, culminating in her dismissal of the slave name "Isabella" in favor of one that was God-ordained. Truth makes it clear that during her years as a slave she had been a hard worker and superior to any man in the field: "Her master insisted that she could do as much work as half a dozen people, and do it well, too" (31); and "[her master] stimulated her ambition by his commendation, and by boasting of her to his friends, telling them that 'that wench . . . is better to me than a man'" (32–33). Her mother is superior to her father in that she remains healthy, works, and cares for him when he grows feeble as his death approaches: "Her mother was still able to do considerable work, and her father a little" (19). In fighting to regain custody of her son after he had been illegally sold away, Isabella trusts fervently not only in God but also in her own legal steps. Her self-assurance at this point in her account rises to rapturous heights: "I know'd I'd have him agin. Why, I felt so tall with-in—I felt as if the power of a nation was with me" (45).

Her unusual height for a woman (nearly six feet, two inches) and her deep voice and darkness of complexion made her an imposing physical presence, and "she most assuredly jolted the finer sensibilities of the era."[33] As Olive Gilbert relates in a typical aside, "The impressions made by Isabella on her auditors, when moved by lofty or deep feeling, can never be transmitted to paper, (to use the words of another,) till by some Da-guerrian art, we are enabled to transfer the look, the gesture, the tone of voice, in connection with the quaint, yet fit expressions used, and the spirit-stirring animation that, at such a time, pervades all she says" (45). That description stresses a presence and stature usually reserved—in America during the 1850s—for men. Stowe, in her tribute to Truth, also notes her stature and compares Truth to a "work of art": "I do not recol-lect ever to have been conversant with any one who had more of that silent and subtle power which we call personal presence than this wom-an. . . . Her tall form, as she rose up before me, is still vivid to my mind."[34] Perhaps the most telling aspect of Stowe's description is the assertion that she had never met "any one" with more "silent and subtle power which we call personal presence," quite a claim for the well-traveled author who had visited with such preeminent male icons as Emerson, Hawthorne, Longfellow, and Lincoln.

Yellin, however, has criticized Stowe's depiction of Truth as being "static, mysterious, and inhuman," a "mutilate," and thus a "contradic-tion" of what Truth stood for as a woman.[35] Although charges of racism have historically, and to some degree rightly, dogged Stowe, such perva-sive cultural attitudes cannot be judged too harshly. Clearly, Stowe of-ten demonstrated a halting ambivalence regarding race, but her descrip-tion is admiring and contradicts any assertion of being "inhuman."[36] Yellin's critique ignores Stowe's obvious praise and admiration in the face of the rampant racism among northern women.[37] To the contrary, Stowe, in making such comments, seemed clearly cognizant of that rhetorical "power of enactment" Campbell has described as a central feature of Truth's influence.[38]

In the context of Truth's argument for co-equality and even superi-ority to men, the heart of the *Narrative* lies in the discussion of her in-volvement with a religious sect that came to be called the Kingdom of Matthias (or the Matthias delusion), her rejection of that sect, and her subsequent call by God to walk about the countryside (thus, "Sojourn-er") and preach (thus, "Truth").[39] Although Robert Matthews, the leader of the sect, at first seemed to espouse equality and fellowship, he began to teach other doctrines (he claimed to be the "Father, or to possess the spirit of the father" while Elijah Pierson, his partner, was proclaimed to be the resurrected "Elijah the Tishbite") once many people had fallen under his charismatic spell (92). Much of his teaching can be characterized as misogynistic: "Every thing that has the smell of woman will be destroyed. Woman is the capsheaf of the abomination of desolation—full of all deviltry" (94). In the end, the sect was publicly exposed when Pierson's mysterious death led to accusations against Matthias.

Truth's extensive treatment of her involvement with what she came to believe was a sadly misguided and deceived group underscores her later conviction concerning the treachery and manipulative greed of the male leadership of much of American religion. Her rejection of the male-dominated church culminated in the personal, mystical experience of being named and sent forth by God, a remarkable moment suggesting that women did not require the agency of male leadership and a reminder that the gift of prophecy and evangelism were no longer reserved for men: "She had learned much that man had never taught her" (112).

Truth's reliance on the personal priesthood of the believer can be compared with Harriet Beecher Stowe's claims that *Uncle Tom's Cabin* emerged from a vision that came to her during a communion service. Stowe's assertion that the book was written under the influence of God verifies and authorizes her prophetic mission in the same way that Truth's claims of divine guidance, holy mission, and receiving her name from God do.[40] In addition, their moral stances as ministers of the Word marked them as woman's rights advocates through their claim to equality before God and their inherent ability to employ prophetic voices. Truth rejected male interpretive autocracy and chose to depend fully on her own biblical interpretations. When she was examining the Scriptures, "she wished to hear them without comment. . . . She wished to compare the teachings of the Bible with the witness within her" (108–9). And her version of Christian theology, based on a personal vision of Jesus (67), was replete with idiosyncrasies, including an affinity for deeply sexual imagery in describing the saint's marital relationship with God (69–70). Moreover, she often mixed elements of Native Africanisms (such as "Nommo," which Carla Peterson describes as "the Word as the productive life force") with the biblical Christianity she ostensibly was preaching.[41]

Despite her doctrinal beliefs, however, the boldest features of Truth's rhetorical claims concerning the superiority of women to men were her actions in real life. Beginning on June 1, 1843, she felt called by God to "leave the city" of New York and walk about as an itinerant preacher in

Massachusetts, which she did, off and on, for nearly the next decade (99). It was her personal move to gain independence from the oppressive masters of her past, including her former owners and Matthias, that marked Truth's active declaration. Her bold exploits as an independent woman provide one of the most significant enactments of the woman's rights movement during the antebellum years. The incidents surrounding Truth's experience with Matthias and his group function in her narrative as did Frederick Douglass's description of his declaration of in/dependence from Covey. They are both moments of full entrance into the American metanoia.

Truth's goal of demonstrating her superiority to men was the focus of her most famous public moment, the brief "Ar'n't I a Woman?" speech of 1851, delivered extemporaneously to the Woman's Rights Convention in Akron, Ohio. As Yellin describes the event, "The chair had to plead for silence as Sojourner Truth stood, tall and black, to deliver a speech that redefined womanhood. Her subject was power: the lack of power that men ascribe to womankind and the presence of her own power and the power of all women." Campbell, too, characterizes the same goal of rhetorical forms of enactment: "power."[42]

The fragments of the speech that remain suggest the power of enactment as Truth expertly developed it here and throughout her career.[43] Its down-home and folksy style, exemplified by its title, illustrates Truth's exploitation of a highly "democratic idiom."[44] Early in the speech, she asserts that enactment was her emblem: "I am a woman's rights" (xxxiii). That statement conflates her existence with the abstract ideal of the woman's movement and echoes the numerous proclamations of Jesus, all beginning with the divine "I am," in the book of John. Douglass used a similar rhetorical strategy, as did Emerson. Throughout the speech, she refers to her body. "I have as much muscle as any man," she said, holding up her arm. "I can carry as much as any man, and can eat as much too. . . . I am as strong as any man that is now."

As Campbell points out, the speech as a whole was "refutative," responding to various claims men have made against women: intellectual inferiority, lack of legal recognition, and the assertion that women's limited sphere was ordained by God.[45] Truth denies and pointedly refutes such claims. Among the many biblical references she marshals as support was one of the most cutting lines of reasoning in the history of women's rhetoric: "And how came Jesus into the world? Through God who created him and woman who bore him. Man, where is your part?" In linking womanhood and motherhood with salvation, Truth foregrounds a prominent feature of the feminizing tendency of the nation during the 1850s, what Elizabeth Ammons has termed "Stowe's Dream of the Mother-Savior."[46] More important, however, is the subordination of the male gender to the agencies of God and woman. The exclusion of man from the culminating soteriological process of God for the history of the world is a tour de force and one of the great achievements of women's rhetoric. It was perhaps even more significant in the antebellum years because of the race of its speaker.

The striking and wonderfully unpretentious manner and presence of Truth is hard to capture from the vantage point of contemporary culture, but it was a key element in the success of her rhetorical project to advance the cause of women. One of the most convincing (and bizarre) testimonies of the power of enactment as it resided in the physical presence of Truth during these years, for example, was the little-known event surrounding a series of meetings she held in Koskiusco County, Indiana, in 1858. At the close of the third meeting, a "Dr. T. W. Strain, the mouthpiece of the slave Democracy . . . stated that a doubt existed in the minds of many persons present respecting the sex of the speaker, and . . . that a majority of them believed the speaker to be a man" (138). In light of that accusation, the doctor "demanded that Sojourner submit her breast to the inspection of some of the ladies present." Confusion and a great uproar followed that request, but when asked why such a submission should be made, he replied, "Your voice is not the voice of a woman, it is the voice of a man."

Truth, despite the uproar, was nonplussed. In what was certainly one of the oddest public moments of nineteenth-century America, after assuring listeners that her breasts had suckled numerous white children, "she quietly asked them, as she disrobed her bosom, if they, too, wished to suck!" Truth, apparently, had succeeded so fully in demonstrating her equality with the masculine through her unquestioned power of enactment that she was required to enact her womanhood by "[exposing] her naked breast to the audience" (139), which she promptly did. Her act was fraught with the spirit of independence from social norms or fears of public ridicule and further evidence that she had helped alter permanently antebellum America's inscribed idea of what a woman should do or how a woman should be defined.

The profound influence of such women has been greatly underplayed and for many years was strangely and unjustly ignored, even though they were some of the most prominent and influential figures of their time. Equally underplayed, however, may be the differences in emphasis that marked women's rhetoric. In general, despite such differences, their religious fervor and Endicottean rhetoric, marking them as revivalists of the American myth and champions of the tenets of the Declaration and its inherent power of enactment, remain important registers of the spirit of the age. As revivalists, each of the women under discussion developed and deployed the rhetorical strategy that Kenneth Burke has termed "identification," a strategy that should lead to a culmination of consensus called "consubstantiation." As James R. Andrews has explained,

> For Burke, rhetoric is a means of using language to overcome the divisions that exist between people. He sees "the use of language as a symbolic means of inducing cooperation in beings that by nature respond to symbols." *Identification* . . . is promoted when language is used to reduce divisiveness and to bring the speaker and listener closer together in their conceptions and perceptions of the world around them, with the ultimate achievement being a psychological fusion that Burke calls *consubstantiality*.[47]

The women that have been discussed were not content that the public would only know intellectually their concerns regarding ensuring human rights. In the role of prophetesses of God, they powerfully commanded Christian auditors to rise up, go forth, and enact the healing and redemption for which they were called. The women all shared a desire to produce a rhetoric that might initiate "psychological fusion" among the American people. They all worked to employ rhetoric as "a means of using language to overcome the divisions that exist between people."[48] That burden informed their writing and public acts and constitutes a firm belief in the regnant myths of America and a zealous affirmation of the creed inherent in the Declaration. Moreover, the burden consistently involves a symbiosis of the religious and civil realms and combines and equates beliefs in the Bible and the Declaration. The combination being advocated, and the subsequent commitment to it, issues in the American metanoia.

That cultural effort culminated in the rhetorical documents produced by two individuals associated with each other for other, possibly mythologized, reasons: Harriet Beecher Stowe and Abraham Lincoln. Stowe was the author of *Uncle Tom's Cabin*, the chief articulation of the American metanoia. Her aim was nothing less than to achieve the consubstantiation of belief that might finally close the sanctification gap then plaguing antebellum American life. And Lincoln, although clearly influenced and shaped by any number of other sources, willingly and genuinely shared the burden of Stowe and the earlier women commentators as he advanced his visionary agenda. It was a somewhat different version of the American metanoia but still one by which he hoped to save the Union.

4 Closing the Sanctification Gap

Doing the Word in *Uncle Tom's Cabin*

The two previous chapters of this book have described how African Americans drew upon and fostered essential aspects of the emerging mythos of antebellum America, particularly in their shared focus on the idealism of the Declaration and on the biblical directive to become doers of the Word. Moreover, the impulses to perform personal American declarations resulted in enactments carried out in largely gendered forms as men and women worked out salvation in perceptively different ways and with different emphases despite the obvious affinities in precept. Similarly, Harriet Beecher Stowe's *Uncle Tom's Cabin* (1852) illustrates two primary ways in which slaves might react to the slave system and appears to suggest that one should be favored over the other.

The first of these two paradigms is typified in Stowe's portrayal of George Harris and might be termed a "masculine solution" to the system. In George, Stowe depicts a fall into agnosticism and perhaps atheism that is the result of degrading treatment at the hands of an inhumane master. In spite of his desperate situation, Stowe was reluctant to depict George giving full vent to his rage. She never allows his anger or strong self-will to undercut her own version of his plight. Instead, Stowe tempers George's rage throughout the novel with the feminine impulses represented by numerous women characters, a leavening that results in his return to a Christian moral commitment.

The contrasting approach to the slave power would be the "feminine solution," a heightened state of grace illustrated by a variety of female characters. Ironically enough, however, it is probably best depicted among the slaves in the saintly Tom, the suffering servant. In most ways he is the opposite of George: passive, mild, gentle, simple, and rarely shaken in his faith. As some critics have suggested, such a contrast can be partially attributed to the racial difference separating the two men. Tom is fully African American, and George is apparently at least half white through his unidentified father. That racial discrepancy might lead to the conclusion that the two characters inhabit different worlds that can never intersect. They are so diametrically opposed, for example, that they never appear together during the course of the narrative, as if any contact might result in a terrific "explosion of immeasurable force."[1] Stowe seemingly favors the feminized example of Tom, as several critics have suggested.[2] Indeed, Jane Tompkins has even argued that the foregrounding of the feminine versus masculine tension constitutes the heart of *Uncle Tom's Cabin*. Tompkins maintains that the novel's "totalizing effect" and "political purpose" are designed "to bring in the day when the meek—which is to say, women—will inherit the earth."[3]

Yet such a complete privileging of the feminine was unequivocally not Stowe's central political purpose, and such a view greatly reduces and simplifies her aims. As with the African American men and women discussed in the earlier chapters, it would be just as easy to focus on their mythic similarities as it would be to magnify their differences. To foreground gender differences is to miss the more important rhetorical purpose of either the African American community or of Stowe as documented in *Uncle Tom's Cabin*. All of these agents desired to fashion a consensus concerning the American idea.

In constructing a fiction to further her sensational designs upon society, Stowe was more a revivalist of the American civil religion than of the feminine. In particular, she asserted in *Uncle Tom's Cabin* that women and men alike are not merely called to make the right political statements but are urged to perform exploits. Again, Tompkins has famously contended that the "real message of the book is emphatically not quietist . . . it instructs [women] to go act—if necessary covertly, but to act."[4] Yet the novel also instructs men "to go act" as well. The initiatives Stowe envisioned involve both sexes jointly in a symbiosis of effort. She understood and illustrated the very different contributions that would be necessary from both sexes if the Union were to perpetuate itself.

On still another level, *Uncle Tom's Cabin* complicates categories of gender by suggesting the possible benefits of men becoming more like women and vice versa, a tendency exemplified in the form of the titular character. Thus, the novel transcends issues of gender by subordinating them to Stowe's central political and rhetorical purpose: the building of a cultural consensus with regard to America's hegemonic myth of concern, a sublime goal to be fully embraced by male and female alike. She desired to foster a social paradigm by which the Union might perpetuate itself, one that featured the Declaration and its concomitant call to the practical action of doing the Word and did not rule out subversive disobedience or even physical violence. In so doing, Stowe worked to revive the founding vision as she conceived it.

Moreover, the call to action was predicated largely upon religious innovations—a call to Christian holiness and a closing of the sanctification gap—that also subordinated gender to other categories. Stowe agreed with the prevailing religious sentiments of her era and then wrote her masterpiece. Hers was a firm belief that social wrongs, including but not limited to chattel slavery, would "disappear when enough people had been converted and rededicated to right conduct."[5] As Theodore R. Hovet has argued, Stowe clearly adhered to certain aspects of the doctrine of Christian holiness, defending them, for example, in two New York *Evangelist* reviews of books written by her friend Thomas Upham. In one, she asserted an awareness of and tacit consent to the concept of the Wesleyan second blessing: "Christians . . . appear to themselves and others to have experienced a kind of second regeneration, and the change in their own eyes and in that of others, is almost as great as the first conversion."[6] Stowe was sympathetic to the charismatic elements of various African American autobiographies and familiar with them, as a passage from *The Key to* "Uncle Tom's Cabin" (1853) demonstrates: "We are not surprised to find almost constantly, in the narrations of their religious histories, accounts of visions, of heavenly voices, of mysterious sympathies and transmissions of knowledge from heart to heart without the intervention of the senses, or what Quakers call being 'baptized into the spirit' of those who are distant."[7] One wonders, in reading that passage, whether Stowe was familiar with the writings of Maria Stewart and Jarena Lee and perhaps was alluding to them.

Elsewhere in the *Key*, Stowe describes the Methodist camp-meeting moment of metanoia as experienced by a slave named Josiah Henson, who became a primary model for Tom: "Henson grew up in a state of heathenism, without any religious instruction, till, in a camp-meeting, he first heard of Jesus Christ, and was electrified by the great and thrilling news that He had tasted death for every man, the bond as well as the free. This story produced an immediate conversion, such as we read of in the Acts of the Apostles, where the Ethiopian eunuch, from one interview, hearing the story of the cross, at once believes and is baptized."[8]

Although Stowe's vision of the American mythos included Christian principles of sanctification directly linked to the traditions of holiness and contemporary Methodist revivalism, those explicitly Wesleyan principles and their impact on *Uncle Tom's Cabin* and other of her novels, particularly *The Minister's Wooing*, have received far less scholarly attention than the more commonly cited influence of traditional Edwardsean Calvinism.[9] What Carla Peterson has shown to be the burden of numerous antebellum African American women can be expanded to include Stowe. What constitutes that burden is the overpowering desire that all Americans, both male and female, become not only hearers but also doers of the Word.[10]

For Stowe, the call to entire sanctification transcended the issue of gender. God beckoned (and an American millennium required) both male and female, and Stowe's rendition of practical action and the power of enactment is as clearly exemplified in the novel by male characters, including George Harris, Tom, Simeon Halliday, and Phineas Fletcher, as by the female characters, especially Rachel Halliday and Little Eva, frequently analyzed by feminist critics. Significantly, male and female characters also draw upon the liberatory rhetoric of the Declaration in their speech and actions.

Rather than simply viewing George and Tom as symbols of gender differences, they can be identified as preeminent poles of a cultural dialectic pitting concern against freedom. In this view, Tom exemplifies concern and orthodoxy, and George symbolizes freedom and progressivism. Not only can George and Tom (or at least that which each embodies as an archetype) intersect but they should also, and must, intersect with and activate one another symbiotically. Such an analysis would feature their similarities more than differences. Both Tom and George enter into the typical American act of the individual declaration of in/dependence and share the central experience: the American metanoia. Tom's concern-centered approach must be counterbalanced with the more violent call to arms and practical action of George's freedom-centered approach.

Rather than excluding the possibility of Tom and George intermingling, Stowe argues for the value of them tempering and shaping one another. Thus, by associating Tom with a feminized, mythic concern and George with a masculinized, mythic freedom, she insists that concern needs freedom, freedom needs concern, and the Union and the American idea need them both. As in the American metanoia, both conservatism and radicalism are central, a combination Eric Sundquist has termed the "radical conservatism" of the novel.[11]

Stowe embraced and incorporated into her masterpiece a balanced view of America's myth of concern that attempted to conjoin the two aspects being posited, for example, by Frederick Douglass and Sojourner Truth during the same period (1851–55) in their autobiographical works. In a sense, *Uncle Tom's Cabin* ably attempts to bring together harmonically the revolutionary enactment of African American males and the faith enactment of African American females. Stowe, Truth, Douglass, and numerous others shared a desire to build a consensus to save the Union, and that common religious mission was the objective of their work as revivalists: "to sustain the reality of the culture myths" and "to reinterpret them to meet the needs of social change."[12] For these revivalists in the decades before the Civil War, as Timothy L. Smith has observed, "Wesleyan Christianity proved better suited than any other system of religious thought to incorporate and reinforce the social and moral aspirations of a nation."[13]

~

Uncle Tom's Cabin introduces the dilemma of George Harris almost immediately. The third chapter depicts him conversing with his wife Eliza, and an emotional discussion begins when he states, "I wish I'd never been born."[14] Throughout the chapter Stowe provides reasons for George's justification in revolting against his master and running away, a rhetorical strategy directly comparable to the catalog of grievances listed in the original Declaration. George tells Eliza that their marriage is meaningless in the eyes of the law and that his master wants him to take another bride. He describes how his master forced him to tie a heavy stone to his beloved dog Carlo and toss it into a pond to die. "My life is as bitter as wormwood," he says, invoking the biblical term for cursedness. Eliza, the first person in the novel to challenge his reasoning, argues that he must endure and serve his master. At that, George storms out, "My master? and who made him my master?" (13). He describes how he considers himself a better man than his master, and the facts suggest that he is correct in that judgment. George had done admirable work in a factory and invented a device for hemp-cleaning. The master, apparently jealous of his success, had then yanked him from that secure position and made him return to the fields. Stowe's portrayal of the injustices George suffered convinces readers that he is unable to endure his enslavement, that superficial protests such as Eliza's are inadequate, and that George is therefore justified in running off.

George's acts of rebellion culminate most obviously in his escape, during the course of which he voices a number of exemplary arguments against slavery in antebellum American culture, including arguments applying republican ideals. As he is disguised and making his way north, George encounters his former supervisor from the factory, Mr. Wilson. Able to pass as a white, George draws Wilson aside and lets him in on his secret, but Wilson, shocked, urges George to return to his master at once. His arguments draw heavily upon the Scriptures and typify the standard rhetoric used by Christian apologists to support slavery during the antebellum period. "Don't quote Bible at me" (95) is George's response to Wilson's facile use of scripture. Even after that bitter outburst Wilson continues to exhort George to go back. He again quotes the Bible, showing the vast cultural authority accorded to it by pro-slavery advocates: "Let everyone abide in the condition in which he is called" (a reference to I Corinthians 7:20). George rejects Wilson's argument by placing him in an equal situation: "I wonder, Mr. Wilson, if the Indians should come and take you a prisoner away from your wife and children, and want to keep you all your life hoeing corn, if you'd think it your duty to abide in the condition in which you were called" (95).

Wilson's counter-arguments throughout this dialogue rehearse the rhetoric of those who blindly acquiesce in the status quo. Shocked and dismayed by his encounter with a typological embodiment of the American myth of freedom, he appeals to the law of the land: "Why, George, this state of mind is awful; it's getting really desperate, George. I'm concerned. Going to break the laws of your country!" (95). Debunking Wilson's arguments, George is cooly rational: "My country again! Mr. Wilson, *you* have a country, but what country have *I*, or any one like me, born of slave mothers? What laws are there for us? We don't make them,—we don't consent to them,—we have nothing to do with them; all they do for us is crush us, and keep us down. Haven't I heard your Fourth of July speeches? Don't you tell us all, once a year, that governments derive their just power from the consent of the governed?" (96). It is an implicit reference to the Declaration of Independence. One of George's primary moves is to distance himself from American society through his use of the second person: "You have a country, but what country have I?"

At almost the same time, Frederick Douglass often used the second-person device to distance himself from hypocritical homage to American idealism, perhaps most memorably in a speech entitled "What to a Slave Is the Fourth of July?" (1852): "This Fourth of July is yours, not mine. You may rejoice, I must mourn . . . your celebration is a sham; your boasted liberty, an unholy license; your denunciation of tyrants, brass fronted impudence."[15] The rhetoric of the political hegemony, represented by George as "your Fourth of July speeches," is empty and deceptive and constitutes a blasphemy of the original principle celebrated on that sacred holiday.

Well before the 1850s, George and Douglass emphasize, community celebrations of Independence Day had become "religious observance[s]" featuring public readings of the Declaration as "a religious text, and the oration in lieu of the sermon."[16] By lamenting in jeremiadic form the lost ideals of the Declaration, the true meaning of the Fourth, and the political notion of popular sovereignty—as the Declaration puts it, "governments derive their just power from the consent of the governed"—George advances a view of America's rapidly evolving myth that is rooted deeply in the founding vision, including the Constitution and the Declaration. His rebuke also indicates that by the 1850s the Declaration had become a central point of contention among commentators and writers desirous not only of abolishing slavery but also of elevating it as a central symbol of the national myth.

George also relates several critical personal experiences that powerfully seal his declaration of in/dependence from Wilson. The most critical concerns the story of his older sister, "a pious, good girl" and a "member of the Baptist church." George sadly describes how she was unable to live a godly life because of the wickedness of her master and how he would often hear her being attacked: "Sir, I have stood at the door and heard her whipped, when it seemed as if every blow cut into my naked heart, and I couldn't do anything to help her; and she was whipped, sir, for wanting to live a decent Christian life" (96–97). The indelible mark of that memory evokes a poignant story told by Frederick Douglass about his Aunt Hester at the beginning of his 1845 *Narrative,* again suggesting the parallel between "real" and fictive rhetors at the time Stowe was writing.[17]

Finally, George returns to the republican ideals in what serves as a peroration of his rhetorical appeal: "I'll fight for my liberty to the last breath I breathe. You say your fathers did it; if it was right for them, it is right for me!"[18] Such ideals are worth dying for, claims George, bringing to mind the words of the fiery patriot Patrick Henry: "I'm a *freeman!* . . . *I'm free!* . . . All men are free and equal *in the grave,* if it comes to that" (98, emphasis in the original). Thus, George (and Stowe) explicitly connects his personal rebellion against slaveholding America with the struggle of the revolutionary founders of the nation: "In his rhetorical crusade against slavery . . . or even in his millenarian uprising against it . . . the slave rebel, one could say, became most American."[19] Consequently, George convinces Wilson that he is justified in his revolutionary act, and as the two men part Wilson gives George money as a token of support.

The encounter illustrates Stowe's belief that white Americans like Wilson would ultimately be convinced by the power of enactment as typified by George's personal declaration. The justification has been made for his escape, as in the original Declaration, and thus George, like the Founders, has not only announced but also begun to act out his independence.

After the encounter with Wilson, George begins to change because of the practical actions of others. The critical influence is the Quaker household of Simeon and Rachel Halliday, who reunite George with his wife and son. The peaceful godliness of the Hallidays is symbolized in the opening passage of the chapter by the rocking-chair in the shiny and inviting kitchen: It is a "real comfortable, persuasive old chair," and in it sits "our old friend Eliza," George's wife (116). Throughout the episode, Simeon not only quotes from Psalm 73 and encourages George to seek God but also testifies to his own convictions through practical action. Meanwhile, Rachel reigns as archetypal "mother-savior" of the perfect Christian household, peppering her gentle speech with the stylistics of the King James Version: "Thee knows thee can stay here. . . . Where's thy baby, Ruth? . . . Mary, thee'd better fill the kettle, hadn't thee?" (117–18).[20]

Rachel, like Jesus, is able to "put a spirit into the food and drink she offered" (122). She "enacts the redeemed form of the Last Supper," and the communal spirit found in her kitchen "exemplifies the way people will work in the ideal society."[21] George, for the first time in his life, "sat down on equal terms at [a] white man's table."[22] In contrast to Wilson, Simeon's and Rachel's dependence on the Scriptures brings about real behavior and results in the true power of enactment. Although George continues to question the religion of the Hallidays—"Is God on their side?" (165)—his "doubts" and "despair" "melted away before the light of a living Gospel, breathed in living faces" (122). He responds to the living ministry of these "living faces," whose power of enactment finally compels him to concede, "I'll try to feel like a Christian. . . . and read my Bible, and learn to be a good man" (161).

George is clearly being refined by Christian agents of the American myth of concern very similar in spirit to Tom, characters whose manifestation of the practical action inherent in Christian love is tangible and real, and who, in Longfellow's words, "act in the living present, / Heart within, and God overhead." As Stowe says of Simeon, arguments increase dramatically in rhetorical power when they are wedded to practical action: "If these words had been spoken by some easy, self-indulgent exhorter, from whose mouth they might have come merely as pious and rhetorical flourish . . . perhaps they might not have had much effect; but coming from one who daily and calmly risked fine and imprisonment for the cause of God and man, they had *a weight that could not but be felt,* and both the poor, desolate fugitives found calmness and strength breathing into them from it" (166, emphasis added).

When the time comes for George to continue his journey, Simeon arranges for his friend Phineas Fletcher to escort him and his family to Canada: "Phineas Fletcher will carry thee onward to the next stand" (123). As Phineas claims, invoking a Wesleyan emphasis, "What we do, we are conscience bound to do; we can do no other way" (165). Phineas, formerly a "hearty, two-fisted backwoodsman" (164), has undergone a radical conversion experience and thus is the perfect guide for George's continuing journey. The climax of the escape comes when the slave traders Tom Loker and Marks trap the party, led by Phineas, on top of a ridge. George, ordered to surrender, "stood out in fair sight, on the top of the rock, as he made his declaration of independence; the glow of dawn gave as a flash to his swarthy cheek. . . . and, as appealing from man to the justice of God, he raised his hand to heaven as he spoke" (172). The melodramatic scene invoking the Declaration of 1776 is transformed to mythic significance by being steeped in images of God and the "glow of dawn" and by George's culminating assertion: "We don't own your laws; we don't own your country; we stand here as free, under God's sky, as you are" (170, 172). As in George's dialogue with Wilson, and as Frederick Douglass wrote, the use of the second person emphasizes the distance and tension between the poles of we and you.

The apparent glory of the moment is deflated, however, as Marks cocks his pistol and smirks, "Ye get jist as much for him dead as alive in Kentucky" (172). Phineas, aware of Marks's intentions, sums up the rhetorical value of George's exalted declaration: "Thee'd better keep out of sight, with thy speechifying . . . they're mean scamps" (172). In the final analysis, such "speechifying" and public enactment by a black man proves to be not only ineffective but also dangerous and perhaps even fatal for George. Statements only become rhetorically persuasive insofar as they are joined by practical action. Thus, when the slave traders advance upon the trapped party it is Phineas who intercedes: "'Friend,' said Phineas, suddenly stepping to the front, and meeting him with a push from his long arms, 'thee isn't wanted here'" (173). Loker is thrown down the chasm, severely injured but not lost, and again the power of enactment of Christian charity is played out through the healing care of Quaker women. If Loker stands for the decadent extremes of slaveholding culture, then his salvation is assured through the agency of both male and female sensibilities steeped in enactment. He symbolizes a fallen, backslidden society yet discovers redemption through the violent practical actions of men such as Phineas, whose physical resistance initiates the redemptive process that leads to the agency of women and finally results in Loker's conversion.

George does fire a shot at Loker and the bullet "entered [Loker's] side" (173), but the scene demonstrates Stowe's ambivalence about the ability of any black man to enact fully the Declaration of Independence. George, when he tries to make his stand, is shot at and almost killed. Even when Loker approaches him, George is unable to finish him off and relies instead on the intervention of Phineas. Such ambivalence exemplifies Stowe's handling of race throughout *Uncle Tom's Cabin*. Later in the novel, the endorsement of George's revolutionary actions is further deflated when Stowe insists that he not only be reconciled to God but also that he relocate himself and his family to Africa. Her call to action, typified in George, is undercut and qualified and reflects the deep racial biases of which Stowe and most of her society were often guilty. The hesitation regarding race indicates the limits the era placed on the ability of Stowe and many other whites to envision a black person as an enacter of the Declaration of Independence. To put it another way, she simultaneously could and could not envision such a thing.

The fact that George's mother was a black slave and his father a white master explained for antebellum readers his powerful intellect and passionate desire for freedom. That his father was white also gives credence to George's early rejection of Christianity, because such an act conflicted with then-popular views of full-blooded African Americans as naturally passive and docile Christians. That view was most popularly espoused by the Ohioan Alexander Kinmont and later described as the "Romantic Racialism of the North."[23] Stowe knew Kinmont's writings and possibly attended his lectures when she lived in Cincinnati in 1837 and 1838.[24] More important, she clearly accepted the major premises of Kinmont's theories of race, the most influential of which was the concept that races could be identified according to traits and characteristics. Sections of *The Key to "Uncle Tom's Cabin"* illustrate her concept of the "negro" personality, which she compared to the "Oriental" race. Both contrast sharply with the "Anglo-Saxon race—cool, logical, and practical."[25] Stowe's racial theories thus informed the construction of her novel. For example, the obvious contrast between the revolutionary mulattoes (George, Eliza, and Cassy) and the docile, full-blooded Africans (Tom, Chloe, and Sam) has frequently been the topic of some of the most heated and even belligerent criticisms of *Uncle Tom's Cabin*.[26]

Largely as a result of the confusion surrounding George's racial identity, his rhetorical position is problematic. As one critic suggests, his "speechifying" signals the inherent contradictions of a character who "simultaneously ridicules American ideals and calls for their realization."[27] Stowe carried out the same rhetorical strategy that is at the heart of many American jeremiads, both past and present. In *Uncle Tom's Cabin* she sought to join social criticism to spiritual renewal, which made the novel a classic expression of the jeremiad mode. The major burden of jeremiadic speech is to engender repentance among listeners and exhort them toward fulfillment of their destinies as dictated by the American civil religion. One need only read the novel's "Concluding Remarks" to understand the earnestness of Stowe's Old Testament-like appeal. As Jane Tompkins has put it, *Uncle Tom's Cabin* "provides the most obvious and compelling instance of the jeremiad since the Great Awakening."[28]

Yet Stowe, Douglass, and other transcendentally inclined thinkers did not ridicule America's ideals any more than Cotton Mather or Jonathan Edwards ridiculed the biblical ideals to which they appealed. Passages from various miscellaneous writings demonstrate Stowe's enlistment of, and high regard for, republican ideals, particularly the moral philosophy of the Declaration. In other writings she testified to her uncompromised allegiance to the Declaration. In *Men of Our Times* (1868), she asserted that "the American government is the only permanent republic which ever based itself upon the principles laid down by Jesus Christ. . . . The Declaration of American Independence chrystalized a religious teaching within a political act." And in *Dred* she argued that the ideals of the Declaration are merely articulations of God's divine word as elaborated in the Scriptures. These pregnant ideals, according to Stowe, instigated the morally acceptable revolutionary acts of Denmark Vesey.[29]

For Stowe, the Declaration was a political expression of divine origin and could thus be the ultimate ground for American consensus. Following this view, Jeffersonian egalitarianism was regularly employed as an important sub-argument to support Stowe's central political and rhetorical agenda: the building of a cultural consensus. Stowe's work as revivalist of the founding vision as she conceived it depended on the viability of the founding ideals to bring about a consubstantiation by which the Union would be saved.

Thus, rather than attacking the ideals, antebellum commentators ridiculed the shoddy, hypocritical attempts of Americans to enact fully, or to "do," the pious and patriotic works suggested by those ideals. They also frequently parodied the rhetoric of those unwilling to embody their proclaimed ideals and thus become doers of the Word. George Harris, for example, does not so much ridicule the ideals of the American myth of concern as much as he calls attention to the useless, seemingly endless rhetorical enunciations of those principles in the face of their vast un-fulfillment in everyday social life—the sanctification gap.

Elsewhere in the novel Stowe builds on that rhetorical distinction. As evidence that she is occasionally willing to ridicule the rhetorical invocation and subsequent lack of fulfillment of American ideals, she creates the flamboyant slave Sam, whose shenanigans aid greatly in al-lowing Eliza to escape the slave trader Haley early in the narrative. Sam is the most accomplished slave trickster in the first part of the book until Cassy makes her appearance near the novel's end. Rhetorically, Stowe's inclusion of Sam underlines what had become by the 1850s a common social spectacle: parodies and burlesques of republican and egalitarian rhetoric. It was a mode of speaking practiced by many of the nineteenth century's most famous comedic personalities, including John Phoenix, Artemus Ward, Petroleum V. Nasby, Bret Harte, Lucretia P. Hale, Bill Nye, and, later, Mark Twain. In such parodies, solemn nationalistic pride be-came "a string of stereotyped, meaningless phrases and misplaced plati-tudes."[30] Bill Nye, for example, asked:

> But, fellow-citizens, how can we best preserve the blessing of freedom and fork it over unimpaired to our children? How can we enhance the blood-bought right, which is inherent in every human being, of the people, for the people, and by the people, where the tyrant foot hath never trod nor bigot forged a chain, for to look back from our country's glorious natal day or forward to a glorious, a happy and a prosperous future with regard to purity of the ballot and free speech. I say for one we cannot do otherwise.[31]

Considering such remarks, it is instructive to notice what seems to be a relatively insignificant detail of *Uncle Tom's Cabin:*

> one of Sam's especial delights had been to ride in attendance on his master to all kinds of political gatherings, where . . . he would sit watch-ing the orators, with the greatest apparent gusto, and then . . . he would edify and delight [other slaves] with the most ludicrous burlesques and imitations. . . . it not infrequently happened that [the slaves listening] were fringed pretty deeply with those of a fairer complexion, who lis-tened, laughing and winking, to Sam's great self-congratulation. In fact, Sam considered oratory as his vocation, and never let slip an opportuni-ty of magnifying his office.[32]

Thus Sam's function is to highlight and mock the inherent inconsis-tencies and hypocrisies of much public rhetoric. The ring of listeners at his feet during his burlesques includes slaves as well as whites. Like read-ers, they laugh and wink at Sam's justifiable ridicule of the earnest ora-tors of the antebellum south. Stowe undercuts Sam's mockery of Amer-

ican ideals, however. Unlike George, he is a full-blooded African slave—
"three shades blacker than any other son of ebony on the place" (37)—
and his attack on lofty nationalistic jingoism is restrained and jovial compared with George's more severe examinations. His acts of revolution are
all meant to be humorous; for example, he places a "sharp little nut"
under the saddle of Haley's horse (39).

The most consequential debate in the novel regarding the Declaration is the lengthy exchange between Augustine St. Clare and his twin
brother Alfred. That exchange is preceded by one of the book's more
horrifying episodes, the violent beating of the slave Dodo by Henrique,
Alfred's spoiled, twelve-year-old son. Henrique, the logical result of slave-
holding philosophy and parenting, provides a startling contrast to Little
Eva, who is his cousin and Augustine's daughter. The messianic Little
Eva's deathbed appeal, one of the century's most enduring literary moments, is saturated with pathos and selfless Christian love. In all that she
says and does, lily-white Eva epitomizes the Christian commission to
become a doer of the Word.

Significantly, the slave who is beaten before the argument with Henrique is given the name Dodo, a doubling of the verb in question, and the
chapter contains numerous other puns that rely on an understanding of
Stowe's emphasis on doing. When Eva asks him to love the slave whom
he has savagely and openly whipped, Henrique replies, *"Love* Dodo?"
(237, emphasis in the original), suggesting that loving equals doing and
that true virtue means loving to do. Henrique is shocked by Eva's prop-
osition that he take seriously the biblical commands to love everyone.
He counters by stating the obvious: "O, the Bible! To be sure, it says a
great many such things; but, then, nobody ever thinks of doing them,—
you know, Eva, nobody does" (237). The punning reaches its height when
Eva first confronts Henrique about his cruel actions.

> "How could you be so cruel and wicked to poor Dodo?"
> "Cruel,—wicked!" said the boy, with unaffected surprise. "What do
> you mean, dear Eva?"
> "I don't want you to call me dear Eva, when you do so," said Eva.
> "Dear Cousin, you don't know Dodo." (231)

Not only does the doubling of "to do" sound amusing, but the very act
of violence against "poor Dodo" also suggests the deeply ironic humor
of a culture doing violence, literally, to the ideal of doing. Henrique, the
representative child of a fallen aristocratic culture, remains blind to his
hypocritical acts of violence to Dodo as well as Christian and republican
idealism.

The brothers witness the scene, and the debate begins with August-ine chiding, "I suppose that's what we may call republican education, Alfred?" Drily, he suggests Henrique's failure to live up to the "first verse of a republican's catechism, 'All men are born free and equal.'" "Poh! . . . one of Tom Jefferson's pieces of French sentiment and humbug," Alfred retorts. "It's perfectly ridiculous . . . I think half this republican talk sheer humbug. It is the educated, the intelligent, the wealthy, the refined, who ought to have equal rights and not the canaille" (233). Later, Albert pro-vokes Augustine by asking, "Why didn't you ever take to the stump;—you'd make a famous stump orator! Well, I hope I shall be dead before this millennium of your greasy masses comes on" (234).

That the twins act as two sides of the same coin is also apparent in George's character. His simultaneous idealism and cynicism demonstrate Stowe's enlistment of, and high regard for, republican ideals, particular-ly the moral philosophy of the Declaration. They also show her sense of strong disapproval for those such as Augustine St. Clare who are never able to take a stand. Ironically, it is Alfred who brings their lengthy ex-change to a close when he says, "Well, there's no use in talking, Augus-tine. . . . What do you say to a game of backgammon?" (235). Discredit-ing both Augustine and Alfred St. Clare, who merely "talk the talk," Stowe wished to foster a social paradigm that featured the right use of rhetoric. It would be dependent on an action-oriented gospel and Decla-ration and a call to practical action and doing the Word.

Given its emphasis throughout the narrative, it is important to ex-amine the motif of performing virtuous acts, a central organizing feature of *Uncle Tom's Cabin.* Maria Stewart, Jarena Lee, Sojourner Truth, and numerous others also attempted to become doers of the Word in accor-dance with that most action-oriented section of the New Testament, the Book of James, and encouraged others to do likewise. Stowe also placed a great deal of emphasis on the minute acts of daily doing, by which, through the persevering faith of one such as Tom, the ultimate act of martyrdom might become thinkable.

"Faith without works is dead" (James 2:26), one of the most common-ly quoted scriptures, is thoroughly tested and finally proven true through-out *Uncle Tom's Cabin.* Attention to the book's language suggests that an insistent attention to doing was one of Stowe's major artistic impera-tives. It is an imperative that comports with some of Jesus's most mem-orable words in the Sermon on the Mount: "Everyone who hears these words of Mine, and *does* them, may be compared to a wise man" (Mat-thew 7:24; emphasis added).

Throughout the narrative, Stowe makes clear that, as Alfred puts it, "there's no use in talking" (235). The character most useful in illustrating this motif is Augustine St. Clare, who remains good in "talk" but obviously deficient in "walk." Again and again, that weakness is apparent. When discussing the plight of Prue, for example, Ophelia (who embodies Yankee initiative) asks him, "an't you going to *do* anything about it?" (191, emphasis in the original). Ophelia often proclaims immediate action in the present tense, telling Augustine several times that "now is the only time there ever is to do a thing in" or "Now is all the time I have anything to do with" (268, 272). She frequently confronts St. Clare in a similar fashion: "And what are you going to do?" (268). In a satirical aside, the narrator notes that "St. Clare, like most men of his class of mind, cordially hated the present tense of action" (268). During the belabored argument with his twin brother, Albert directly challenges that lack of initiative: "I tell you, Augustine, if I thought as you do, I should do something" (235). "One man can do nothing, against the whole action of the community" (235), Augustine replies evasively. Of course, that sad hypocrisy is the focus of the episode and exactly what Stowe seeks to condemn. Her focus is on Augustine's lack of doing in his one genuine discussion with Eva about her own innocent faith:

> "What is being a Christian, Eva?"
> "Loving Christ most of all," said Eva.
> "Do you, Eva?"
> "Certainly I do." (253)

Although Augustine frames the question with his concept of "being," Eva quickly turns the emphasis onto doing, in this case on loving—what John Wesley termed the "perfect love" that results in virtuous Christian behavior. Being a Christian becomes emphatically what "I do." Significantly, the episode concludes with Eva growing "fervent, radiant with joy," something Augustine "had seen before in his mother" (253) and an indication of the presence of the second blessing of holiness.

Similarly, Eva's deathbed appeal is saturated with pathos, selfless Christian love, and the exhortation to do the Word and be Christ-like: "I want to speak to you about your souls. . . . You are thinking only about this world. . . . there is a beautiful world, where Jesus is. . . . But, if you want to go there, you must not live careless, thoughtless lives. . . . You must be Christians. . . . If you want to be Christians, Jesus will help you" (251). The emphasis on being a Christian prefigures her dying words: "O! love,—joy,—peace" (257), which suggest Christian sanctification in that they are the first-listed "fruit of the spirit" (Galatians 5:22). The rest of the passage from Galatians is also worthy of quotation: "Now those who belong to Christ Jesus have crucified the flesh with its passions and desires. If we live by the Spirit, let us also walk by the Spirit" (24–25). Thus, in their scriptural context, Eva's last words point directly to a fullness of sanctification among believers. The fruit of the spirit are so called because they are the logical issue of true biblical Christianity.

Eva's deathbed motivations, which touch her auditors and result in the salvation of the seemingly reprobate Topsy, illustrate the same virtues that guide Uncle Tom's moral activities while contrasting sharply with George's pragmatic, self-serving ends. These virtues signal Stowe's version of Christian heroism, which she believed might save the Union. Tellingly, Tom's closest relationship is with Eva, and his moral gravity is most easily compared with hers. George Harris's masculine impulses toward dissent, freedom, and independence by any means including violence contrast sharply with Tom's more pacifistic and Christ-like motivations.

Uncle Tom is feminized, solemn, and gentle. He is also a "good, faithful creature. . . . a sort of patriarch in religious matters. . . . he was looked up to with great respect, as a sort of minister among them; and the simple, hearty, sincere style of his exhortations might have edified even better educated persons" (28, 26). Rather than taking matters into his own hands, Tom habitually abstains from violent behavior in the face of the most oppressive and unjust activities of the slave system. He appears to refrain from anger of any sort. For those reasons he has often been considered feminized, too-docile, and even emasculated, criticisms given classic expression by James Baldwin that still inform many commentators' views of the novel.[33]

Such a reading, however, tends to underestimate the rhetorical power and purpose of Tom's almost transcendent restraint and self-sacrifice. It also sadly neglects the social impact of the major precepts (especially enthusiasm and the quest for the supernatural) of early American Methodism, which by 1850 had attained a 34 percent share of church membership in the United States.[34] Accordingly, it is an error to characterize Tom and Eva as sentimentalized, cardboard characters. As Ann Douglas has argued, "Uncle Tom and Little Eva appear ridiculously exaggerated only to constricted secular minds. . . . only secular culture in a serious state of impoverishment could permanently equate Uncle Tom's faith with impotence."[35] And yet for many years Tom has been just so equated. In reality, Tom's enactment of his moral beliefs is more hard-hitting and effective than George's or virtually anyone else's in the narrative. They are shown to affect those who surround him, and it is evident that

Stowe made a special effort to underline their rhetorical power. Perhaps the most moving section of the book, where Stowe demonstrates Tom's power of enactment as well as the connection of his death to Eva's earlier demise and ultimately to the death of Jesus, is the chapter entitled "The Martyr," which reports the elevation of Tom beyond heroism to the ultimate status afforded by Christianity. As he is attacked and then killed for his faith, he relies upon the Scriptures: "Into Thy hands I commit my spirit!"[36]

These words echoing the dying Jesus constitute Tom's declaration of in/dependence from the domain of darkness and death. He copies the readiness to die and the lack of bitterness of Jesus and even tells the demonic Simon Legree that he is ready to die for him. "A higher voice was there," softly whispering to Tom, the narrator states (350), and there "stood by him ONE,—seen by him alone,—like unto the Son of God" (see Hebrews 7:3 and Daniel 3:25) to comfort him in his misery. Tom boldly preaches the need of repentance to Legree: "My troubles'll be over soon; but, if ye don't repent, yours won't *never* end!" (358). Others present recognize his courage, and the episode ends with Sambo and Quimbo so deeply moved that they must cry out, "O Tom! do tell us who is *Jesus*, anyhow?" (359). Sambo and Quimbo, perhaps the most degenerate blacks in the novel, are the ready accomplices of every whim of their reprobate master Legree and often participate in his drunken debaucheries. For Stowe, the enactment of true Christian sacrifice reverberates and affects others. Tom's enactment of Christian suffering, in a manner similar to Eva's, results in the salvation of Sambo and Quimbo and thus can also be viewed as a rhetorical act achieving clear consequences through the power of enactment.

The redeeming value of a true enactment of Christian suffering and service—exemplified in the selfless martyrdom of Tom and the simpler everyday acts of Rachel and Simeon Halliday, Phineas Fletcher, Eva, and others—contrasts sharply with George's actions. But these separate acts share a key affinity: They all are acts and add weight to words spoken. They all also constitute declarations of independence from the ossified, weightless platitudes of a decadent authority. All are demonstrations of how doing is much better than merely talking, and all constitute individual declarative acts that can be distinguished from the backslidden state of most citizens who have fallen away from the grace of the true American metanoia.

In foregrounding enactments that are powerful because they demonstrate "a weight that could not but be felt," Stowe illustrated a central emphasis of America's myth of concern as it had developed by midcentury. Rather than merely privileging the feminine, she saw male and female agents as equally important to the redemptive work promised by the American idea. Further, as seen in the depictions of George and Tom, Stowe insisted that elements of both radicalism (George) and conservatism (Tom) are needed to temper each other. As in Frye's model of myth, concern and freedom must be allowed free expression and full participation in America's public realm.

As a result, Stowe highlighted not so much the differences between gender, as many have asserted. Rather, in concert with the tradition of African American antebellum women's rhetoric that foregrounds doing the Word and the tradition of African American men forced to violent, physical resistance when all else failed, *Uncle Tom's Cabin* champions practical actions that would close the sanctification gap plaguing American society. Such actions would thereby heal a culture, founded on Christian perfection, that might ultimately save the Union. Stowe's focus on doing the Word, specifically on her repetitive use of forms of "to do," is affirmed in the novel's "Concluding Remarks": "Do you say that the people of the free states have nothing to do with [slavery], and can do nothing? . . . what can any individual do?" (384, 385). In response to such rhetorical questions, Stowe insists that northerners "have something more to do" and then lists numerous acts as examples: "They can see to it that *they feel right*. . . . you can *pray!* . . . [you should aid the] poor, shattered, broken remnants of families. . . . [who] seek a refuge among you; they come to seek education, knowledge, and Christianity" (385). In support of such remedial services, Stowe tells of a "body of men at the north . . . who have been doing this" (386).

Stowe also spends considerable effort recounting the stories of more than seven emancipated slaves, all of whom had found success in the North through persistent and virtuous doing of the Word. She describes, for example, "K—. Full black; dealer in real estate; worth thirty thousand dollars . . . member of the Baptist church; received a legacy from his master, which he has taken good care of, and increased" (387). These individuals are "but few . . . among multitudes which might be adduced, to show the self-denial, energy, patience, and honesty, which the slave has exhibited in a state of freedom" (387). Further, argues Stowe, such action should motivate free northerners to aid them further: "If this persecuted race . . . have done this much, how much more they might do, if the Christian church would act towards them in the spirit of the Lord!" (388). Echoing the Lord's Prayer, she reminds readers that God's will was "to be done on earth as it is in heaven." Finally, Stowe's peroration emphasizes her contention that the Union is "to be saved . . . by repentance" (388).

This salvific repentance includes both personal baptism into the Spirit as well as a civil religious act culminating in an American metanoia. Thus, the Word that is to be done includes both the Scriptures and the sacred words of the Republic written by the Founders. The benediction of the story, delivered at the end of chapter 44, "The Liberator," as a eulogy for the martyred Tom by the young George Shelby, is significant in this regard: "Think of your freedom, every time you see UNCLE TOM'S CABIN; and let it be a memorial to put you all in mind to follow in his steps, and be as honest and faithful and Christian as he was" (380). The purpose of that directive is to transform Tom's original shack into a kind of temple. That sacred memorial would be on the one hand a temple of the Holy Spirit. On the other hand it would also be a temple of the Republic, as suggested by a detail from the opening passage describing it: The "wall over the fireplace was adorned with some very brilliant scriptural prints, and a portrait of General Washington, drawn and colored in a manner which would certainly have astonished that hero, if ever he had happened to meet with its like" (18). Washington, as commander-in-chief of the Continental Army during the War for Independence, was the quintessential doer of the originating declaratory Word. Suggestively, the passage does not make clear the exact or full manner in which his visage had been altered. What is important, however, is the fact that Washington has been "colored" and made to represent more closely the African heritage of the home. Such an act stunningly re-shapes the nation's first president to fit more closely the image of the home's inhabitants. He has been co-opted as authorizing agent of an African American agenda of freedom and social assimilation.

The president's altarlike (and altered) presence is obviously nuanced, as at least one critic has pointed out.[37] Yet the problematic theoretical undertones suggested by the presence of a blackface General Washington are more the rule than the exception in a novel grappling with issues of race in antebellum America. It is clear that Washington has taken his rightful place in the homes of those seeking revolutionary independence. As such, his elevation alongside the Scriptures in Uncle Tom's home exemplifies the joining of the social and the sacred that is the classic mark of the jeremiad mode in American history. As George Shelby laments, Tom's home should remain "a memorial to put you all in mind to follow in his steps." The centerpiece of that home, as sketched by Stowe, was itself a memorial to the American civil religion built on the Bible, the Declaration, and doing the Word.

5 *Abraham Lincoln as America's Revivalist*

On February 11, 1861, Abraham Lincoln boarded a train from his home of many years, Springfield, Illinois, to what would become his new home, the White House in Washington, D.C. His inauguration as the sixteenth president would take place less than a month later, on March 4. By that time, however, the state of the Union had declined significantly since his election in November 1860. Seven states had declared their intention to leave the Union, beginning with South Carolina's radical ordinance of December 20 that dissolved its ties with the remainder of the states. Other Deep South states followed in rapid order, and all seized federal property and assets within their borders, including forts, arsenals, mints, post offices, customhouses, and port facilities.[1] Lincoln's election had been the straw that finally broke the back of hard-line southern Democratic leaders, boding ill and destruction for their cherished institution of slavery.

The speeches Lincoln delivered during his whistle-stop journey to Washington were generally short and seemingly simple and unimportant, although he did speak in many of the most important northern cities as well as in a number of smaller towns.[2] In addition, the trip was undertaken despite the apparent risk posed by assassination plots, rumors of which had already surfaced not only in the press but also in the form of numerous threats Lincoln received in his personal mail. He insisted on carrying out the tour, but in light of any possible danger decided that Mary Lincoln and their sons should not accompany him. The journey, "all Seward's idea," was an important rhetorical event designed to "expose [Lincoln] to the public and to rally Union morale."[3]

On most such occasions Lincoln avoided governmental policy state-ments.[4] He preferred to focus instead on the ideological foundations he would make even more prominent in his inaugural address. He also un-derstood the inherent power of the American myth and used it expertly to gain support for and devotion to his effort to solve the impending civ-il crisis. Far from being characterized by banality or evasion, these speech-es exemplify the mythic and ideological formulations Lincoln would use in fashioning a national consensus he hoped capable of saving the Union. As Garry Wills has argued, he shaped an American mythical ideology that still remains resonant for many Americans. Wills calls Lincoln a "great artist of America's Romantic period" who accomplished, virtually sin-glehandedly, the "recontracting of our society on the basis of the Decla-ration as our fundamental charter."[5] The speeches Lincoln made on his way to Washington demonstrate such artistry as well as the rhetorical skills and ideological force that would mark his presidency. Like his fa-vorite speaker Henry Clay, Lincoln aimed to ensure that all public mo-ments "were made for practical effect"; the support he intended to gar-ner would result in a consensus necessary to save the Union.[6]

In his speeches, Lincoln foregrounded personal responsibility and sought to foster the enactment of ideals, as did many female commenta-tors before him. Putting it in Sacvan Bercovitch's somewhat sinister (and notably Geertzian) terms, Lincoln invited listeners to embrace fully "the web of rhetoric, ritual, and assumption through which society coerces, persuades, and coheres."[7] It was not he alone, Lincoln insisted, who would save the Union: "Let me say that it is with you, the people, to advance the great cause of the Union and the constitution, and not with any one man. It rests with you alone. This fact is strongly impressed on my mind at present. In a community like this, whose appearance testifies to their intelligence, I am convinced that the cause of liberty and the Union can never be in danger."[8]

Here as elsewhere Lincoln sought to foster a consensus by appealing to the common ground that forms the basis of what he called "a com-munity like this." Although he never defined what he meant by that term, he flattered listeners by describing the community as one "whose appearance testifies to their intelligence." By so doing, he encouraged them to participate in their community. Lincoln's hope was not merely that the community would save the Union but that it would "advance the great cause of the Union," suggesting millennial progression. Final-ly, in an assertion similar to Harriet Beecher Stowe's and Sojourner Truth's claims of supernatural intervention, Lincoln said that his posi-tion was "strongly impressed on my mind at present," conveying additional urgency and suggesting prophetic inspiration from God. More generally, it also appealed to the growing Protestant emphasis on enthusiasm. Thus, Lincoln's strategy in this passage, prominent among the women commentators discussed in earlier chapters, resembles Kenneth Burke's notion of "identification." He was a master of what Burke described as "the use of language as a symbolic means of inducing cooperation in beings that by nature respond to symbols."[9]

All the way to Washington, Lincoln repeatedly applied the strategy of identification in an attempt to reduce division and bring listeners closer to him:

> In all the trying positions in which I shall be placed . . . my reliance will be placed upon you and the people of the United States—and I wish you to remember now and forever, that it is your business, and not mine. . . . It is your business to rise up and preserve the Union and liberty, for yourselves, and not for me.

> the working men are the basis of all governments. . . . I hold that while man exists, it is his duty to improve not only his own condition, but to assist in ameliorating mankind.

> I cannot but turn and look for the support without which it will be impossible for me to perform that great task. I turn, then, and look to the American people and to that God who has never forsaken them.[10]

The emphasis in each excerpt is on individual responsibility. Almost pleading, Lincoln argued that "it [the preservation of the Union] is your business, and not mine," that it was a "duty," and that he was turning "to the American people and to that God who has never forsaken them."

Lincoln's move to associate the American idea with the New Testament's Kingdom of God was a recurring strategy in his speeches, suggesting a consensual civil religion incorporating the traditional mythic qualities of America as redeemer nation. As Garry Wills explains, "A belief in our extraordinary birth, outside the processes of time, has led us to think of ourselves as a nation apart, with a special destiny, the hope of all those outside America's shores. This feeling, of course, antedated Lincoln. . . . But Lincoln's was the most profound statement of this belief in a special American fate. His vision of it was not pinned to a narrow Puritanism or imperialism, but simply to the declaration itself. Its power is mythic, not sectarian."[11]

Wills's analysis is charged with the religious and mythical language that marks Lincoln's speeches. In the passages just cited, for example, Lincoln identified aspects of "our extraordinary birth, outside the processes of time," a genesis much like that of Jesus and the church. Conceiving of America as "a nation apart, with a special destiny, the hope of all" seems much like the Christian concept of the function and role of the church in world events. As with the earlier antebellum rhetoric, a heavy dependence on biblical imagery and allusion as well as the conflation of church and state are frequent features of Lincoln's rhetoric. Furthermore, aspects of these mythic constructs "antedated Lincoln." Many others, including women, had roles in shaping the idea of the Declaration. Lincoln's rhetorical power derived in part from his success in incorporating a mythical view of the Declaration into his speeches that had achieved great resonance by the outbreak of the Civil War.

Wills is correct in claiming that Lincoln's major achievement was not merely to tap into the power already inherent in the myth but to elaborate upon it. He did so, like some had done before him, by tying the myth of America directly to the Declaration. His emphasis on America's "extraordinary birth," for instance, can be compared to the tendency of Fourth of July orators to "[fix] a specific, pivotal moment in the past from which to date a national existence. . . . [and which] proclaimed an essential unity and collective destiny born of an overwhelming, shared experience."[12] Lincoln's attachment to the Declaration has been discussed frequently. James M. McPherson, for example, has described his commonalities to a hedgehog. A hedgehog "relates everything to a single issue," and Lincoln's single issue during that time of crisis was the centrality of the Declaration.[13]

The image of the Declaration is recurrent in Lincoln's thought and speech. The Declaration is not only exalted but in some instances also endowed with scriptural authority. In the speech at Independence Hall in Philadelphia, for example, Lincoln reverently spoke as if at a church ceremony and as if the original patriots surrounded him and his audience as he venerated the "sacred" and "holy" Declaration:

> I am filled with deep emotion at finding myself standing here in the place where were collected together the wisdom, the patriotism, the devotion to principle, from which sprang the institutions under which we live. . . . I have never had a feeling politically that did not spring from the sentiments embodied in the Declaration of Independence (Great cheering). . . . I have often inquired of myself, what great principle or idea it was that kept this confederacy so long together. It was . . . *something* in that Declaration giving liberty, not alone to the people of this country, but hope to the world for all future times. (Great applause).[14]

Many of the mythic elements described previously are present in these lines. A sense of holy awe and sincere reverence pervades the opening. A trinity of wisdom, patriotism, and devotion is associated with the Declaration, all terms echoing traditional Christian faith ("patriotism," in the sense that the word originally invoked fatherhood, from the Greek *pater*). Twice Lincoln uses forms of the verb "spring," invoking not only conception and birth but also the seasonal sense of new beginnings. First, "the institutions under which we live" "sprang" from that trinity of wisdom, patriotism, and devotion. Second, and more important, Lincoln claims that he "never had a feeling politically that did not spring from the sentiments embodied in the Declaration of Independence." The image magnifies the power of those sentiments to multiply and bring ideals to life, and listeners signaled allegiance by breaking into "great cheering."

Lincoln also chose to highlight an amorphous word in this long excerpt. He suggests that there is "something" in the Declaration "giving liberty," not merely to those within his hearing in Philadelphia on February 22, 1861, but "to the world for all future time." The words "great applause" are significant, because crowds inevitably responded when Lincoln would rise to the heights of his ideological expression of the mythic qualities he saw in America. Moments of great applause can often be considered as successful engagements with the "mystic chords" binding audience and speaker. Lincoln and his listeners entered some level of a consensual agreement with the evolving myth of America as redeemer nation, a mission that would continue to resound and bear hope. By suggesting that something in the Declaration provided the impetus for such ameliorative effects, however, Lincoln introduced an aspect of that document, its meaning, and perhaps its sacred source that McPherson either ignores or overlooks.

Lincoln made similar suggestive statements about that mysterious "something" in other speeches. When speaking before the New Jersey Senate in Trenton, he invoked the founding of America through bitter revolution:

> I recollect thinking then, boy even though I was, that there must have been *something* more than common that those men struggled for. I am exceedingly anxious that that *thing* which they struggled for; that *something* even more than National Independence; that *something* that held out a great promise to all the people of the world to all time to come; I am exceedingly anxious that this Union, the Constitution, and all the liberties of the people shall be perpetuated in accordance with the original idea for which that struggle was made, and I shall be most happy indeed if I shall be an humble instrument in the hands of the Almighty, and of this, his almost chosen people, for perpetuating the object of that great struggle. (209, emphasis added)

Four times in this passage, Lincoln referred to a "thing" or a "something." Rhetorically, it was in his interest to avoid being specific about what the something was, because its ambiguity placed it beyond clarity and made it a mystical abstraction to which listeners would assent more readily than to a concrete definition. Whatever the ambiguous something was, it likely could be associated with the similar statement from the Independence Hall speech: "It was . . . *something* in that Declaration giving liberty" (213). The something in the speech can be associated with the prevailing idea or myth of America. Lincoln then identified that something with "the original idea for which that struggle was made." As Wills has stated, "America is the American idea for Lincoln, and that idea is contained in the Declaration."[15] The idea is not identical to the Declaration, and Lincoln referred to a distinct "object of that struggle." Rather, the Declaration should be understood as a singular, even sublime, expression of that idea.

As countless examples make clear, from the women writers discussed previously, to slaves and former slaves, and to labor organizers whose activities are described by Philip S. Foner, the view of the essence of the Declaration as the central premise of American freedom and civil order became established over many years and through a substantial number of spokespersons and organizations.[16] The process of doing so, however, culminated in the rhetorical brilliance of Lincoln, whose breathtaking "re-clothing" of that document permanently inscribed it as a fundamental part of the American civil religion. It is important that the "original idea," which for Lincoln might perpetuate the Union and all for which it stood, be consistently depicted in religious or spiritual language. The something consists primarily of the general spiritual and moral elements Robert Bellah has identified as America's "civil religion."[17]

Lincoln powerfully invoked such elements throughout his cycle of speeches. For example, the speech at Trenton incorporated numerous references that described the consensual civil religion of his day. What he described was "more than common," suggesting a special, perhaps ideal, realm. Four times, Lincoln refers to the past, present, and future "struggle." The American idea also offers "a great promise to all the people of the world to all time to come," suggesting a millennial vision typical of national myth. "Perpetuate" and "all time to come" assign the idea a timeless quality. Lincoln also invokes the humility of Christ and other exemplary servants of God when he fervently hopes to "be an humble instrument in the hands of the Almighty." Finally, as an illustration of Lincoln's brilliant control of images, he calls Americans the "almost chosen people," which hints at an apocalyptic fulfillment. "Chosen people," of course, is a biblical figure of speech for not only Israel but also the New Testament church, and it brims with mission and promise.

It seems clear that civil religion, in addition to invoking consensus, also has a rhetorical purpose. As Bellah notes, "The American civil religion was never anticlerical or militantly secular. On the contrary, it borrowed selectively from the religious tradition in such a way that the average American saw no conflict between the two. In this way, the civil religion was able to build up without any bitter struggle with the church powerful symbols of national solidarity and to mobilize deep levels of personal motivation for the attainment of national goals."[18] In Bellah's terms, Lincoln often "borrowed . . . religious tradition" in the form of numerous "powerful symbols" in order to foster an American consensus. In particular, he conflated the idea of America with a traditional Christian view of the mission and role of the church and the importance of rising "in masses" and living out beliefs. The most explicit example of that, in the speech at Indianapolis, came as Lincoln stated, "When the people rise in masses in behalf of the Union and the liberties of their country, truly may it be said, 'The gates of hell shall not prevail against them.'"[19] The quotation is derived from Jesus's words in Matthew 16, which come directly after Peter's confession of the real identity of Jesus. Jesus responds by agreeing and promising that "upon this rock I will build My church; and the gates of hell shall not prevail against it" (Matthew 16:18). In his use of the allusion, Lincoln associates the revelation of the American idea with a true understanding of the identity of Jesus and ascribes both to an invisible God. By conflating the Union with the church and the forces of light, he implies that any who might oppose the Union (i.e., secessionists) were comparable to the guardians of hell. Thus, the struggle is framed in terms of a cosmic battle between light and darkness. Numerous other passages suggest the association of the Union and the Christian church. In his farewell at Springfield, Lincoln asserted, "Without the assistance of that Divine Being . . . I cannot succeed" (199). Elsewhere he claimed that with regard to "the salvation of this Union there needs but one thing—the hearts of the people" (199), putting the mission in soteriological terms demanding spiritual ("hearts") assent by every citizen.

Lincoln's political cause was not merely for America. It was the "political cause. . . of the whole world" (201), and each American's duty was "to assist in ameliorating mankind" (203). The power of Lincoln's rhetoric frequently rose to rapturous heights as he described the country's special place among other nations: "I wish you a long life and prosperity individually, and pray that with the perpetuity of those institutions under which we have all so long lived and prospered, our happiness may be secured, our future made brilliant, and the glorious destiny of our country established forever" (207). Again, the nation is similar to the church and presented in four temporal modes: the past ("under which we have

all so long lived and prospered"), the present ("our happiness may be secured"), the future ("our future made brilliant"), and eternity ("our country established forever"). Those final words, "established forever," reso-
nated strongly for his Bible-reading listeners. They were a common
phrasing from the King James Version and described the eternal nature
of the salvation of believers. His point was that the nation possesses a
destiny that is implicitly devised and overseen, like the church's, by providence, and that destiny is indeed "glorious."

Powerful albeit brief images joining the idea of America with the role,
purpose, and perpetuity of the Christian church marked Lincoln's rhetoric before he was inaugurated. Thus it is not surprising that many listeners
were alarmed by what they heard in such speeches. Although Lincoln
remained evasive, his insistence on the eternal nature of the American
destiny bode ill for secessionists. Undoubtedly, many people were able
to read between the lines and realize that he was preparing ideologically
for governmental policies that would ensure the perpetuation of the
Union. As Robert G. Gunderson points out, the Indianapolis speech
"aroused much tense speculation." Although "he made no categorical
statement of policy, he nevertheless asked some rather tantalizing rid-
dles." The headline of the following day's *Cleveland Plain-Dealer*, for
example, was "Lincoln Has Spoken. He Goes for Taking the Southern
Forts—War Inevitable!"[20]

Thus, the speeches of the train tour, far from being banal, unprepared
ramblings, were critical foreshadowings of the central focus and themes
of the subsequent inaugural. They provided attentive listeners with a way
to identify Lincoln's central policy announcement of the Inaugural Address: that he was passionately and undeniably committed to the perpetuity of the Union. "I hold, that in contemplation of universal law, and
of the Constitution, the Union of these States is perpetual. Perpetuity is
implied, if not expressed, in the fundamental law of all national governments. . . . the Union will endure forever—it being impossible to destroy
it, except by some action not provided for in the instrument itself" (217).
Again, divine sanction ("universal law") is associated closely with the
American project ("the Constitution"). Lincoln asserted that if Americans held to the "express provisions" of the Constitution, "the Union will
endure forever—it being impossible to destroy it." His was a resolute faith
worthy of the most pious believer. Later, he admitted faith in "intelligence, patriotism, Christianity, and a firm reliance on Him, who has never
yet forsaken this favored land" (223). That statement reiterated the close
association of American self-reliant responsibility ("intelligence, patriotism") with the church's reliance on God ("Christianity, and a firm re-

liance on Him"). Finally, Lincoln emphasized that America is not common but "favored."

Elsewhere in the First Inaugural he was even more willing to place the matter completely in the hands of God, in the fashion of seventeenth-century Calvinists: "If the Almighty Ruler of nations, with his eternal truth and justice, be on your side of the North, or your side of the South, that truth, and that justice, will surely prevail, by the judgment of this great tribunal, the American people" (223). The sentence is filled with suggestive religious terminology ("eternal truth and justice," "judgment," and the "great tribunal"), all of which amplify and extend the visionary conflation of nation and church.

Other passages from the First Inaugural are strikingly similar to the train tour speeches. For example, Lincoln again depended heavily upon a Burkean identification from listeners:

> While the people retain their virtue, and vigilence, no administration . . . can very seriously injure the government . . .
> My countrymen, one and all, think calmly and well, upon this whole subject . . .
> In your hands, my dissatisfied fellow countrymen, and not in mine, is the momentous issue of civil war. (223)

As Waldo Braden explains, the famous closing lines of the First Inaugural, like other parts of the speech such as those discussed previously, also "contain elements of what Kenneth Burke spoke of as identification."[21] "We are not enemies, but friends," Lincoln says. "We must not be enemies. Though passion may have strained, it must not break our bonds of affection. The mystic chords of memory, stretching from every battle-field, and patriot grave, to every living heart and hearthstone, all over this broad land, will yet swell the chorus of the Union, when again touched, as surely they will be, by the better angels of our nature."[22] Lincoln's strategic attempt to form consensus through identification, an attempt initiated in the speeches given during his journey to Washington, culminated here. Surely it is one of the finest rhetorical passages in American history, but Lincoln's other speeches that led to this moment were also replete with related imagery and at times nearly as powerful. Further, the lines were shaped by the same cultural concerns that moved the women commentators and anti-slavery writers of the same period.

To integrate the diverse aspects of the American heritage, Lincoln invented the metaphor of the "mystic chords of memory" as a central image to unite the rest. These chords literally appear to stretch from place to place, forming a massive, weblike network by which all true Americans are joined. The image can usefully be related to Lincoln's description of Henry Clay: "[Clay] truly touches the chords of human sympathy. . . . All his efforts were made for practical effect. He never spoke merely to be heard."[23] For both Clay and Lincoln, in order to be a successful speaker and thereby bring about "practical effect," it was necessary to connect somehow with those mystic chords. Because they are also "bonds of affection," society is forcibly held together but in a positive manner ("affection").

The bonds or chords invoke two aspects of the common American heritage as it has been understood and transmitted. First, Lincoln clearly suggests religious elements in these passages with words and phrases such as "mystic," "living heart," "swell the chorus," and the "better angels of our nature." The majestic closing images of the First Inaugural demonstrate hope that is religiously inspired. Lincoln's conviction was that if Americans could stay connected to those mystic chords they would "yet swell the chorus of the Union," which invokes an image of the myriad singers glorifying God described in the Book of Revelation. A sweeping panorama of all history is depicted by moving linearly, in this magical final sentence, from the past ("memory, stretching from every battle-field, and patriot grave"), to the present ("to every living heart and hearthstone, all over this broad land") and into the future ("will yet swell the chorus of the Union"). Such panoramic views of eternally ordained institutions, typical of Lincoln, associate nation and church.

Second, traditional American mythical elements are brought together by the mystic chords, including "battle-field," "patriot grave," "hearthstone," and "this broad land." Again, mixing these images with religious elements suggests a conflation of nation and church. The "masculine" ("battle-field," "patriot grave") is just as important as the "feminine" ("living heart," "hearthstone"). The mystic chords, like the earlier image of a national fabric, somehow connect and integrate the two aspects, secular and religious and masculine as well as feminine. But the list of historical images suggesting the founding and settlement of America is also important. As Michael Kammen has pointed out, "In the United States, more often than not, memory has provided a bulwark for social and political stability—a means of valorizing resistance to change."[24] These mystic chords are emphatically of memory, and their chief aim is "social and political stability." The polarized mythical aspects of the common heritage include the religious and the cultural/historical as well as the masculine and feminine; they are all enmeshed. Lincoln's breathtaking finale to his great speech includes tributes to the feminized version of American soteriology when it invokes the "bonds of affection," "every living heart and hearthstone," and "the better angels of our nature." These appeal to the necessary inclusion of the feminine for their support and cohesion and demonstrate the profoundly feminine aspect of Lincoln's rhetorical program.

In 1855 Sarah Josepha Hale suggested that "to bring about the true Christian civilization, which only can improve the condition of our sex, the men must become more like women, and the women more like angels."[25] It was that feminine segment, ruled by hearts and "better angels," that would be the decisive factor in promulgating Lincoln's version of the American gospel as contained in the Declaration. To cement the national ideology by which the Union might prevail into immutability, Lincoln appealed to the feminized segment of society, recognizing that any appeal to consensus must take the feminine sensibility into account. Well before the war, what Ann Douglas has labeled the emerging "feminization of American culture" had begun to exert considerable market force in literature, religion, and education. Women writers had a strong tendency to mythologize the role of the mother-savior, as was the case in Stowe's depiction of the Quaker women in *Uncle Tom's Cabin.* Men, however, participated in this ideological view as well. As Nathaniel Willis asserted at midcentury, "It is the women who exercise the ultimate control over the Press." Many even maintained that it would be best if the rapidly expanding, highly competitive American society took on a more feminine aspect. Sylvester Judd, in 1839 for example, complained of there being "little of the genuine emotion in our [sex]. . . . Women are the bonds of society," and William Ellery Channing reportedly focused his attention on the conversion of women because he believed them to be "the powers that rule the world, and that if they would bestow their favor on the right cause only and never be diverted . . . triumph would be sure."[26]

Thus, it is not surprising that Lincoln's version of the American myth of concern incorporates themes and motifs similar to those the sentimental revivalists of the antebellum period espoused. As a "period during which old symbols are clothed with new meaning," the American awakening beginning in the 1850s rivals the other awakenings of American history.[27] And perhaps the key "new meaning" consisted of a turning to the Declaration as central symbol in the emerging national myth that might help American society to sustain and uphold its codes and render them coherent. The Declaration of Independence became inscribed as the common mythical element that united all the mystic chords that might allow America to save itself from ruin, through the rhetorical acts of revivalists ranging from Stowe to Frederick Douglass and including such women as Maria Stewart, Jarena Lee, and Sojourner Truth as well as men like David Walker, Nat Turner, and Abraham Lincoln. In advancing that mythic creed Lincoln built on strategies that others had earlier developed and deployed. In doing so, he recognized and embraced them all as central players in the construction and implementation of America's regnant myth of concern.

Lincoln's final train trip, the solemn funeral procession that deposited the slain president back in Springfield in 1865, reflected and fostered the mythic quality he had attained since his death. Of course, a number of historical details helped ensure that the horrific news was received in an atmosphere of awe, not the least of which was that the president had been shot on Good Friday. Almost immediately, a massive effort began to refigure the work and accomplishment of Lincoln, and preachers, poets, journalists, and artists all undertook the task of mythologizing him to such an extent that revisionary historians have done little since to undermine or challenge their work. Some scholars have felt that the "redefinition of Lincoln's place in American thought, his swift transcendence from history into folklore, was one of the more remarkable cultural phenomena of our history. . . . Lincoln the man was swallowed by the myth."[28]

Historical investigations of the weeks following Lincoln's death have demonstrated the outpouring of emotion by Americans throughout the North. New York City, for example, like many others, was awash with funereal decorations. Almost every building was festooned with drapery, ribbons, and crepe, and most people wore mourning badges.[29] At the White House, the line of mourners stretched out until more than twenty-five thousand had viewed the dead president. The train journey westward, departing on April 21, took twelve days and allowed mourners in a number of major cities to pay their respects and pass by the open coffin. At least sixty thousand turned out in New York, 120,000 in Chicago, and on May 3 and 4 more than seventy-five thousand silently passed by the bier in Springfield.[30]

But the reaction was not all so orderly and solemn; sometimes the grief turned ugly. Some southern sympathizers were mobbed, arrested, and in a few cases murdered for lack of outward mourning or for making at times minor negative comments about Lincoln. James Urian of Philadelphia, for example, was arrested for reacting gleefully to the news of the assassination, and a Maryland mob killed Joseph Shaw, editor of a Democratic newspaper, who had previously written critically of Lincoln. Buildings not decorated with proper funereal garb were often defaced. Even former president Millard Fillmore was not overlooked, as an angry crowd sprayed ink on his house when he refused to display what were deemed the proper emblems of mourning. Overall, a "study of 21 newspapers revealed over 120 instances of mob actions and arrests within the first three days after Lincoln's death."[31] Alarming as these facts appear, such prevalent mob violence supports a view of intensive, even irrational adulation and grief of a sort that bordered at least for some on religious idolatry.

Not surprisingly, many prominent American politicians, authors, and ministers spoke in glowing terms about the dead leader. Ralph Waldo Emerson, for example, explained at the Unitarian church in Concord on April 19 that "Serene Providence" is able to create "its own instruments" and suggested prophetically that Lincoln "may serve his country even more by his death than by his life." Henry Ward Beecher, speaking in Brooklyn on April 23, compared Lincoln to Moses, both of whom could only approach the Promised Land—for Lincoln, likely a reunited Union—without actually entering it.

Beecher's appeal mirrored a common feature of church eulogies. In a detailed analysis of 372 sermons delivered by northern preachers in the weeks following the murder, Charles J. Stewart has shown that Beecher's Old Testament allusion was normative: "Nearly half of the sermons" compared Lincoln directly to Moses.[32] In Philadelphia on April 23 (the same day Lincoln's body rested in Independence Hall, scene of his most memorable speech on the train journey to Washington in 1861), Phillips Brooks, like many preachers from Maine to Illinois, claimed that Lincoln's death was "no accident, no arbitrary decree of Providence." Something in his "character," said Brooks, "produced the catastrophe of his cruel death." Lincoln was, in fact, the "type-man" of the country, and his character was "the character of an American under the discipline of freedom." He was "the anointed and supreme embodiment" of "the American truths." Brooks enjoined listeners to "thank God forever for his life and death," suggesting like so many others that Lincoln's death was an act of providence. Brooks's appeal was commonplace; 92 percent of the sermons "stated that God had allowed the assassination."[33]

For Brooks and many others, a correct interpretation of Lincoln's death would issue in an American metanoia: "The new American nature will supplant the old. We must grow like our president, in his truth, his independence, his religion, and his wide humanity. Then the character by which he died shall be in us, and by it we shall live."[34] Thus would Americans be imbued with the dead leader's spirit, just as Christians are filled with the Holy Spirit: "If you abide in My word, then you are truly disciples of mine; and you shall know the truth, and the truth shall make you free," and, "You know Him because He abides with you, and will be in you" (John 8:31–32; John 14:17). In all, Lincoln's meteoric rise as mythic hero is a striking transformation that surely owes much to the suggestive and somewhat mystical quality of his most famous public speeches. Specifically, the mythologization of Lincoln and his canonization as patron saint of the American myth within a mere six weeks of his death testify to the popularity of his political thought as he expressed it through finely wrought public speeches.

Just as the eulogies turned typically to the religious aspect of the dead president, so did numerous pictures and prints. He became engraved (quite literally) almost overnight as a martyr and saint.[35] That transformation is best illustrated by considering several examples of the print art created directly on the heels of his assassination. John Sartain's *Abraham Lincoln: The Martyr Victorious* (fig. 1), is a glorification of Lincoln being welcomed into the heavenly realm by George Washington, "father" of America. They are both surrounded by numerous angels, several of which are playing harps as one adorns the saintly Lincoln with what appears to be a laurel wreath "symbolizing triumph and eternity."[36] The same angel waves a palm branch over Lincoln, and it is clear that he, like Jesus, is meant to be proclaimed savior and martyr. The image of *In Memory of Abraham Lincoln—The Reward of the Just* (fig. 2) by D. T. Wiest is the apotheosis of Lincoln, who is shown being carried heavenward by two angels, his hands spread outward like the crucified Jesus. A solemn angel and a mourning Indian sit in the foreground, sadly viewing what appears to be Roman garb, again suggestive of Jesus. A bald eagle also stands at attention in the picture, apparently saluting the risen Lincoln and thus again bringing together the civil and the religious. Finally, two color lithographs, Currier and Ives's *Washington and Lincoln / The Father and the Saviour of Our Country* and Kimmel and Forster's *Columbia's Noblest Sons* (figs. 3 and 4), join the two presidents as both political and quasi-religious forebears of the American idea. In the former, Washington and Lincoln join hands before a flame of liberty, by this time the preeminent American religious and political ideal and suggestive of the language of the Declaration. The latter has Liberty ("Columbia") herself placing her hands on oval portraits of the two men, marking an equality of status and implying an anointing through the biblical laying on of hands. A document streams forth under each portrait: under Washington, the Declaration; under Lincoln, the Emancipation Proclamation, both statements that ostensibly abolished slavery and could serve as America's most vaunted scriptures. In the foreground, a lion sleeps peacefully, recalling the millennial sabbath of the prophet Isaiah. As the title of the Currier and Ives lithograph indicates, viewers could rightly call Lincoln the saviour of the country, co-equal with Washington as the preeminent incarnations of American mythic ideals.

Figure 1. John Sartain,
*Abraham Lincoln, The
Martyr Victorious*
(The Lincoln Museum,
Fort Wayne, Ind., #3324)

Figure 2. D. T. Wiest,
*In Memory of Abraham
Lincoln—The Reward of
the Just* (The Lincoln
Museum, Fort Wayne,
Ind., #3282)

Figure 3. Currier and Ives, *Washington and Lincoln: The Father and the Saviour of Our Country.* (Harry T. Peters Collection, Museum of the City of New York)

Figure 4. Kimmel and Forster, *Columbia's Noblest Sons* (The Lincoln Museum, Fort Wayne, Ind., #3452)

Such depictions demonstrate the almost immediate recognition of not only Lincoln's greatness but also his strangely religious qualities and status as a mystical and spiritual leader. The pictures, like the many sermons and speeches memorializing Lincoln, show him as "an American icon deified in the classical tradition of the dying god, martyred symbolically, on the anniversary of history's most famous martyrdom, linked by deed to Washington, and by virtue and violent death to Jesus Christ."[37] Thus, Lincoln (and his most cherished words) became forever the direct link between the religious and the political realms of the Union. His life, and perhaps most important his death, sealed him in public memory as the embodiment of the nation's mythic civil religion. Coincidentally, his best public speeches exemplified that religion to a degree that has not yet been, nor perhaps ever will be, surpassed.

PART 2

Misreading the Myth

Introduction

Emerson as Myth

Jefferson's document of 1776 has ably served as the representative anecdote of American political and cultural myth, a claim that has been my central argument. The remainder of this book will argue that it became common to view specific cultural moments as embodying elements of the original Declaration, and in turn these moments were mythologized as symbols of central importance for understanding the broad sweep of American literary and cultural history. The mythic re-reading of these events commonly emphasized the striking dissent of a particular individual against corrupt, powerful, and largely reified institutional hierarchies. In each of the cases to be discussed, an individual who was at first vehemently attacked for espousing radical ideas that ostensibly challenged traditional homespun values and beliefs was transformed, primarily through hindsight, into an American hero of dissent and a prophetic voice of the American metanoia.

My model for this phenomenon is the moment almost universally thought to be the quintessential religious, intellectual, and cultural variant of the colonists' act of declaring independence. From 1837 to 1839 Ralph Waldo Emerson gave a series of public declarations of in/dependence that included not only the legendary "American Scholar" oration and the "Divinity School Address" but also two less well-known yet equally important speeches. "Literary Ethics," the Dartmouth College oration, was delivered in July 1838, and "The Protest" on January 16, 1839, in Boston's Masonic Temple. Taken together, these speeches are commonly explained as having rhetorically performed a feat nearly identical in the cultural realm to that of Jefferson's Declaration in the political realm. Just as the Declaration reprimanded the tangible political and economic tyrannies imposed by the king of England, Emerson rebuked the conformity and cowardice he witnessed among his ostensibly democratic and Christian fellow citizens in the new nation. His anger seethed against the patriarchal, deadened formality of the Unitarian religious tradition and also against his peers who feared to speak out and foster the healthy individualism imagined by the Founders.[1] According to Joel Porte, Emerson had long suffered from a "sublime discontent" that finally provoked, in the summer of 1838, his "self-definition through defiance and dissent."[2]

Emerson's most famous public moments in 1837 and 1838, however, must be recognized for what they have become in American cultural history: preeminent examples of representative anecdotes which, through a process of mythologization and reductionism, have come to stand as the foremost symbols for complex historical developments. Interpretations such as Porte's are valid in that they show how these public moments exemplify Emerson's emotional and intellectual development. But the far less valid intent of many critics is to depict the experiences of a great author like Emerson as exemplifying not only his inner conflicts and tensions but also those of society as a whole. Emerson's struggles, or Mark Twain's or Sinclair Lewis's, thereby become America's struggles. In Emerson's case the seminal instance of mythologization was Oliver Wendell Holmes's *Ralph Waldo Emerson*, published in 1885, nearly fifty years after his orations. In it Holmes claimed that "this grand Oration ["The American Scholar"]" was not merely Emerson's personal act of declaring independence but "our intellectual declaration of independence."[3]

Holmes's troublesome use of the first person ("our") hardly needs to be deconstructed here, and yet that reductionist pronouncement characterizes the way a majority of teachers continue to discuss Emerson's speeches of 1837 and 1838, regardless of the claim's dubious historical veracity. Observations from several prominent literary historians and critics over a number of decades confirm this characteristic. Ernest Erwin Leisy, for example, wrote in 1929 that "in 'The American Scholar,' the new leader sounded the nation's cultural declaration of independence."[4] Ludwig Lewisohn in 1932 referred to "The American Scholar" as "a declaration of independence from literary colonialism."[5] In *The Oxford Companion to American Literature* (1948), the second sentence of the entry on "The American Scholar" noted that the speech was "called 'our declaration of independence' by Holmes."[6] For Arthur Hobson Quinn in 1951, "The American Scholar" was "a declaration of independence against 'the courtly muses of Europe.'"[7] Theodore L. Gross emphasized in 1971 "the famous declaration of cultural independence in 'The American Scholar.'"[8] Larzer Ziff has also joined this growing consensus. Referring once again to "The American Scholar," he observes, "More than sixty years after the United States had declared its political independence, here at long last, observers felt, was the declaration of intellectual independence."[9] Ziff, however, fails to cite any of the speech's "observers" in support of his assertion. Finally, *The Cambridge History of American Literature* (1943) stated that "The American Scholar" is "called our intellectual Declaration of Independence. With far more fundamental truth [Emerson's] little volume, *Nature,* might be called our religious Declaration of Independence." That claim is made despite the fact that earlier in the same book William Cullen Bryant's article on American literature (published in the July 1818 *North American Review*) was termed America's "first declaration of intellectual independence, antedating Emerson's 'The American Scholar' by nineteen years."[10]

One begins to wonder how many declarations America has produced. In any case, a striking feature of all those cited is that none with the exception of the entry in *The Oxford Companion to American Literature* mention the primary source of the comparison, Oliver Wendell Holmes's book. That omission suggests that the idea had moved from assertion to myth. The original source had seemingly been forgotten or ignored. It is as if Holmes's concept has achieved widespread credence, thereby becoming unexamined common sense in the teaching of American literary history.

Elsewhere and in more general terms, critics have often noted the revolutionary and/or religious spirit of "The American Scholar." In 1927 Vernon Parrington called the speech the "quintessence of transcendental individualism. . . . [containing] the same revolutionary conception . . . that Jefferson had come upon."[11] And in 1935 Fred Lewis Pattee was equally enthusiastic: "But here was a new spirit. Here was a John the Baptist preacher . . . laying axes at the foot of trees."[12] Frederic I. Carpenter maintained that "the millennial hope of an ideal new world . . . inspired the Declaration of Independence and the Bill of Rights, Emerson's address to 'The American Scholar' and Whitman's *Leaves of Grass.*"[13]

What they suggested is that a common spirit somehow has animated all great American works of revolution and religious repentance, one of the most significant of which was Emerson's famous speech. For these critics and many others, Emerson's most renowned declaratory moment leaves the staid arena of the historic and magically rises to the level of the mythic American metanoia. Such critical moves are not altogether to be despised. Mythological reductionism is a highly useful teaching and

critical apparatus that helps students and scholars understand the sweep
and trajectory of an endlessly complex cultural system. The move to locate points of historical origin may also be vitally important for society
because beginnings satisfy, in Edward W. Said's words, a "primordial need
for certainty."[14] Still, such mythologizing should be recognized for what
it is. The moment of Emerson's "declaration," whether in 1837 or 1838,
was a culmination of his personal intellectual process, as well as of
American religious, literary, and cultural developments that had begun
during the 1820s.

If the public performance and subsequent reception of "The American Scholar" have been largely mythologized, surely a similar conclusion
can be reached about Emerson's other primary public moment of this
period. The heated discord generated by the "Divinity School Address"
featured others besides Emerson. Andrews Norton, the dean of Harvard-
style Unitarianism, was pitted against Orestes Brownson, George Ripley,
and William Ellery Channing. Norton's well-known attack on the so-
called New Divinity in his pamphlet *A Discourse on the Latest Form of
Infidelity* (1839) was concerned only tangentially with Emerson's speech
at the Divinity School. Norton also aimed at other enemies, generally the
theological "opinions now prevalent, which are at war with a belief in
Christianity"—opinions of which Emerson was only one advocate of
many. He was also concerned with more vocal critics such as Brownson,
whose attacks on Norton's recently published Christian apologia *The
Evidence of the Genuineness of the Four Gospels* (1838) exemplified the
conflict.[15]

These facts also underline other considerations that are often under-
emphasized. His audience understood Emerson primarily as a religious
thinker, and his speeches were originally perceived as religious in nature.
They should most properly be analyzed within the context of the hegemonic Christian milieu in which they were delivered. The foregrounding of Emerson's "intellectual," "literary," or "cultural" legacy rather
than his religious legacy is more after the fact than it was contemporary
to the audiences of 1837 and 1838 and thus worthy of careful critical
scrutiny.[16]

Likewise, mythologizing the "Divinity School Address" as a religious
declaration tends to give short shrift to the context of the massive changes
in American Protestant religion that had commenced well before the
summers of 1837 and 1838. Moreover, the shift in American Christianity was but one prominent example of an even broader shift in Western
philosophy that has been summarized as "the movement . . . towards the
positing of some dynamic and practical version of what Schopenhauer

calls 'the will.'"[17] For example, the powerfully influential work of theologians such as Lyman Beecher and Nathaniel William Taylor in Presbyterian churches that extensively reformulated the concepts of repentance, revival, and the role of the individual will took place not in Boston but in New Haven and not during the 1830s but during the 1820s. Taylor's legacy was his conviction that for evangelism to succeed in a democratic America, self-accountability and the agency of individual will power must be emphasized rather than a sinner's dependence on God. Sin and guilt, according to Taylor, were not primarily part of humanity's moral nature but were to be attributed to voluntary choice.

Such a view had a profound impact on Taylor's chief disciple, Charles Grandison Finney, who was the nation's most famous evangelist by the time of Emerson's speeches. In 1831 Finney had made this new type of revivalistic religion well-known in a speech entitled "Make Yourselves a New Heart," delivered in Boston, Emerson's backyard and the citadel of Unitarianism. The sermon had been widely known and reviewed, and Emerson surely knew about its tone and content.[18] Like Emerson, Finney worked and preached for many long years within the confines of his original tradition, Presbyterianism, before leaving it in 1836.

There is a world of difference between Finney and Emerson theologically, not the least detail of which was Finney's insistence on the historical claims of Christianity, including miracles, which constituted the core of Emerson's highly original attack on Unitarianism. Nonetheless, at least a decade before Emerson's momentous speeches Taylor, Finney, and others emphasized Emerson's central principles, including the priesthood of the individual, the human soul's direct and unmediated encounter with the divine, and the need for each believer to experience God and the spirit realm personally.[19]

On an even broader scale, the highbrow theological innovations of thinkers such as Taylor, Beecher, and Emerson followed in the wake of the innovative populism of a variety of middlebrow or even lowbrow preachers during the first three decades of the nineteenth century. Often highbrow and populist preachers found themselves at odds. Overall, religious populism contributed momentum to what Nathan Hatch has called the "democratization of American Christianity" throughout the early nineteenth century, a movement to which Emerson's contribution was surely noteworthy but not of the first order. Hatch argues:

> Turbulence and bitter struggles for authority . . . characterize[d] American Christianity from 1790 to 1820. . . . To the consternation of respectable clergymen, the terms of that debate were set largely by people who had not known status, influence, or power. This stringent populist chal-

lenge to the religious establishment included violent anticlericalism, a flaunting of conventional religious deportment, a disdain for the wrangling of theologians, an assault on tradition, and an assertion that common people were more sensitive than elites to the divine.[20]

The populist preachers of the early nineteenth century spoke to the lower and middle classes in their own vernacular, or what one scholar has labeled "democratic eloquence," often using Jeffersonian and anti-Federalist rhetoric to enhance their messages.[21] They tended to flaunt their dissent before the more learned "backslidden" theologians and church councils, championing youth, ecstatic spiritual immediacy in worship and preaching, and a heightened individualism that created a level of free thought and expression the church had not known. A characteristic figure would be the itinerant Methodist preacher Lorenzo Dow, often labeled as crazy by mainstream religious leaders, who tirelessly tramped up and down the East Coast. He "cultivated the image of John the Baptist, and a radical Jeffersonian, who could begin a sermon by quoting Thomas Paine. Dow sought the conversion of sinners at the same time that he railed at tyranny and priestcraft and the professions of law and medicine." Numerous others are also worthy of serious consideration as leaders in the march toward democratic religious sentiment in America. Elias Smith, Barton Stone, and Alexander Campbell, for example, "all found traditional sources of authority anachronistic and groped toward similar definitions of egalitarian religion" a full two decades before Emerson's ostensibly original proclamations. Smith, who resigned from the Baptist church in 1800 "as a manifesto of his own liberty," challenged followers in 1809 to "be republicans indeed. . . . Many are republicans as to government, and yet we are but half republicans . . . in matters of religion. . . . Venture to be . . . independent in things of religion." Stone characterized his resignation from the Presbyterian denomination as the "declaration of our independence." And Campbell, the colorful and extremely influential church leader who founded the Disciples of Christ, asserted in 1830 that July 4, 1776, was "a day to be remembered as was the Jewish Passover. . . . This revolution, taken in all its influences, will make men free indeed."[22]

Thus, it seems misleading historically to fix so much value on Emerson's contributions to the evolution of democratic religion in America. Instead, the emphasis that literary and cultural historians place on his speeches of 1837 and 1838, as well as the emphasis on Jefferson's Declaration, may be symptoms of what Terence Martin has rightly called "America's need for beginnings."[23] As Robert Spiller argued, however, it is more accurate to claim that Emerson's pronouncements served not

primarily as the beginning but more accurately as the end of a long process of cultural change in America.[24] And yet Emersonian dissent through
public speech has achieved unequaled mythic resonance as a symbol of
democratic individualism and as the prophetic culmination of a long and
steady philosophical sweep, so much so that, for all practical purposes,
Holmes's proclamation is true for most students and scholars of American literary and cultural history.

The same is true for the three cultural moments to be analyzed in
the following chapters. Each has come to symbolize important conflicts
that stood ostensibly at the heart of the culture in which they occurred
and was subsequently mythologized into a representative anecdote by
which important cultural shifts could be easily explained. Each featured
a public literary figure who seemingly stood for a radical version of the
myth of freedom and against an outdated public ideology. And each figure came to be attacked, at times viciously, by spokespersons who stood
for whatever patriotic American values and ideologies they accused the
prophet of freedom to be destroying. Like Emerson in 1837 and 1838 (as
later formulated and mythologized by numerous critics and American
culture at large), these refigured moments became "true" enactments of
"real" American cultural conflict. Thus, each is now regularly viewed,
and often taught, as an enactment of the American metanoia.

The following chapters deal with three public speeches that generated a great deal of social reaction: Mark Twain's comic speech at Whittier's birthday celebration in 1877, Sinclair Lewis's Nobel Prize acceptance speech in 1930, and Lionel Trilling's 1959 speech at Robert Frost's
eighty-fifth birthday celebration (coupled with Frost's participation in the
inauguration of John F. Kennedy in 1961). Each event can be studied (and
is often presented) as representative of the deep cultural tensions between
the parties of concern and freedom. All of the speeches constituted mythic
declarations of in/dependence that set the speakers apart from a substantial and ossified consensus and were viewed as such by a variety of contemporary and subsequent commentators. In addition, because many
people interpreted the speeches as attacks against the regnant American
myth, these moments triggered a deeply felt national urge to defend the
myth of concern against subversive interventions, an urge to which I have
referred as "Endicott's ghost."

Before being too congratulatory about the radical daring of such authors as Emerson, Twain, Lewis, Trilling, and Frost, however, it is necessary to consider the vexed nature of labeling any one of them as heroic
and revolutionary. Each can also be analyzed as a deeply conservative
thinker who maintained thoroughgoing allegiance to America's myth of

concern. Emerson, for example, was not always and merely a radical prophet of freedom. Moreover, an insistent focus on his early work, including *Nature* and the various orations discussed previously but ignoring the troublesome early sermons of the 1820s, underplays the strong currents of conservatism and old-fashioned civil religion throughout much of his thought.

Oddly enough, given the apparently radical nature of his growing outrage against the institution of slavery, a tell-tale sign of Emerson's political and cultural conservatism—and one of the most notable public engagements of his later career—was his outspoken support and glorification of John Brown. In his almost sensational and relentless mythologization of Brown in the months after the Harpers Ferry raid of October 1859, and more generally throughout his anti-slavery writings of the 1850s, Emerson not only demonstrated continued allegiance to aspects of mythic freedom and the transcendental will to power that mark his most famous romantic masterpieces but also to his conservatism. He became the quintessential priest of the American political religion and the conservative myth of concern as represented by the American metanoia. His conservative vision of the American myth, as developed in his speeches about Brown, or, more generally, the abolitionist cause, developed in three ways.[25]

First, Emerson insisted that Brown was a Puritan New Englander. It was a misrepresentation, however, which Thoreau also accepted and propagated uncritically, to state that Brown's ancestor, Peter Brown, had come over on the *Mayflower* in 1620.[26] As one historian has noted, it is just one of a long "series of exaggerations and extrapolations which leads Emerson to 'transcend' the historical facts toward his ultimate apotheosis of John Brown, the transcendental hero."[27] Emerson went on to call Brown's courage an example of "perfect puritan faith," much the same as the faith that brought "his fifth ancestor to Plymouth Rock."[28] These comments found precedent in a reverence for Puritan New England, a thematic seen throughout Emerson's antislavery speeches, and were noticeable as early as his sermons of 1826–32. His connection to and development of the Puritan tradition can be seen throughout much of his career, particularly the use of the jeremiad, and his ardent inclusion of a fictive Puritan connection in his defense of Brown would only seem to reemphasize that connection.[29]

Emerson's jeremiadic scorn regarding the fallenness of Boston as symbol is a central aspect, for instance, of his "Address to the Citizens of Concord" in 1851: "The fame of Boston. . . . the eloquence of the Christian pulpit, the stoutness of Democracy, the respectability of the Whig party, are all combined to kidnap [the runaway slave]."[30] The strong emphasis on the wedding of civil and religious law, a major thematic of the jeremiad mode of Puritan rhetoric, is also evident throughout his anti-slavery speeches: "[America is] a Republic professing to base its laws on liberty, and on the doctrines of Christianity" (92); "[Boston is] the heart of Puritan traditions in an intellectual country" (93); and "every man of worth in New England loves his virtues. . . . we confide the defence of a life so precious, to all honorable men and true patriots, and to the Almighty Maker of men" (110). In summary, said Emerson, Brown was "a fair specimen of the best stock of New England. . . . Our farmers were Orthodox Calvinists, mighty in the Scriptures." Archetypal Brown, like David and several other Old Testament prophets, as a boy was "set to keep sheep . . . bareheaded and barefooted, and clothed in buckskin" (122, 121). In describing Brown, Emerson drew upon the "cult of the Puritan Fathers," and in so doing he succeeded in revitalizing "the Puritan prophecy of America redeemed in time and place: He declares that 'the fear of God in the community . . . is the salt that keeps the community clean' and is the very 'foundation' of society."[31]

Second, and related to the concept of Brown as Puritan New Englander, Emerson developed his conservative view of the abolitionist cause by emphasizing that Brown spoke for American political religion and underscoring his prophetic office as defender of the Declaration. In his speech of November 18, "To Aid John Brown's Family," Emerson claimed that Brown believed in only "two articles—two instruments, shall I say—The Golden Rule and the Declaration of Independence." A short time later in the same speech, Emerson invited listeners to identify strongly with Brown's political and religious philosophy, appealing to "every man who loves the Golden Rule and the Declaration of Independence." Emerson's conjoining of the preeminent creed of the New Testament with the fundamental dogma of the nation is another rhetorical act of political religion. It is worth noting the cagy use of the term *instrument* with regard to the Declaration. It is a legal term suggestive of the philosophical battle at the time over the Declaration's status as a legal instrument, an argument being made by various important affirmers of the Declaration, including Abraham Lincoln. "Instrument" is also suggestive of Brown's frequent claim that he was an "instrument in the hands of God."[32]

Finally, the speech ended with a third reference to the idealistic document of liberty and equality. Emerson praised "a Vermont judge, Hutchinson, who has a Declaration of Independence in his heart."[33] By ascribing to a particular person the characteristic of having fully internalized the Declaration, Emerson was suggesting that it, like the gospel, could be "inscribed" on a person's heart: "I will put My Laws upon their heart, And upon their mind I will write them" (Hebrews 10:16; see also Jeremiah 31:34).

Earlier in his career, Emerson had also emphasized the Declaration. For example, in his magnificent July Fourth oration delivered on July 5, 1829, at Second Church in Boston he said:

> It has pleased God in His providence to distinguish our country in great and important respects. Fifty three prosperous years have elapsed since the Declaration of American Independence. . . . the Christian has peculiar reason to rejoice in an event that he can't help regarding as the fruit of Christianity. . . . I cannot but rejoice that our anniversary is full of honour, is the memorial of virtue of a self-devoted Christian struggle, where a whole people sympathized and suffered, and many a noble martyr gave up the ghost—*for a principle.*[34]

Perhaps Emerson's most powerful reference to the Declaration, and certainly a passage that is a tour de force among his antislavery writing, is in "The Fugitive Slave Law" oration of 1854: "You must be citadels and warriors, yourselves Declarations of Independence, the charter, the battle, and the victory."[35] It is a classic Emersonian figure and similar to one often employed by former slaves such as Frederick Douglass in naming the practical actions slaves took to free themselves and assert their humanity. Runaways were frequently depicted not as outlaws but as patriots who "acted out the Declaration of Independence."[36]

Finally, and again like the original Declaration, Emersonian ideals must issue in action, often violent in nature. As Bertram Wyatt-Brown puts it, for Emerson, Brown had "reanimated the spirit of Yankee idealism by violence." Brown's raid had "endowed antislavery with a virility that its long association with Sunday school ethics, missions to the 'heathen,' women's causes of temperance and equality, and the New England 'priestcraft' had seemed to deny."[37] That virility, or what one historian has called Brown's association with a "cult of martial virtues," is best exemplified by his obsession with several heirlooms he had commandeered from Lewis Washington, great-grandson of George Washington's half-brother: a sword presented to the first president by Frederick the Great and several pistols given by Lafayette. Brown clung to these items, hoping thereby to be associated with the revolutionary hero.[38] That "veneration of the martial virtues . . . created myths from historical events . . . [and] had a profound impact on the historiography of Brown's raid, elevating the untutored, distracted author of that military fiasco into a symbol of martial heroism."[39]

Thus, much of Emerson's response to Brown derived from a veneration of violent action and martial virtue. He was hardly alone in that response. Countless other northern commentators lamented Brown and his doomed raid, including the most prominent abolitionists of the day—Douglass, Wendell Phillips, and William Lloyd Garrison—as well as literary figures such as Bronson Alcott, Henry Thoreau, Lydia Maria Child, and William Ellery Channing. Elizabeth Cady Stanton, for example, claimed that she was ready to "consecrate" her own sons "to martyrdom, to die, if need be, bravely like a John Brown." Perhaps Douglass put it most succinctly: "How shall American slavery be abolished? . . . The John Brown way."[40]

Emerson, again like Douglass, admired Brown as a personification of moral action, which he considered the essence of Christianity. He had long since rejected historic Christian dogma but "continued to find great importance in the 'uses' of his first hero—and still representative 'great man'": Jesus.[41] Emerson's direct comparison of Brown with Jesus was the most controversial aspect of his material on Brown. In his Boston lecture of November 8, 1859, entitled "Courage," Emerson was reported to have said of Brown, "[He is] the Saint, whose fate yet hangs in suspense, but whose martyrdom, if it shall be perfected, will make the gallows as glorious as the cross."

In fact, it is not altogether clear what Emerson actually said. The key words, however, whatever they were, foregrounded Emerson's comparison of Brown to Jesus on the cross. It was widely reported that he said "as glorious as" the cross. As most early historians had it, however, Emerson said that Brown would make the gallows "glorious, like a cross."[42] For most contemporary readers the offense of the metaphor seems slight, but for staid New Englanders and other northerners in 1859 such remarks were cataclysmic. Emerson, when challenged by an acquaintance for the exact wording, evasively replied, "That's about what I said." He seemed to understand the significance of the allegation and couched his response accordingly.[43]

Emerson's remark initiated a highly inflammatory attack from many quarters against the already controversial public figure. He was labeled an "anti-slavery fanatic" by the *Boston Post*, and his well-known comparison of Brown with Jesus brought him much notoriety during a lecture tour in Ohio and Indiana during February and March of 1860.[44] The February 1 *Cincinnati Enquirer* considered Emerson's elevation of Brown "blasphemous," "traitorous," and "a public scandal" and demanded a boycott of his lecture in that city.[45] His appearance in Lafayette, Indiana, later in the same week raised a similar ruckus: "A disposition to startle by clap trap and *ad captandum* expressions is charged upon him. It will be recollected that his glorification of John Brown, in which he asserted . . . that his execution had rendered the scaffold no less sacred than the cross, called forth some very severe rebukes from the press of the country."[46]

The upshot was that Emerson's remarks became widely publicized throughout the North, marking him as a key witness of the work of John Brown. Furthermore, his mythologized version of Brown had become widely associated with a questionable, perhaps even blasphemous, attempt to raise Brown to the level of religious hero. Significantly, Emerson's rhetorical constructions were severely attacked in many news accounts and seen by many as little more than "clap trap and *ad captandum* expressions." For Emerson, however, the association of his hero with Jesus was central to an understanding of Brown's greatness as romantic symbol of moral action—or as champion of practical action and doing the Word.

More generally, Emerson's cumulative remarks about his fallen hero characterized Brown as the incarnation of the American political religion, and to that end he defended Brown in christological terms as the quintessential Unionist. Brown was able, unlike most men, to "use [his] eyes to see the fact behind the form," a point that emphasized his spiritual sight through revelation: "buy from me . . . eyesalve to anoint your eyes, that you may see" (Revelation 3:18; see also I Corinthians 2:10). Brown typified "the love that casts out fear," an allusion to John's claim that "there is no fear in love; but perfect love casts out fear" (I John 2:18).[47]

Finally, Emerson compared Brown's teachings favorably with those of Jesus in a passage about Brown's reverence for "The Golden Rule and the Declaration of Independence." Regarding these as co-equal codes, Brown often taught that it is "better that a whole generation of men, women and children should pass away by a violent death, than that one word of either should be violated in this country."[48] He was alluding to the Sermon on the Mount, wherein Jesus argued that he "did not come to abolish the Law, but to fulfill it. . . . not the smallest letter or stroke shall pass away. . . . Whoever then annuls one of the least of these commandments, and so teaches others, shall be called least in the kingdom" (Matthew 5:17–19).

The effect of Brown's revision and expansion of this gospel passage (and of Emerson's deployment of it) was to elevate the Declaration to a position comparable to God's law and prophecy that the violation of the Declaration, like the violation of God's law, would bring about God's vengeful wrath. Tellingly, the promise of bloody reprisal showed that "even in a hotbed of transcendentalism such as Concord, the American taste for violence was evident."[49] In Emerson's view, the joining of the sacred words of Jesus and the by-then sacred Declaration of Independence constituted the ultimate task of a patriotic practitioner of American political religion: "There is a Unionist," he declared. Thus Brown, now "happily" mythologized into "a representative of the American republic," "the founder of Liberty" who like Jesus was to be honored for his "singleness of purpose," and a "romantic character absolutely without vulgar trait; living to ideal ends," was metamorphosed into a new messiah who exemplified all other incarnations of the American political religion.[50]

These mythic depictions of John Brown encompass a rhetorically sophisticated elaboration of Emerson's view of an American political religion. It is a view that highlights a sublime combination of both radical and conservative elements and introduces other enactments of the quintessentially American metanoia. Like his depiction of Brown, of course, Emersonianism in general can also be seen as a sublime combination of seemingly oppositional categories, including the myths of concern and freedom.

Given the paradoxical aspect of such figures as Emerson and John Brown (or at least of their poetic depictions) it would be wise to remember a theory advanced by Robert Bellah and his associates: A primary feature of American individualism is its "intrinsic ambivalence/ambiguity."[51] As a result, a dialectic that pits autonomy and self-reliance against a desire for community and tradition is not aberrant but endemic. Bellah's theoretical opposition can be used to inform an analysis of ongoing attempts to define major authors such as Emerson. Contemporary scholarship, for example, has been preoccupied with the paradox of the transcendental Emerson compared to the social Emerson, a conflict that broaches the question of whether Emersonian dissent can have social consequence—whether, that is, such an attitude is merely aesthetic dissent with no social effect. A "de-transcendentalized" version of Emerson would stress his desire to engage directly with society and its ills, thereby transforming it. That version, of course, is in direct contrast with the more traditionally transcendental Emerson of introspection, disengagement, and mystical individualism.[52]

John Carlos Rowe, however, has stated that "transcendentalism reveals itself to be at fundamental odds with the social reforms. . . . Emersonian transcendentalism and political activism in mid-nineteenth-century America were inherently incompatible." Specifically, he rejects Sacvan Bercovitch's concept of an "enabling, fundamentally poetic 'paradox' at the heart of Emerson's thought." More generally, Rowe brings up what has become a fundamental obsession of Emerson studies and an issue at the heart of my argument. Although the dispute will continue, my suggestion for retreat from this seeming quagmire of critical paradox is suggested in another of Rowe's comments: "Emerson's political writings from 1844 to 1863 remain so profoundly divided internally between transcendentalist values and practical politics as to be practically useless, except as far as the value of their political rhetoric might be measured."[53]

Rowe is understatedly correct in seeking the value of Emerson's political rhetoric. Rather than trying to solve what appears to be a false dilemma regarding whether Emerson was a transcendentalist or a social reformer, it would be better to embrace the ambivalence itself as inherently American and inherently Emersonian. In that sense, Emersonian wrestling with the sacred versus the secular or the transcendental versus the practical and social is like the much earlier "Puritan dilemma" encountered by John Winthrop, sketched by Edmund Morgan, and suggested even later by Wesley Mott as a key to understanding Emerson.[54] As Mott has argued, it is not too much to claim that the "sermons and their legacy reveal that Emerson's place in the Puritan tradition is even more central than has been supposed."[55] Much the same can be stated about Emerson's defense of—and poetic obsession with—the beleaguered Capt. John Brown.

A view of Emerson that focuses on his de-transcendentalized nature is no more accurate than one that focuses on his transcendental aspects. Instead, both poles of the dialectic are necessary and perhaps even sacred if the American metanoia is to make sense and remain viable. Thus, the rampantly disparate versions of American authors such as Emerson, Twain, Lewis, or Frost comport with a dialectical mode of viewing American culture. Frost, for example, as quintessential American practitioner of the pastoral mode, qualifies as what Leo Marx has called a "liminal figure" who constantly moves between nature and civilization and freedom and concern, the two poles of the dialectical tension. Pastoralism, for Marx, is grounded in the "opposition between the realm of the collective, the organized, and the worldly on the one hand, and the personal, the spontaneous, and the inward on the other. . . . If this world view can be said to have a constant feature, it may well be a recognition of the ineradicable, ultimately irresolvable nature of the conflict at its heart."[56]

Frost may be the most obviously pastoral writer discussed in this volume, Emerson and Twain notwithstanding. And yet in other ways each author I will describe should also be understood as liminal. They are on the border, moving constantly between the two poles, however they might be defined, of the paradox at the heart of American culture. Mark

Twain is likely the quintessential liminal figure in American literary history. He was either a brash and brilliant genius championing a proto-postmodern multivocality or a dark and troubled figure caught up in a world of oppression and capitalistic greed too big for him to see properly. Wherever readers might position themselves along that continuum, Twain, and, to a lesser extent, William Dean Howells, were surely caught somewhere in the middle between the competing poles of those traditional structural oppositions that have performed constant service for English teachers bent on explaining American literature of the late nineteenth century: East versus West, the text versus the voice, the romantic versus the real, and the classical versus the colloquial. Sinclair Lewis, asserting an inclination for freedom even as he was constantly drawn by the allure of mythic concern, was in his heyday also heartily liked and disliked, depending on the political proclivities of the reader.

Thus, each of the figures to be discussed in the following chapters can be considered as liminal because each illustrates the dynamic of the broader culture and "the ineradicable, ultimately irresolvable nature of the conflict at its heart."[57] Twain, Lewis, and Frost, and the public events associated with them, created some of the most influential and widely remembered moments in American literary history since the Civil War. Moreover, they were responsible for unusually prolonged and even heated cultural response from a wide array of sectors within American culture and have become central to the institutional teaching of American literature at the college level in the United States.

Given the chameleonlike nature that this dynamic assumes, it is fitting to begin the following discussion with an account of the Whittier birthday speech of 1877. On that occasion, an older and somewhat benign (or even senile) Ralph Waldo Emerson sat at the dais, no longer the fiery prophet of radical individualism of 1837 and 1838, but one more ossified relic of an earlier declaratory moment. In what would become surely one of Amerian literature's "primal scenes," he had become witness to his own successor, a newer and quirkier voice of freedom: Mark Twain's.[58]

6 *The Myth of the Oppositional West*

Mark Twain's Declaration of In/Dependence at Whittier's Seventieth Birthday Celebration

Unity within American culture, Philip Fisher has argued, has most often been a postwar phenomenon reflecting the desire among most citizens "to fuse a new identity" of consensus and concern and get back to the business of everyday life.[1] After the Civil War, and largely in response to that conflict's massive destruction described aptly by Walt Whitman as a "butcher's shambles," the desire to forge a cultural harmony fostered what has been described as "the closest thing to a coherent national literary culture that America has ever had."[2]

That hegemony was illustrated in the activities of the literary institutions under control of the gentry and based in Boston. Among the Brahmins were the "Schoolroom" or "Fireside" poets Henry Wadsworth Longfellow, Oliver Wendell Holmes, James Russell Lowell, and John Greenleaf Whittier. They approached literature with a sense of religious mission and hoped to provide America, once more, with a revived vision of being a land of destiny and utopian promise. Typical of their didactic themes, and perhaps the masterpiece of the Fireside poets, was Whittier's "Snow-Bound: A Winter Idyll" (1866):

> Large-brained, clear-eyed,—of such as he
> Shall Freedom's young apostles be,
> Who, following in War's bloody trail,
> Shall every lingering wrong assail;

All chains from limb and spirit strike,
Uplift the black and white alike. . . .

A school-house plant on every hill,
Stretching in radiate nerve-lines thence
The quick wires of intelligence;
Till North and South together brought
Shall own the same electric thought,
In peace a common flag salute,
And, side by side in labor's free
And unresentful rivalry,
Harvest the fields wherein they fought.[3]

Here, the Christian mission of earlier days was transformed into the more secular notion of "Freedom," its "young apostles" going forth to "assail" "every lingering wrong." The work of these agents of freedom transcended racial boundaries ("uplift the black and white alike"). The institution of change had become the "school-house." Whittier's purpose was to bring "North and South together" by supplying them with "the same electric thought" and "a common flag" so they might go forth "side by side" to "harvest the fields."

Whittier's ideological agenda in "Snow-Bound," a work exemplifying the cultural mission being advanced by the cohort of Schoolroom poets, featured a strenuous effort at cohesion in the wake of the terrible War of Secession. The harvest is one not only of agricultural products but also of souls, presumably to the cause of "freedom," a seminal characteristic of the American myth of concern. To that end, the poem invokes a nostalgic time before the war when the American myth of concern ostensibly reigned supreme and unchallenged.

The reverence and adulation accorded to the Boston sages in the decades just before and following the war are illustrated by the recollections of younger literary figures of the period, such as William Dean Howells's account of his first visit to Boston as a young writer from the Midwest in 1860.[4] Howells's memoirs suggest the attitude of one willing to prostrate himself before the high priests of culture, who deserved a "species of religious veneration. . . . I suppose there is no question but our literary centre was then in Boston, such was the literary situation as the passionate pilgrim from the West approached the holy land of Boston." His initial meetings with Lowell and Holmes were experiences that "so far transcended my home-kept experience that it began to seem altogether visionary. . . . the great authors I had met were to me the sum of greatness."

Howells was not alone. Other young writers of the period, including Rebecca Harding Davis, were similarly overwhelmed. When she first came to Boston "as a young woman from the backwoods" of Virginia, she esteemed Emerson "the first of living men, . . . the modern Moses who had talked with God apart and could interpret Him to us." As she awaited his entrance at their initial meeting, Davis remembers that her "body literally grew stiff and my tongue dry with awe."[5]

The cultural moment that has come to symbolize this attitude of reverence was the public ceremony honoring John Greenleaf Whittier's seventieth birthday, held on December 17, 1877, and sponsored by the staid *Atlantic Monthly*, the nation's most esteemed periodical.[6] Letters of regret from eminent men unable to attend the dinner were read aloud and bespeak an obeisance that may never again be matched. One such letter, from Clarence Cook, for example, brimmed with millennial splendor in referring to the poets: "We of this generation have lived in a happy time, and we have fleeted the time carelessly, as they always do who live in the golden world. . . . We have seen Longfellow and Bryant, Lowell and Holmes . . . and whatever the future may have in store for our successors, it can never bring flowers of sweeter smell, nor fruit of better taste than these. They are wet with the dew of the morning and shine with its grace."[7] Another letter, from the editor of *Scribner's Monthly*, Josiah Gilbert Holland, also indicated a level of reverence that "must have been taken for granted by many if not most of the guests."

> I wonder if these old poets of ours—Mr. Dana, Mr. Bryant, Mr. Emerson, Mr. Longfellow and Mr. Whittier—appreciate the benefit they confer upon their fellow citizens by simply consenting to live among them as old men? Do they know how they help to save the American nation from the total wreck and destruction of the sentiment of reverence? Why, if they only live and move and have their being among us from seventy years to a hundred, and consent to be loved and venerated, and worshipped and petted, they will be the most useful men we have in the development of the better elements in the American character.[8]

Mark Twain was one of many in attendance who spoke to honor Whittier, and his remarks must be considered in light of such reverence, decorum, and cultural adulation.[9] Twain's speech has been portrayed in similar terms by academics and literary historians for many years, so much so that one critic has described the event itself as a "locus classicus" and a "primal scene of Twain criticism."[10] Traditionally, the speech has been depicted as a dramatic enactment of the confrontation of the conservative hegemony as represented by Emerson and the Schoolroom poets present, including Whittier, Holmes, and Longfellow, against the ridicule and effrontery brought to bear upon cultural institutions by the more liberalized and democratized sensibilities Twain represented.[11]

Twain's speech, which places hobos purporting to be Emerson, Holmes, and Longfellow in the wilderness of the Far West, lampoons the highly romantic and didactic verse of those saintly poets by having it vulgarized by the impostors who recite it. Further, the behavior of the hobos is described as base and indecorous; they drink whiskey, cheat at cards, and tyrannize the frightened homesteader who is their host. Most obnoxiously, the perpetrators of the hoax try to mask their ignoble behavior with romanticized versifying.

According to most of the later accounts provided by literary critics, those who heard Twain sat in stunned silence, offended that a wild young whippersnapper, an upstart from the Far West, would dare to challenge or satirize refined gentlemen on such a solemn occasion.[12] Grant C. Knight, for example, wrote in 1932 that "the Cambridge Group, revolving about what Holmes called the hub of the universe, was more or less isolated from the rest of America. . . . They did their best to ignore the brawling realities of their own Nineteenth Century, and the stony silence with which they received Mark Twain's mid-western humor during a famous birthday dinner was symbolic of their whole attitude."[13] And Alexander Cowie claimed in 1948 that Twain "burlesqued" the poets present "in a humorous speech which was delivered amid ghastly silence to a distinguished assemblage of literati. . . . The reception of his speech was the measure of New England's initial coolness toward Western brashness."[14]

Both accounts derive argumentative weight from the assumption that Twain was met with "coolness" and a "stony silence." What is disconcerting, given such a scenario, is the lack of clarity about what really happened, as evidenced by newspaper accounts written about the event. Henry Nash Smith, in the most definitive version of the dinner and speech so far recorded, cites several newspaper accounts published immediately after the event that indicate that participants thoroughly enjoyed Twain's burlesque. For example, the *Boston Advertiser* reported on December 18 that "the amusement of the audience was intense, while the subjects of the wit, Longfellow, Emerson and Holmes, enjoyed it as much as any," and the *Boston Daily Globe* claimed that Twain "produced the most violent bursts of hilarity . . . and Whittier seemed to enjoy it keenly."[15]

Other newspaper accounts of the dinner included brief descriptions of Twain's participation, yielding evidence that his performance was not immediately an object of controversy but rather considered inconsequential. The *New York Herald*'s report on the day following the event, "Honor to a Poet," mentioned Twain's participation with no implication of its being indecorous: "Mark Twain, when called upon, related one of his experiences on the Pacific coast, in which Messrs. Holmes, Whittier and Longfellow were the chief subjects of his humorous allusions."[16] That short notice is remarkable for its subtle errors. It makes it appear as though Twain's speech involved a true story, and the writer also confuses the focus of his burlesque (substituting Whittier for Emerson), a suggestion of how facts had already become distorted into mythic accounts. In the *Herald*'s and many other accounts, there was little immediate indication of trouble. As Kenneth Eble has argued, "Newspaper reports did not single out the speech as the disaster it seemed to be to Clemens and Howells."[17]

Yet as time went on some evidence of controversy began to surface. For example, an account in the *Chicago Tribune* by the newspaper's Boston correspondent, published on December 30, 1877, related that "the criticisms upon the Whittier Dinner have grown into mightier proportions than I anticipated in my last, where I recorded my mild protest after the information I received that Mark Twain's extraordinary speech was out of order. Everywhere, upon all sides, there has arisen a cry of disgust and reprobation. The fact is, Mark Twain has been made too much of for Mark Twain, and he slops over and we get a little of the Ohio or Mississippi bilge-water."[18]

The comment that cries of disgust had "arisen" suggests that scandal was not immediate but instead grew slowly, like the tide. Smith identifies other newspapers stirring the flames of the apparently enlarging controversy. In an angry letter to the editor of the Springfield, Massachusetts, *Republican*, for example, an unnamed writer belabored his offended sense that Twain had done great damage not just to Whittier but perhaps to all that was holy and righteous about American genteel society:

> No one caring in the least for the "fitness of things" can read without a sense of pain the words of "Mark Twain" at the late *Atlantic*-Whittier dinner. Imagine the scene, the really brilliant company, bright in the best sense of that suggestive word. . . . Into this China shop burst a wild California bull. True gentlemen bear insult in silence. . . . Literary men in America, where so much is tolerated, ought to aim higher than the gutter, no matter what they have of talent, or even genius. American social life, upon which, by God's aid, must be built the mighty fabric of the future state, is in the formative period, and, jealous as we might have been of our political honor, a thousand times more jealous must we be of that most precious possession—reverence for that which is truly high.[19]

For this emotional defender of the didactic moral nature of the Fireside, Twain's "gutter" approach clearly posed a threat to the "fitness of things."

Other sensationalized reports written at some distance from the fact also demonstrate how gossipy renditions aided in multiplying the belief that Twain's speech should be regarded as outrageous behavior and irreverent effrontery. One example is the distorted report by Edwards Roberts published some seven years later in the San Francisco *Chronicle:*

> [I] do remember of Mark Twain being present and of his making a sad failure of a speech he made in which he coarsely parodied some of the poetical efforts of Longfellow, Holmes, Whittier and others. I can remember distinctly the misery depicted on Longfellow's face as Twain continued his uncouth antics before the almost holy group of men. In vain the venerable Whittier tried to smile at the questionable wit of the speaker, and Longfellow at last left the room, remarking, as he did so, "Mr. Twain is very funny tonight—very; but I believe that I must get away from the close air of the room." There was a good deal of gossip for a time regarding that "Whittier dinner speech," as it was called, of Mark Twain, but his friends covered up the failure as soon as they could.
> . . . one may be sure that in the works of the Hartford author he will find no mention of the evening when the creator of "Huckleberry Finn" made fun, before their faces too, of the Boston Gods.[20]

From the best evidence available, Longfellow did not grimace in "misery" or walk out of the room during the speech; such details were mentioned by none of the attendees. Indeed, and despite his ostensibly authoritative tone, the record does not indicate that Roberts himself attended the event, making his claims mere hearsay at best. Perhaps the source of his fable, framed neatly as a confrontation pitting Twain and his "uncouth antics" against the Boston Gods, is precisely where Roberts most tellingly alludes: the "good deal of gossip" that "for a time" immediately following the event circulated concerning Twain's "sad failure."

A notable aspect of the many newspaper accounts is the fact that they conflict so sharply. Most early reports made no mention of scandal, whereas later ones demonstrated the growing perception of one. In light of such inconsistencies, many critics doubt the existence of immediate misgivings or offended sensibilities among the dinner's guests. John Lauber concludes that "the speech had not been the disaster that Twain and Howells believed it to be," and Louis J. Budd concurs: Twain "imagined too many crises, overestimating—for example—the fuss at his speech at the Whittier dinner."[21] The view of the event's effects that Lauber's and Budd's conclusions anticipate holds that the chief actors in the drama initiated the worry and scandal to such a sublime extent that they were largely responsible for its mythologization. According to such a reading, however, Twain and Howells did not overreact at all. They recognized the overarching mythic ramifications of the event more perceptively and quickly than virtually any of their contemporaries.

Correspondence indicates that both Howells and Twain immediately perceived that the speech had created tensions and that both envisioned serious public scandal. Clearly, both men suffered emotional stress over the event, and their letters written during the weeks just after the event demonstrate their sense of a growing scandal. Twain remarked to Howells on December 23, 1877, "My sense of disgrace does not abate. It grows. I see that it is going to add itself to my list of permanencies—a list of humiliations that extends back to when I was seven years old. . . . I must have been insane when I wrote that speech & saw no harm in it, no disrespect toward those men whom I reverenced so much. And what shame I brought upon you, after what you said in introducing me! It burns me like fire to think of it."[22] He seemed to understand that the event, as one of his "permanancies," not only would haunt him personally but also would become a symbolic act forever linked with his emerging cultural legend.

Howells, in responding on December 25, told Twain, "I don't pretend not to agree with you [about the speech]. Everyone with whom I have talked about your speech regards it as a fatality."[23] In a note to Charles E. Norton on December 19, Howells illustrated his deepest feelings about "that hideous mistake of poor Clemens's": "he felt the awfulness of what he was doing, but was fatally helpless to stop. He was completely crushed by it . . . his performance was like an effect of demonical possession. The worst of it was, I couldn't see any retrieval for him."[24] Despite such convictions, however, Howells assured Twain in the note of the twenty-fifth that he should not "exaggerate the damage. . . . while I think your regret does you honor . . . I don't want you to dwell too morbidly on the matter."[25]

Howells suggested writing letters of apology to the main players of the drama, which Twain proceeded to do. He told Howells that he had wanted to send a copy to Whittier as well, "since the offense was done also against him" and against the "well nigh sacred place" that Whittier held in the American "people's estimation." He was unable to bring himself to approach Whittier with such a letter, however, and finally did nothing. Twain's letter to Howells ended in a lament for the desperate state of his emotions a full eleven days after the event:

> I haven't done a stroke of work since the Atlantic dinner; have only moped around. But I'm going to try tomorrow. How could I ever have—
> Ah well, I am a great & sublime fool. But then I am God's fool, & all His works must be contemplated with respect.[26]

Thus, the written records suggest two highly sensitive men acutely aware of their participation at the center of what appeared to them to be a significant, perhaps even "permanent," cultural dispute. Their deeply held views of the event are apparent in the somewhat exaggerated accounts of the dinner published more than thirty-five years after the event.[27] Equally important, virtually all subsequent commentary has been based on these three accounts. Consequently, the intensity of feeling and the cognizance of the underlying cultural tensions must be taken as solid evidence that the moment represented a cultural flashpoint despite ambiguous newspaper accounts of the evening.

It is likely that Howells and Twain beheld the mythical resonance of the cultural moment with more clarity, insight, and historical acuity than did the other contemporary commentators. Both must have internalized a conflict that was then common to the culture as a whole. They were aware of being central players in a dramatic conflict, because each was drawn, to different degrees, by competing sides of the cultural divide. Consensus and freedom, East and West, and romanticism and realism were prominent aspects of both men's subjectivities. They reflected simultaneously both poles of the paradox then vying for cultural supremacy. Despite being typecast by the eastern establishment as westerners, for instance, Twain and Howells identified strongly with the East and made their homes in New England for a major portion of their adult lives. Each imagined himself caught in the middle precisely because each did occupy a middle ground. Twain, as Susan Gillman has put it, found himself "suspended between two roles: the California humorist mocking the institution of the Men of Letters while being accepted as a member of that institution."[28]

Thus Twain, and to a lesser extent Howells, can usefully be considered an embodiment of the mythic struggle that the moment of Twain's speech has come to exemplify. Certainly he was keenly aware of inhabiting a tenuous cultural position in relation to the Schoolroom poets. From December 1867 through his wedding in February 1870 he had spent considerable time and effort to convince the Jervis Langdon family of Elmira, New York, that he was a worthy suitor for their beloved daughter Olivia.[29] His nearly obsessive desire to be accepted as famous, well-to-do easterner is by now a commonplace and perhaps best symbolized by his extravagant life-style and close associations in later years with powerful Gilded Age figures such as Andrew Carnegie and Henry Rogers.

And yet despite his aspirations Twain throughout his career often demonstrated a strong desire to declare independence from what he was fond of publicly denouncing as the decayed, oppressive, elitist eastern hegemony. Moreover, he often could be oppositional through his humor. George Bernard Shaw recognized this special gift and said so in 1907, near the end of Twain's life: "[Twain] is in very much the same position as myself. He has to put things in such a way as to make people who would otherwise hang him believe he is joking."[30]

Considering Shaw's insight, Twain's speech at the Whittier birthday celebration can be read simultaneously as a personal declaration of in/dependence and an earnest jeremiad masked as humor. It can rightfully take its place as another in the long line of those moments of social and cultural repentance that constitute manifestations of American metanoia. A desire to interpret the speech as an enactment of such epic proportions has prevailed almost from the moment of its delivery and throughout its existence as one of the quintessential American anecdotes.

In retrospect, it is not difficult to envision how the scene became so radically mythologized for its central participants or how it resulted in keen emotional stress in the days following the dinner. Both Howells, originally from Ohio, and Twain, born and raised in Missouri but associated with a number of western locales such as San Francisco, were aware of their roles as outsiders among the cultural elite of New England. Referring to his affinity with Twain, Howells commented, "We were natives of the same vast Mississippi valley; and Missouri was not so far from Ohio but that we were akin in our first knowledges of woods and fields, as we were in our early parlance."[31] Both were keen on being embraced by the eastern establishment and cognizant of the tension caused by their geographical differences with New England society. Lauber surmises that personal sensibilities, especially the underlying geographical tension, led to the perception of disaster: "Very likely the timid Howells, himself an outsider from Ohio and never quite sure of his own standing in the New England literary establishment, convinced his friend that the speech had been a frightful blunder. And Mark Twain, trusting Howells's judgment and prone to self-blame, was always ready to flagellate himself to real or imagined misdeeds, to turn blunders into crimes, embarrassments into catastrophes."[32]

Howells and Twain were not alone in sensing condescension at the hands of easterners. Other writers of the period described similar geographical tensions between East and West, many in comments predating the Whittier dinner. In 1852, for example, Alice Cary asserted the worthiness of literary attention on recently settled territories, including her native state of Indiana:

> The pastoral life of our country has not been a favorite subject of illustration by painters, poets, or writers of romance . . . in the interior of my

native state, which was a wilderness when first my father went to it, and is now crowned with a dense and prosperous population, there is surely as much in the simple manners, and the little histories every day revealed, to interest us in humanity, as there can be in those old empires where the press of tyrannous laws and the deadening influence of hereditary acquiescence necessarily destroy the best life of society.[33]

Voicing similar sentiments in 1871, Edward Eggleston explicitly criticized New England:

It used to be a matter of no little jealousy with us, I remember, that the manners, customs, thoughts, and feelings of New England country people filled so large a place in books, while our life, not less interesting, not less romantic, and certainly not less filled with humorous and grotesque material, had no place in literature. It was as though we were shut out of good society . . . perhaps, our Western writers did not dare speak of the West otherwise than as the unreal world to which Cooper's lively imagination had given birth.[34]

Eggleston's complaints are much more direct than those of Cary's, which were antebellum and more properly feminized. They are similar, however, in the authors' sense of remaining "shut out of good society." As one critic has argued, Eggleston, Howells, and Twain wrote in a time of crisis marked by several fundamental issues, "the most immediately important" being the opposition of "East and West": "In this split is to be found the decline of one cultural cycle and the rise of a second. The battle between 'idealists' and 'realists' which provided the major issues of American literary history from 1870 on, is readily identified with the East-West geographical division."[35]

Contemporary critics often regard Robert Spiller's account as being dated in its tendency toward categories that are too vague and characterizations that are overly reductionist; virtually all writers of the period had, for example, both idealistic and realistic tendencies. Spiller's insight into the "East-West geographical division" characteristic of cultural life in America, however, clarifies a key tension underlying the works of Cary and Eggleston and, later, Howells and Twain. His concept could be expanded by noting that the categories were in the process of being reified into complex signifiers that implicitly included a great deal of additional information. The West, for example, stood for much more than its explicit geographical location. It had become associated with a number of cultural modes such as the popular idiom, the realistic, the local, the legendary, and the anecdotal as well as with such popular cultural forms as minstrelsy, burlesque, satire, and other aspects of platform humor.[36]

The West was also quickly becoming the locus for a renewed hope in such American ideals as democracy and individualism that had suffered from disuse and hypocrisy in the corrupt and now elitist East. Through a complicated cultural shorthand the West slowly but surely came to symbolize opposition after the Civil War. As Richard S. Lowry notes, such categorical theorizing is simplistic; nevertheless, the general tendencies within American culture to reduce grand abstractions to shorthanded oppositional terms should not be underestimated.[37]

Numerous authors drew upon and fostered the image of the "oppositional West." Howells, for example, shared Cary's and Eggleston's concerns regarding the chasm between East and West. During his editorship of *The Atlantic* (1871–81), he devoted much energy to opening America's literary terrain to both the western and realist tendencies Spiller has identified. The division between East and West was also a prominent theme of Howells's literary achievement well before the Whittier event.[38] His second novel, *A Chance Acquaintance* (1873), focuses on the relationship between Kitty Ellison, representative of the lively, vigorous, democratic West, and Miles Arbuton, symbolic of the effete, stuffy, aristocratic East. The author's sympathies lie primarily with the vibrant and radiant Kitty. As Kenneth Lynn has argued, her background is strikingly similar to Howells's.[39]

Readers were aware of the tension between East and West in the novel, and there was controversy over the accuracy of Howells's depiction of the characters in *A Chance Acquaintance*.[40] Arbuton's name suggests Miles Coverdale, the similarly impotent and psychologically troubled representative of Bostonian culture in Nathaniel Hawthorne's *The Blithedale Romance* (1852). Arbuton betrays his coldness and lack of feeling early in the novel when Kitty mistakenly slips her arm through his at their first chance meeting at Niagara Falls. Her bold act, a move not proper among Boston's refined, is threatening to Miles and causes him to want to pull away and avoid her touch.

In general, Howells was highly critical of Arbuton's version of Boston gentility. Kitty originally holds Boston in high esteem as the sacred birthplace of the abolition movement and every other positive byproduct of democratic thought. That mythic view is captured in a letter she receives during the opening pages of the story from her Uncle Jack, venerating the city as "the birthplace of American liberty, . . . the yet holier scene of its resurrection. . . . a city where man is valued simply and solely for what he is in himself, and where color, wealth, family, occupation, and other vulgar and meretricious distinctions are wholly lost sight of in the consideration of individual excellence" (8).

Upon experiencing the milieu of Boston as typified by Miles, however, Kitty reexamines her views. He "isn't the Bostonian of Uncle Jack's imagination, and I suspect he wouldn't like to be" (81). Miles "talks about the lower classes, and tradesmen, and the best people, and good families, as I supposed nobody in *this* country *ever* did" (81). Discussing Miles later with a friend, Kitty complains that he is from "a world where everything is regulated by some rigid law that it would be death to break. . . . he seems to judge people according to their origin and locality and calling, and to believe that all refinement must come from just such training and circumstances as his own" (85–86).

Kitty eventually becomes highly critical of Boston: "This new Boston with which Mr. Arbuton inspired her was a Boston of mysterious prejudices and lofty reservations; a Boston of high and difficult tastes, that found its social ideal in the Old World, and that shrank from contact with the reality of this; a Boston as alien as Europe to her simple experiences . . . a critical, fastidious, and reluctant Boston, dissatisfied with the rest of the hemisphere, and gelidly self-satisfied in so far as it was not in the least the Boston of her fond preconceptions" (91). In the same way that Miles originally shrank from Kitty's attempt to touch him, she claims that Arbuton's social scene "shrank from contact with the reality of" any milieu other than its own. Just as Miles remains coldly detached and shallowly prideful of New England as unchallenged and supreme, Boston is "gelidly self-satisfied." After Kitty's eyes have been opened to what the ideal Boston of her uncle's letter has become, she rejects Arbuton's proposal of marriage. The cultural tension between East and West is finally irreconcilable. According to this reading, it is clear that, for Howells, the West represented a reified oppositional figure calling for the repentance of a corrupt and decadent East.

In his suggestive role as a prophetic Jeremiah calling America back from Boston's backslidden state as represented by Arbuton and to her original founding vision of democratic equality, as symbolized by the vibrant and radiant West, it is natural that Howells would be drawn so strongly to Twain. Of course, Twain was willing to go far beyond what the more conventional and decorous Howells contrived in works such as *A Chance Acquaintance*. Whereas Howells wrote a novel of mannered society that implicitly criticized Boston gentility, Twain attacked cultural icons and historical sites explicitly and at times savagely. In *The Innocents Abroad* (1869), a popular success, for example, he laments of European art museums, "[I am] weary with looking."[41]

As a result of his earlier works and his even more ridiculous satires and burlesques published in various newspapers or delivered from lecture-hall podiums, Twain had developed a wide audience and a substantial reputation well before his appearance at the Whittier dinner in 1877. In the autobiographical travelog *Roughing It* (1871), for example, he used vernacular English that betrays breathless, teenaged innocence meant to represent areas far west of literary Boston. By insisting on the viability of such everyday language, Twain demonstrated that romanticized and sentimental prose was rarely the most effective way to communicate the realistic West.

The tension resulting from pitting the gelid East against the effervescent West, typified by Eggleston's comment in 1871 and worked out in Howells's novel of 1873, found important symbolic manifestation in the Whittier event of 1877. Twain, who represented vernacular speech, boyhood innocence, frontier independence, and democratic egalitarianism, had established a solid basis for his claim to being the premiere symbolic manifestation of the oppositional nature of the American Far West, the "oppositional West incarnate." Careful consideration of the text of his speech and, more generally, of the tall-tale form itself, reveals Twain's attempt to foreground East-West tension and foster a concept of himself as oppositional West incarnate by framing himself and his humor and rhetoric as western.[42] His use of a humorous albeit oppositional stance in the speech and exaggerated response to the speech's fallout invited subsequent commentators to recount the episode as a singularly provocative manifestation of a quintessentially American mythos. Much of that commentary emphasized Twain's role as a revolutionary declarer of independence, thus creating one of the most tried and true mythic enactments of the American metanoia in the nation's literary history.

The birthday speech opened with a bang. Twain remarked upon the occasion by describing himself as "standing here on the shore of the Atlantic and contemplating certain of its largest literary billows" (230). That suggests his geographic differences with the audience and associates the location with its most famous denizens, the Boston Gods. Twain called the poets "billows," however, ambiguously evoking both the majestic natural power of ocean waves and the stilted, overbearing fluff of conventional rhetoric.

Immediately Twain launched into a bogus anecdote in which he told of asking a lonely Nevada miner to give him food and lodging for the night. The miner is taken aback by the presence of the fourth "littery man that has been here in twenty-four hours." The others, he claims, were Longfellow, Emerson, and Holmes—"consound the lot!" (231). Twain openly punned on the word *literary* by having the miner mispronounce it as "littery," a mistake linking literature with garbage, and the miner's "consound," a variant of "confound," condemns the impersonators. The miner's description of the three frauds is funny and bold: "Emerson was a seedy little bit of a chap . . . Holmes was as fat as a balloon; he weighed as much as three hundred, and had double chins all the way down to his stomach . . . Longfellow was built like a prize-fighter. . . . They had been drinking, I could see that. And what queer talk they used!" (231). These comments, especially the brisk ridicule of Holmes's notorious obesity, are among the speech's most pointed, and the opening lines all exemplify what one scholar has referred to as Twain's "performative masculinity . . . the performance of pugnacious self-display."[43]

Twain's principal concern, however, was with the "queer talk" of the perpetrators. He juxtaposed the diction of the Fireside poets with the everyday vernacular of the simple miner. Ten times the fraudulent guests offer stylized and sometimes slightly altered verses from the works of the Fireside poets, and each occurrence marks that language as irrelevant and superficial in the context of the various mundane activities typifying the life of the western frontiersman. As the miner prepares a dinner of "bacon and beans" for his guests, for example, Emerson laments poetically the sad state of the meal:[44]

> Give me agates for my meat;
> Give me cantharids to eat;
> From air and ocean bring me foods,
> From all zones and altitudes.[45]

The miner begins to resent the romantic yearnings of his guests: "If you'll excuse me, this ain't no hotel. You see it sort of riled me—I warn't used to the ways of littery swells."[46] After the meal, when the miner brings out a jug of whiskey, Holmes desires more refined spirits: "Flash out a stream of blood-red wine! / For I would drink to other days" (232). In response to Holmes's lament, the miner turns to him and says, "Looky here, my fat friend. I'm a-running this shanty, and if the court knows herself, you'll take whiskey straight or you'll go dry."[47] The raw language of the miner, studded with such words as *ain't, rile, warn't, looky,* and *a-running,* clashes with the less-familiar terms the easterners employ: *agates* and *cantharids.*

The three impostors begin to "play euchre at ten cents a corner," but they all apparently cheat, which brings them to their feet to fight. The brawl simmers down immediately, however, when the three "wished they had some more company." At that point Emerson points to the miner and asks, "Is yonder squalid peasant all / That this proud nursery could breed?" (232).[48] That statement, calling the miner a peasant, makes the three charlatans seem condescending and aristocratic. The Boston elite, Twain asserts, does not appreciate the American worker but rather views them as "squalid."

The miner awakens early the next day, head clouded from the whiskey, to discover Longfellow sneaking away. He is wearing the miner's boots and attempting to steal them. Longfellow responds to the miner's accusation (232) with verses from one of the century's most renowned stanzas, the ending of "A Psalm of Life":

> Lives of great men all remind us
> We can make our lives sublime;
> And, departing, leave behind us
> Footprints on the sands of time.[49]

In the context of the ridiculous story, Longfellow's heightened romantic adage becomes the hypocritical dodge of a pathetic con man. By juxtaposing his memorable words of didactic moralism with the petty contrivances of a trickster trying to steal the boots of a man who has graciously been his host, Twain betrays an ambivalence that informs his speech and the performative moment in which it was embedded.

It is significant that he asserts the "distinction" that had been achieved by the Fireside poets.[50] The cheats and scoundrels Twain sketched appear to know the poetry of these sages intimately, and their allusions draw upon some of the best-known poems of the nineteenth century. Thus, the fact that Twain made use of the Fireside poets' work indicates their widespread influence, apparently even on those he depicted, and displays Twain's deep reading of and even admiration for the poetry they created. Yet the juxtaposition of Longfellow's verse with an act of theft by a petty crook suggests that there is something dishonest and even fraudulent about the style and manner of the versifying itself. Twain's authentic esteem for the honored guests is seemingly tempered by his suspicious iconoclasm. His tale is ambivalent about the revered poets and, by extension, the institution of authorship. It simultaneously manifests the consensus and dissensus that are the fundamental marks of the American declaration of in/dependence.

Perhaps the most famous part of the speech is its deeply ambiguous and rather sinister ending, which suggests that the poets (and the speaker) are impostors, as are all writers:

> "Why, my dear sir, these were not the gracious singers to whom we and the world pay loving reverence and homage; these were impostors."
> The miner investigated me with a calm eye for a while; then said he, "Ah! impostors, were they? Are you?"[51]

Here the true genius of Twain's speechifying is most evident. He calls the poets "gracious singers" who receive "loving reverence and homage." That stilted language, however, is also a burlesque of such a view. The profundity of the ending lies in the blurring of the distinction between the actual Boston poets, the apparently fraudulent guests, and the speaker, Mark Twain. All, to some degree, can be counted as various sorts of impostors. Moreover, it is slightly off the mark to say that the poets themselves were the focus of the burlesque. As Richard Lowry has suggested, Twain targeted not so much the men but rather their names as literary trademarks. Holmes, for one, appeared to recognize that. In writing back to Twain, he assured him that "it never occurred to me . . . to feel wounded by your playful use of my name."[52]

Certainly, hearing Twain say in the very presence of the Boston Gods that "*these* were not the gracious singers. . . . *These* were impostors" might have struck some guests as indecorous and disrespectful. Despite the fact that in Twain's tale the poets are only being impersonated, it seems plausible that the speech might have engendered scandalous reaction from some of the more decorous members of the assembly.[53] When properly understood, however, the speech dramatically enacted a central tension of the contemporary culture by depicting the speaker as inhabitant of a highly ambivalent middle ground. Twain simultaneously championed and criticized both east and west, concluding with the haunting possibility that the speaker, like all writers, might qualify as a "co-impostor" with all the rest. By ending the speech with a calm assertion of his role as impostor, he included all authors—and perhaps the entire institution of authorship. It seems sinisterly ironic and yet oddly in keeping with his role as jeremiadic prophet that the speech's ending undercuts as well as deconstructs the mythologized figure of Twain as oppositional West incarnate.

Despite the apparent laughter during the event, Twain's implicit suggestion that the real poets at the dinner were frauds explains why some members of the mainstream interpreted his speech as a breech of decorum and an attack against good manners and right thinking. Conservative writers understood the speech as Twain's way of distancing himself and representing western speech and culture to the cultural hegemony of Boston. The speech attained prominence as an attack on the institution of the author as centered in Boston and focussed on whether any cultural figure (such as the venerated poets present) was worthy of reverence. In suggesting the hypocrisy of such cultural stalwarts of the East, and also recognizing his fallibility, Twain broached a theme that one critic has identified as "bad faith."[54] In doing so before an illustrious audience, he implicitly associated deception and hypocrisy not only with the East but also with Boston and *The Atlantic*'s stellar contributors.

Twain's and Howells's emotional unease resulted from sensitivity to participating in this deep and widening cultural schism and their awareness that such an interpretation of Twain's speech was possible. Certainly Longfellow, writing to Twain on January 6, 1878, betrayed a similar awareness as he attempted to deflate such social tension:

> Dear Mr. Clemens,
> I am a little troubled, that you should be so much troubled about a matter of such slight importance. The newspapers have made all the mischief. A bit of humor at a dinner table is one thing; a report of it in the morning papers is another. . . .
> I do not believe that anybody was much hurt. Certainly I was not, and Holmes tells me he was not. So I think you may dismiss the matter from your mind, without further remorse.[55]

The fact that Longfellow should have even discussed the possibility of a scandal with Holmes, however, reveals that such an embarrassment was possible.

In addition to illustrating Twain's ambivalence, however, the speech served two other important functions. First, it acted as a barometer of the underlying cultural tension that had existed well before the dinner and far beyond the psychological world of Twain or Howells. Second, when such an underlying tension is represented as manifesting itself openly at a highly public event, key participants like Twain tend to be branded as agents of one wing of the dialectical tension. What results are caricatured portrayals of the moment being propagated and reinforced. As a result, Twain became even more prominently associated with one of the parties engaged in the cultural war surrounding this tension: the oppositional West.

The cultural conversation about the Whittier dinner, beginning with the personal unease of Twain and Howells and advancing over many decades through accounts that include the men's memoirs, has produced a mythic representation that illustrates a number of the late-nineteenth century's most important literary and cultural conflicts. Spiller's analysis identifies the most prominent conflict as the opposition of East and West, but it is far more useful and all-encompassing to foreground a different, more enduring conflict—the never-ending, inherently American struggle between concern and freedom. Boston would be cast as headquarters of concern, and the "great confused West," in Barrett Wendell's term, would stand in as mythic freedom.

Thus, Twain's speech, the resulting uproar, and the cultural moment in which both are embedded exemplify Kenneth Burke's notion of the "representative anecdote," marking it as a mythical moment demonstrating the tensions and contradictions inherent in the general culture.[56] In fact, the Whittier dinner has been understood as representative of more than one underlying opposition. For example, the opposition has been depicted as indicative of the subtle shift in literary sensibilities away from the romantic and Bostonian gentility and toward the realistic and regionalized; as pitting the high literary language of the Boston elite against the vulgarized western vernacular (as represented in Twain's actual speech); and, in more general terms, as the renegade forces of the western frontier against the staid eastern elitist establishment. In each version of the conflict, a predominant theme is the opposition of east against west, with Twain becoming cast as sole representative of the West. The predominant view of Mark Twain as oppositional West incarnate evolved as a product of a cultural conversation that spanned many decades. Of course, Twain's association with the West was a feature of newspaper and critical response well before the Whittier event and was at least partly a result of how he presented himself publicly. In addition, long after the Whittier dinner and even well after Twain's death, critics as well as supporters almost universally remarked on his supposed "oppositional westernness" and cast him as the preeminent representative of the American West and of radical opposition and mythic freedom.

Initially, of course, Howells was Twain's foremost critical champion and a seer of his unique and lasting place in American literary history. Howells identified Twain's style as "the American Western."[57] In the long-term conversation defining and reframing him, it appears that Twain became categorically representative of all things western at an early stage of American literary scholarship. Some early histories focus entirely on Twain's geographic roots. William Simonds, for example, called him "a distinctly western product."[58] John Nichol described Twain as western in terms of style, which Nichol found highly destructive: "The master of this degenerate style is a writer to whom it is hard to do neither more nor less than justice: his success is, relatively, so far in advance of his deserts, that we have to resist the temptation to depreciate his really great, though, as seems to me, often misused ability . . . [Twain] has done perhaps more than any other living writer to lower the literary tone of English speaking people."[59] Barrett Wendell agreed in 1900 that Mark Twain was "characteristically American" and "thoroughly American. . . . On the whole, however, we may say of our great confused West, that just as surely as New

England has made its mark in the literary history of America, so as yet this West has not."[60] Wendell, as it turned out, was wrong. Twain certainly did leave a mark, and so did the West. But Wendell correctly noted the opposition between Twain, the West, and the literary establishment of New England. The rather negative perspective toward Twain espoused by critics such as Nichols and Wendell corresponds, not surprisingly, to a view of cultural tradition privileging Boston's genteel tradition.

Howells and Wendell, and later Van Wyck Brooks and Bernard De-Voto, disagreed vehemently about Twain's achievements, and yet they all tended to frame him as characteristic of the Far West—indeed, as representative of the West and in turn of America itself.[61] An extensive map of the cultural conversation concerning Twain would eventually show that the disagreements over him betrayed far stronger general disagreements about the meaning of America and prevailing national myths. Vernon Louis Parrington in 1930, for example, took a highly favorable view of Twain as prophet of democratic egalitarianism warring against the insidious "disease" of New England's genteel tradition:

> Here at last was an authentic American—a native writer thinking his own thoughts, using his own eyes, speaking his own dialect—everything European fallen away, the last shred of feudal culture gone, local and western yet continental. A strange and uncouth figure . . . yet the very embodiment of the turbulent frontier that had long been shaping a native psychology, and that now at last was turning eastward to Americanize the Atlantic seaboard. . . . Twain was indubitably an embodiment of three centuries of American experience—frontier centuries, decentralized, leveling, individualistic. . . . Mark Twain was the child of the frontier past.[62]

The most telling aspect of Parrington's mythic concept is that he turns the tables against the eastern establishment. That is, Twain, as "embodiment of the turbulent frontier," now represented the shifting of literary and cultural power. The final irony of that power shift, for Parrington, was that in figures such as Twain the West "at last was turning eastward to Americanize the Atlantic seaboard." Far from being the moralizing agents of the American dream, New England must now be newly Americanized by the moralizing efforts of the more democratic and individualistic West, as exemplified by Twain.

The glorification of Mark Twain still continues. Shelley Fisher Fishkin's *Lighting Out for the Territory: Reflections on Mark Twain and American Culture* (1996), for example, extends his mythologization. The book, an important contribution to Twain scholarship, nevertheless frames Twain as the central acolyte in the temple of the American metanoia. In a near-hagiographic valorization, Twain is called "our Homer, our Tolstoy, our Shakespeare, our Rabelais."[63] According to Fishkin's repeated formulation, Twain is the quintessential representative American—"the most distinctively American of American authors" (7–8). That theme continues throughout the book: Twain "became the voice of the new land" and "was the embodiment of that most American of traits: the ability to invent—and reinvent—oneself" (8, 127). *Huck Finn*, for Fishkin, should be viewed mythically as America's literary equivalent to the Declaration of Independence. It constituted a "declaration of independence from the genteel English novel tradition"; the book was begun and abandoned "during the summer of 1876, one hundred years after the signing of the Declaration of Independence"; and it has "served as America's literary declaration of independence. . . . [and] is often taught as a model of how one breaks free from the colonizer's culture to create an indigenous national literature" (112, 117, 184–85).

Such readings of Twain are hardly unique, of course. Yet they must also be recognized for precisely what they are: mythologized renditions that are pedagogically useful but theoretically troublesome. Fishkin's assertions about *Huck Finn* echo similar claims made about Emerson's key speeches of 1837 and 1838, which also mythologized them as "America's literary declarations of independence." The merit of either claim is hardly as interesting (and certainly much less empirically determined) as the insistent efforts of the various critics to establish exactly which literary masterwork is most like the original Declaration. Emerson, the key agent of freedom in the earlier version of the myth, was magically transposed to the other side in later versions of the Whittier birthday event. Thus, an ineluctable aspect of the "anxiety of influence" always marks the evolving myth of America: Strong sons ultimately become the strong (and corrupt) fathers who are misread by the champions of the next generation of dissent.[64]

The struggle to define not merely Twain's involvement with the Whittier dinner but also, and much more sweepingly, his accomplishment as a writer and contributor to American culture ultimately can be analyzed as another of the "myriad of self-contained cultural disputes" that "actually amounts to a fairly comprehensive and momentous struggle to define the meaning of America."[65] In such a formulation, Twain, oppositional West incarnate, is cast as an agent of freedom and progressivism against the hegemonic consensus represented by the East. In addition, critical readings of Twain's Whittier dinner speech, his overall literary accomplishment, or even more broadly descriptions of the impact of the oppositional West (or of the "oppositional elsewhere") in

American literary history proceed naturally from any critic's stance toward the overarching mythic struggle underlying the nation's society and culture. Thus do critical depictions of authors, shaped as they inevitably are by a critic's predispositions, become participants in the struggle to define America.

Another issue concerns Twain's fervent embrace of the very Gilded Age values and ideologies that he most famously condemned. To broach the question squarely, Just how oppositional was Mark Twain? Any full reading of the author's life would be remiss without admitting his desperate desire for the public adulation, social status, and prestige that his written works constantly burlesque and condemn. Further, he was overcome by passion for wealth, power, materialism, and the bonanzas just around the corner despite the fact that he regularly denounced them. Beginning in 1871, for example, Twain invested in sending his acquaintance James Riley on a wild goose chase to South Africa in hope of garnering lavish wealth in the rumored diamond mines there. The fall of 1871 also saw his move to the Hartford neighborhood known as Nook Farm, "which was as staunchly committed to liberal Congregationalism as it was to the Republican party." There Twain would spend at least $122,000 over several years to build and furnish his home on Farmington Avenue, a spectacular symbol of effusive opulence that would have been unthinkable for any previous American author. His involvement with James W. Paige, the smooth-talking inventor of a typesetting machine, arguably became Twain's version of the Holy Grail. For nearly a decade he sank at least $250,000 into what turned out to be a futile attempt to perfect and market the Paige Typesetter, a failure that has by now attained a legendary status. He also failed in his compulsive attempt to own a publishing house, which collapsed primarily as a result of the vexed attempt to bring out a ten-volume *Library of American Literature.* During and after the worst financial times of his life in the early to mid-1890s, Twain counted as his closest ally the controversial strongman of the Standard Oil Trust, Henry Huttleston Rogers, who helped bail him out of his monetary miseries. Rogers, an archetypal Gilded Age entrepreneur, was described by Twain in 1902 as "not only the best friend I ever had, but . . . the best man I have ever known." As Justin Kaplan puts it, Twain was "representative of a broad spectrum of paradox . . . as a writer he stood outside American society of the Gilded Age, but as a businessman he embraced its business values."[66]

Moreover, Twain could be inspired by even the most explicitly conservative rhetoric. During his courtship to Livy, Twain used Oliver Wendell Holmes's popular novel *The Autocrat of the Breakfast Table* as a sort of "courting book." Holmes, he considered, stood "at the pinnacle of literary culture."[67] The courtship resulted in his reading (and commenting favorably on) a large number of "sentimental" works such as Coventry Patmore's *The Angel in the House* ("exquisite"). Twain strictly oversaw Livy's reading lest it should "soil [her] purity": "Read nothing that is not *perfectly* pure . . . neither [*Don Quixote*] nor Shakspeare are proper books for virgins to read."[68]

That conservative streak often manifested itself in Twain's public political life. In 1879, when U. S. Grant returned to America from a long stay abroad, Twain participated in a reunion of the Army of the Tennessee in Chicago. Twain, who "worshipped" Grant, was "transfigured by oratory" as he listened to the patriotic rhetoric throughout the course of the evening. As he later wrote to Howells regarding Col. Robert Ingersoll's impassioned speech: "[Ingersoll is] the most beautiful human creature that ever lived. . . . I doubt if America has ever seen anything quite equal to it."[69] It was at the end of that evening of pomp and nostalgia that he gave his well-known "Babies" oration in which he breathlessly invoked America's future greatness: "Think what is in store for the present crop! . . . Our present schooner of State will have grown into a political leviathan."[70]

The millennial splendor hinted at in "The Babies" came to full-blown fruition in Twain's letter "To Walt Whitman," included in a commemorative volume of tributes addressed to the aged poet in 1889. Twain's brief yet enlightening contribution focused on the "greatness" of the Gilded Age era and echoed the fervent patriotic optimism of Whitman's most memorable verse:

> What great births you have witnessed! The steam-press, the steamship, the steel-ship, the railroad, the perfected cotton-gin, the telegraph, the telephone, the phonograph, the photograph . . . those latest and strangest marvels of a marvelous age. . . . but tarry yet awhile, for the greatest is yet to come. Wait thirty years, and then look out over the earth! You shall see marvels upon marvels added to these whose nativity you have witnessed; and conspicuous above them you shall see their formidable Result—Man at almost his full stature at last!—and still growing, visibly growing, while you look. . . . Wait till you see that great figure appear, and catch the far glint of the sun upon his banner; then you may depart satisfied, as knowing you have seen him for whom the world was made.[71]

The exclamation points, the strategic capitalization ("Result"), the repetition of the word *marvels,* and the catalog of inventions all echo the techniques of the great romantic poet to whom he wrote. The biblical allusion is to the millennial return of Jesus, "for whom the world was made." It is hard to write this off as concealing some level of ironic detachment. The passage rings with authentic hope and betrays the fervent cultural optimism fundamental to not only the era but also to Mark Twain himself.

What is evident in these examples is that the man was drawn strongly and relentlessly by concern as much as freedom: "[The] code he detested was also, in part, the one he lived by."[72] For Kaplan, as the title of his biography—*Mr. Clemens and Mark Twain*—suggests, the two "personalities" were so distinct that they could be conveniently named: Mr. Clemens was concern-oriented, and Mark Twain was freedom-oriented. That paradigm for explaining the bedeviled author has become standard. Twain seemingly endorsed such a divided version of himself, but in keeping with the oppositional nature of the western lands of America he drew the two parts of his psyche in typically geographic terms. As he put the issue in his underrated speech "The Pilgrims," "I am a border ruffian from the state of Missouri. I am a Connecticut Yankee by adoption. I have the morals of Missouri and the culture of Connecticut, and that's the combination that makes the perfect man."[73] Thus, to label Clemens/Twain as merely an embodiment of mythic freedom and opposition is as simplistic as it is to label him a conservative lackey of the industrial and cultural machine of the Gilded Age. That is the fundamental irreconcilability of the Twain debate, and it is undoubtedly the key to his status as the nation's most mythic author.

Finally, mythical accounts generally, despite presenting historical problems of accuracy and tendencies toward oversimplification, remain firmly lodged in the lectures and teachings of many Americanists. Teachers of literature are actively involved in reflecting and fostering mythical configurations when such figures prove handy for describing the cultural moments in which they are embedded. The desire to read Twain as being preeminently entangled in cultural conflict is a major trend in Twain studies and continues to mark him as the nation's most representative author.[74] As they always have, Burkean "representative anecdotes," such as the Whittier birthday situation continue to serve teachers and professors as indispensable tools of instruction. At the same time, teaching literature always involves, to some degree, implicit participation in myth-making as well.

7 *Cultural Conflict Makes the Man*

Sinclair Lewis as Pagan, 100 Percent American, and Nobel Laureate

---

In the years immediately after the armistice that ended World War I the United States was plunged into economic turmoil and emotional crisis. Approximately four million former members of the military flooded an already overburdened labor market. Inflation had cut the purchasing power of the U.S. dollar in half in fewer than four years; the average cost of living grew nearly 99 percent between 1914 and 1918. Labor became disgruntled with working conditions, and there were unprecedented outbreaks of civil unrest. In 1919 alone, well over four million workers were involved directly with 3,600 labor strikes.[1]

Such economic conditions only added to the paranoia pervading America during World War I. Frustrated Americans, who had been "whipped into a frenzy of wartime enthusiasm," were left after the armistice with a "directionless belligerence which sought a new outlet." They "needed an enemy, one that could account for the disruptions on the home front."[2] Garry Wills's description of the phenomenon is more concise: "Preachers need devils."[3]

Not surprisingly, a variety of candidates for diabolization emerged in the years following the war. At first, the focus of the initiative that came to be called the Red Scare was upon communist insurgency, resulting in the rhetorical attacks on Bolsheviks and Parlor Reds, epithets aimed loosely at all manner of liberals and radicals, progressives and revolutionaries, and reformers and crackpots. Although the Red Scare subsided rather quickly early in the 1920s, "the crusade for 100 percent Americanism continued through most of the decade." For example, the American Legion, now considered a quietly conservative club for veterans, began just after World War I as a vigilante group of super-patriots who often violently persecuted those suspected of being incompletely patriotic. Their targets were not only members of racial groups (mainly blacks) but also professors, teachers, members of the clergy, and prominent officials, who were often "bullied, smeared, and subjected to outrageous restrictions."[4]

The chief example of a vicious hate group that advocated social cohesion and homogeneity was the Ku Klux Klan. The KKK was openly dedicated to the ideal of the Ku Klux Kreed, a manifesto that "declared simply for white supremacy and 'the sublime principles of pure Americanism.'" The urge toward consensus following World War I helped the KKK evolve into a well-financed and, especially in certain states, politically powerful force for conformist principles as well as bigotry. D. C. Stephenson, for example, could boast that he had become by 1928 "the most powerful man in Indiana," and an estimated two hundred thousand Klan members attended his coronation as the state's Grand Dragon.

The KKK, an extremist manifestation of what I have termed Endicott's ghost, framed itself as defending the conservative myth of concern against any constituencies that might defy its vision of America. Although now known primarily for its persecution of blacks, the Klan also openly castigated Bolsheviks as well as Jews, Roman Catholics, ethnic immigrant groups, modernists, socialists, evolutionists, and any other "enemies" who threatened its mythic concepts. The Klan's alarmist message contributed to an increase in racial and ethnic tensions that resulted in such incidents as the bloody Chicago race riots during the summer of 1919.[5]

In the midst of such growing economic and emotional anxieties, the KKK was thus an extremist expression of the conservative impulse toward what became known as a "return to normalcy." The insistent nostalgia for an idyllic, wholesome life-style, most prominently associated with the homespun values of a typical midwestern village, proved to be a powerful force in solidifying postwar cultural conservatism. Exemplifying that desire for normalcy was the Republican nominee for the presidency in 1920—Sen. Warren G. Harding. The handsome Harding personified himself as patriotic, modest, and home-loving—"Main Street come to Washington"—and was given to conducting interviews and campaign speeches from his front porch.[6] His inaugural speech of March 4, 1921, signaled allegiance to the patriotic rhetoric and vague platitudes that marked his campaign:

Our supreme task is the resumption of our onward, normal way. Reconstruction, readjustment, restoration—all these must follow. I would like to hasten them. . . . We contemplate the immediate task of putting our public household in order. . . . We want an America of homes, illumined with hope and happiness, where mothers, freed from the necessity for long hours of toil beyond their own doors, may preside as befits the hearthstone of American citizenship. We want the cradle of American childhood rocked under conditions so wholesome and so hopeful that no blight may touch it in its development, and we want to provide that no selfish interest, no material necessity, no lack of opportunity, shall prevent the gaining of that education so essential to best citizenship.[7]

Harding's vision of America called for a return to "our onward, normal way" in which real men worked to bring home wages to their hearths and homes, the glorified reward for their daily toil. Here, American mothers were again established as ruling angels of a family's domicile. Under them, America's future, "the cradle of American childhood," would be cared for so as to eliminate any possibility of "blight."

Harding's rhetorical stance, in a sense, offered a toned-down version of the jeremiadic content of the much more violent hysteria promulgated by the KKK. Both appealed to the inherent postwar desire to return to normalcy. Walter Lippmann noted in 1927 that the KKK, and the xenophobia and fundamentalism of which it was the nation's primary manifestation, was symptomatic of the cultural milieu of the early 1920s. It was "an extreme but authentic expression of the politics, the social outlook, and the religion of the older American village civilization making its last stand against what [looked] to it like an alien invasion."[8]

As Frederick J. Hoffman has argued, towns became reified in the minds of supporters as abstract symbols of all things good, pure, and right about American society. Children of the second half of the nineteenth century had been indoctrinated with such a view of midwestern civilization through texts such as the McGuffey school readers. William H. McGuffey, called by one scholar an "apostle of religion, morality, and education," tried to inculcate a small-town ideal in students that might "bolster midwestern civilization against the dangers inherent in pioneering new frontiers." As a result, his texts, approximately a hundred million copies of which were sold between 1850 and 1900, depicted small towns in largely mythical and didactically moralistic terms and asserted the superiority of village and country life over that of the rapidly developing cities of the late nineteenth century.[9]

A similar conservative, although perhaps more genteel, sensibility was manifested as an influential literary institution in the form of the American Academy of Arts and Letters (AAAL) and the National Institute of Arts and Letters (NIAL). The AAAL was formed in 1904 as an upper chamber, or senate, to the NIAL, which had been formed six years earlier. Thanks to significant funding supplied by Archer M. Huntington, its chief benefactor and son of railroad millionaire Collis P. Huntington, the AAAL was able, on November 19, 1921, to lay the cornerstone for a "kind of citadel of learning," a massive edifice at Broadway and 155th Street in New York City. Situated in this luxurious and expensively appointed stronghold, the AAAL "constituted themselves as defenders of the English word and priests of its pronunciation." The AAAL also sought to become the national authority on artistic taste and hoped to represent and advance the cause of literary excellence. As an indication of how it would undertake that agency, the AAAL launched its priesthood with "an elaborate and well-publicized four day festival" honoring the figure one academy member called "the foremost American man of letters" except for Emerson: the Schoolroom poet James Russell Lowell.[10]

The conservative impulses toward normalcy, small towns, and genteel sensibility typified America's postwar myth of concern. Small towns were the most prominent symbol of the whole package, and the AAAL its greatest literary champion. Millions of Americans desired a return to the more stable environment represented by the old and familiar patterns of the prewar years. In response to that desire, a variety of conservative spokespersons ranging from the Ku Klux Klan to the American Academy of Arts and Letters became strange bedfellows by fostering similar cultural positions informed to varying degrees by the continued influence of Endicott's ghost. That is, in jeremiadic tone the conservative supporters of America's myth of concern all advocated a return to previous values and simultaneously called for resistance to encroaching subversive interventionism.

In turn, a number of iconoclastic and often savage critics of middle-class American civilization reached an apogee of influence in the early 1920s and attacked the reified, mythic concept of the town.[11] Carl Van Doren gave this critical stance a name: the "revolt from the village." Opposing the mythical conception of America's Victorian small-town culture as an idyllic and near-utopian environment, the revolt Van Doren described included a depiction of a rural population "sunk in greed and hypocrisy and—as if this were actually the worst of all—complacent apathy." The movement was notable for its "especial candor in affairs of sex": "There is filth . . . behind whited sepulchers." Van Doren discussed numerous writers as leading the way in the revolt, the most important of whom were Edgar Lee Masters, Sherwood Anderson, and Sinclair Lewis. Lewis's best-seller *Main Street* (1920) depicted a small town in Minnesota replete with hidden sins, tireless backbiting and gossip, tedious complacency, and conformity to communal patterns of thought and behavior.[12] In more generalized terms, the revolt had two major themes: a demonstration that village reality comprised a kind of "buried life" (an allusion to Matthew Arnold's poem of that name) and a sustained attack against any sort of conformity and compliance in American public activity.[13]

The literary history of the 1920s can be understood as an ongoing struggle in which conservative spokespersons for the myth of concern found themselves defending their territory against a host of subversive younger writers. According to that premise, the work of numerous writers can be understood as manifestations of an overarching cultural conflict pitting concern against freedom and informing the culture of the entire decade. In that context, Sinclair Lewis was a central figure for several reasons: his popular success by way of the massive sales of his novels; his depiction by a variety of critics, including Van Doren and H. L. Mencken, as a key literary leader; and his openly hostile attitude toward the conservative manifestations of Endicott's ghost, including small-town life and its literary champion the AAAL.

Above all, Lewis's considerable importance during the 1920s can be attributed to his reification as a symbol of rebellion, cutting satire, and devilish subversion. In a sense, he became the preeminent cultural icon of literary iconoclasm, and it is possible to view his seminal and most widely publicized cultural statement, the Nobel Prize acceptance speech of 1930, as an overt articulation of American metanoia. Through the enactment of that public statement Lewis declared his in/dependence from the tyrannies he imagined to be ruling American arts and letters. And a variety of critics and observers received and constructed that moment, in which he ostensibly both announced and initiated a new start in American literature, as a symbolic act of declaring independence.

∼

Conservative backlash attacking Lewis began early in the decade as cultural spokespersons criticized the content of his breakthrough achievement *Main Street.* The Rev. Charles H. Brent, bishop of the Episcopal Diocese of Western New York, made headlines when he excoriated the book in a public address in Rochester in July 1921. Brent's critical comments were picked up by the *New York Times* and then by numerous other newspapers. *Main Street*, for Brent, was distinctly a "pagan book" that featured "little more than sodden depression" and contrasted sharply with the "idealistic character of the great literature of the ages."[14]

A similar backlash came from Meredith Nicholson, whose own books such as *A Hoosier Chronicle* (1912) depicted the sunshine and grace of small-town life in his native Indiana. Nicholson's response to *Main Street*—"Let Main Street Alone!"—was originally published in the *New York Evening Post* in 1921 and then appeared in a book of essays, *The Man in the Street*, later in the same year. The cracker-barrel wisdom of his prose provided a homespun defense of American villages:

> Nothing in America is more reassuring than the fact that someone is always wailing in the market-place. . . . [Yet] happiest are they who keep sawing wood and don't expect too much! . . . There are diversities of gifts, but all, we hope, animated by the same spirit. . . .
> There is, really, something about corn—tall corn, that whispers on summer nights in what George Ade calls the black dirt country. There is something finely spiritual about corn that grows like a forest in Kansas and Nebraska. And Democracy is like unto it—the plowing, and the sowing, and the tending to keep the weeds out. . . .
> It isn't all just luck, the workings of our democracy. If there's any manifestation on earth of a divine ordering of things, it is here in America. . . .
> It's only the remnant of Israel that can be saved. Let Main Street Alone![15]

Several features of Nicholson's comments are worth remarking. America's greatness, illustrated by its honest workers "sawing wood" and its "finely spiritual" corn, is not just "luck." Rather, America, as a "manifestation on earth of a divine ordering of things," prospers through "diversities of gifts . . . animated by the same spirit," an allusion to I Corinthians 12:4 that links the American mission with that of the New Testament Christian church. America's small towns, the "remnant of Israel," are the "manifestation of the Spirit for the common good" (I Corinthians 12:7).

Brent's and Nicholson's attacks illustrate a conservative tendency to focus specifically on Lewis as representative of the radical element threatening their cultural positions, a tendency shared by members of the AAAL. Among the crop of talented writers that emerged during the early 1920s, Lewis became the principal target of the AAAL's attacks. As Charles Fenton has argued, he was the "heaviest cross the Academicians [i.e., the AAAL] bore." Indeed, the emotional remarks of a number of AAAL members initiated a growing feud between them and Lewis. Some of the more astute members of the academy, such as George Woodberry, observed that the literature of America, even as the edifice on Broadway was being erected in 1921, was changing. Lewis's aesthetic style and sensibility were termed cheap, vulgar, and, most important, un-American.

Woodberry's views were alarmist and even horrified: "What if it be true that our older literature was merely a back-flow from Europe, and the future really is rooted in Mark Twain and Missouri!" He lamented the passing of the genteel establishment and feared that perhaps the world as he understood it was about to end and a new medievalism, or what he termed a "New Barbarism," was at hand.[16]

The feud between Lewis and the AAAL simmered over many years, and when Lewis declined the Pulitzer Prize for *Arrowsmith* (1925) in 1926 he explained the refusal in the following manner:

> Between the Pulitzer Prize, The American Academy of Arts and Letters, and its training school, the National Institute of Arts and Letters, amateur boards of censorship, and the inquisition of earnest literary ladies, every compulsion is put upon writers to become safe, polite, obedient, and sterile. . . .
>
> I invite other writers to consider the fact that by accepting the prizes and approval of these vague institutions, we are admitting their authority, publicly confirming them as the final judge of literary excellence, and I inquire whether any prize is worth that subservience.[17]

Above all, Lewis loathed attempts to force upon American literature a conformity championing safety and politeness, which he associated with the Victorian sensibilities of the Fireside poets and William Dean Howells. Lewis's statement rejecting the Pulitzer, by labeling the efforts of literary institutions as the acts of a sinister "authority" attempting to force upon writers an untoward "subservience" through "inquisition," consists of a type of literary declaration of in/dependence. The renunciation of the Pulitzer framed him as champion of America's myth of freedom and a leading representative of the changing direction of much of the cutting-edge fiction then being produced, a move that helps to explain the AAAL's (and Woodberry's) response to his popularity and achievement.

Although he had rejected the Pulitzer Prize, Lewis was giddy with emotion and fully intent on accepting the Nobel Prize when it was announced late in 1930 that he had become the first American to win it. Several members of the AAAL responded to the announcement with displeasure and even anger. Perhaps most significantly, Henry Van Dyke, a cleric and Princeton professor, stated that the fact that Lewis had won the Nobel Prize constituted "an insult to America."[18] In a speech at a Business Men's Association luncheon on November 28, Van Dyke commented on the sad decline of tradition in America: "Nowadays, the modern idea is to scoff at these traditions." Typical of such scoffing were the "unrepresentative" works of Lewis, and in awarding him the Nobel Prize the jury had "given America a very back-handed compliment."[19]

Others also agreed that Lewis should not have been singled out as the foremost American author. It had been a poorly kept secret that Theodore Dreiser and Lewis were the two clear favorites in the balloting, and Dreiser was overwhelmed with depression at the news of Lewis's award.[20] According to W. A. Swanberg, Dreiser, who yearned deeply for the recognition that the Nobel Prize would bring him, was "almost suicidal" at losing the honor, and supporters sent him many notes of condolence, some filled with explicit criticism of Lewis.[21] Sherwood Anderson, for example, wrote that he had won "because his sharp criticism of American life catered to the dislike, distrust, and envy which most Europeans feel toward the United States."[22] Lewis Mumford elaborated publicly on Anderson's private claim: "Lewis's success in Europe has a political as well as a literary aspect. . . . In crowning Mr. Lewis's work, the Swedish Academy has, in the form of a compliment, conveyed a subtle disparagement of the country they honored."[23]

A fervent patriotism typical of the Endicottean impulse to defend the American myth of concern was illustrated profoundly in widespread protest and seething anger in several publications. Coverage of the achievement in the *New York Sun*, for example, was highly critical of the young generation of writers of which Lewis was the prime example. His character types, including George Babbitt, had been, regrettably, "accepted by our intelligentsia, the tired young protagonists of freedom in sin and salvation, as the symbol of America, not themselves. They have put on Lewis's spectacles and smitten Main Street with their typewriters. . . . That Main Street is not America and that *Babbitt* is not a typical American, any well-informed visitor knows."[24]

The concept of the intelligentsia smiting small towns "with their typewriters" suggests Carl Van Doren's framing of a movement of authors revolting from the village. The *Sun*'s writer, who disagreed with Lewis's picture of small-town life and rejected the attacks of "tired young protagonists of freedom," tried to refute Lewis's critique by brushing it aside as a manifestation of ignorance.

The Commonweal described its view of the meaning of Lewis's honor:

> United States literature and life are represented abroad by elements which predominantly emphasize their most sordid and questionable aspects. . . . the work of avowed Socialists, destructive critics of the prevailing social system of this country, together with the work of social satirists and literary muckrakers, stands out above all other types or kinds being done in the United States. . . . the seamy underside of the New World nation whose wealth and material greatness and power have grown so portentously, are welcome to other nations that have become eager to learn its faults and flaws.[25]

Thus, Lewis, along with certain other dangerous subversives (elsewhere the author mentions Upton Sinclair and Jack London), could best be described as one of the more "destructive critics of the prevailing social system" by which America had risen to its greatness as a nation.[26] All of the writers distorted America, charged *The Commonweal*'s writer, by choosing to represent only the nation's "seamy underside."

Many religious leaders also were against Lewis's recognition. Billy Sunday, one of the nation's foremost fire-and-brimstone evangelists, declared that had he been God, "Lewis would have never gotten to Stockholm."[27] The reproach was typical of evangelical reprehension. The alarmist rhetoric of Raymond H. Palmer that appeared in the *Christian Century* also lamented the selection. Lewis's works, said Palmer, constituted "a devastating criticism of our national mind," and the honor was no "cause for rejoicing." His "books contain hardly a character who is not weak and warped, hardly a thought or a philosophy that is not a disgrace to this country in so far as it is a true picture of our national habits." Yet Palmer surrounded such harsh criticisms with assertions that Lewis had produced "the truest picture on a large scale that has been made" about Americans and that his novels, although at times "overdrawn," were nevertheless "essentially true." Palmer mourned the demise of "a whole generation of men and women in America today, men and women who have left the certain road of disciplined Christian living to follow the pied pipers of jazz down the roads marked 'Freedom from restraint!'" Although Palmer recognized that Lewis's novels were most valuable for containing "truthful" depictions of such decline, they were to be shunned as disgraceful and skewed depictions of "people who submit to no discipline, who have no manners, no historical perspective, nor religion worthy of the name."[28] Sunday's and Palmer's comments, like the Reverend Brent's, demonstrate the tendency of religionists to make a whipping boy of realistic fiction that depicted a fallen and backslidden society. By winning the Nobel Prize, a crowning achievement at the end of a decade-long public chastisement from various agents of concern, Lewis cemented forever his reputation as chief pagan whipping boy of a movement.

Yet there was also a great deal of support and approbation for Lewis's literary accomplishments. *The Nation* stated that it was "eminently just" that he be awarded the prize: "More than any other writer of equal or lesser eminence he has set down the spirit of America." Furthermore, Lewis's satirical attacks against American archetypes worked hand in hand with "a kind of inner sympathy and kinship with the worst of them. [Lewis] can laugh at Babbitt because he knows just what a good-hearted,

eager, perplexed fellow he is. . . . This is not by any means a totally sear-
ing picture of America; it is touching and humorous as well."[29] George
Bernard Shaw, awarded the Nobel Prize in 1925, made his support clear.
Americans, Shaw wrote, love criticism like that Lewis exacted. Further,
Lewis had "said just the right thing to the Swedish Academy." He was
correct to judge "the 100 per cent. American as 99 per cent. idiot."[30]

Robert E. Sherwood questioned Van Dyke's charge directly through
the title of a piece that appeared in *Scribner's Magazine:* "Literary Sign-
Posts: Is the Nobel Prize an Insult?" In contrast to Van Dyke's criticism,
Sherwood described Lewis, as a result of his award, as a "legitimate cause
for nationalistic pride" and addressed the cultural conflict surrounding
Lewis directly: "There have been many who have protested with heat that
the action of the Nobel Prize committee is nothing more nor less than a
deliberate, studied insult to these United States. There are fervent patriots who feel that we might do well to dispatch a few battleships to the
Scandinavian peninsula and request those Swedes to apologize. . . . The
fact is that the executors of the Nobel estate . . . could not have chosen a
more representative, more nearly 100 per cent. American than Sinclair
Lewis."[31] What is notable is the reference to certain "fervent patriots"
who seemed directly opposed to Lewis's honor. They misunderstood
Lewis, who was truly "representative" of America and could even be
thought of as representative of the patriots' "intensely personal, preju-
diced and fraternal attitude of a Brother Elk."[32]

Vanity Fair also showed approval of Lewis by publishing a satirical,
nearly full-page drawing coupled with a brief but telling commentary by
H. L. Mencken. The cartoon, drawn by William Cotton and entitled "Mr.
Lewis and the American Eagle," depicts a caricatured Lewis holding a
distraught and suffocating bald eagle by the throat. Lewis threatens the
poor creature with a closed fist, while the eagle, wings raised in protest,
pathetically holds a celebratory ribbon in its beak, as if in a death throe.
The effect is to pit Lewis directly against the glory and mythic power
inherent in one of America's most cherished symbols. Underneath the
caricature, Mencken burlesqued those attacking the Nobel Prize jury:

> The award . . . must have come as gruesome news to the pedagogues who
> have been laboring so shrilly of late to restore sweetness and light to the
> national letters. [Lewis] represents everything that they fear and abom-
> inate—and yet, with the prize in his pocket, he represents American lit-
> erature to the world. The Swedes were not content to choose him above
> Henry Van Dyke, Owen Wister, Hamlin Garland and Robert Grant: they
> also had to rub it in. . . . Altogether, it was a red-letter pair of days for the
> wicked.[33]

Mencken's comments foreground the important conflict over how Sinclair Lewis should be best represented in the American and world press. He repeated the phrase that kept turning up—the notion that Lewis "represents American literature." Numerous other critics, both for and against Lewis, echoed that concept or a broader, even more telling one: the problem of Lewis's representation of America to the world. Lewis Mumford, for example, also broached the question of whether Lewis's novels were "representative of American life" and responded emphatically—"Yes."[34]

Finally, Mencken noted the conflict pitting Lewis against the AAAL, and, specifically, Henry Van Dyke, who were vainly trying to "restore sweetness and light" to the literary scene. Elsewhere the caustic Mencken had conflated the genteel sensibilities of the AAAL with the petty violence of the KKK, both of which he depicted as sharing a commitment to the repression of progressive literature and what Mencken considered good sense. He publicly imagined the "secret conference between the National Institute of Arts and Letters and the Ku Klux Klan," thus associating the two groups as similar conservative agents and smearing the NIAL and AAAL by aligning them and their representation of America with evil and malignant visions of the KKK.[35]

Van Dyke's assertion that Lewis's award was an insult commenced a cultural debate about how Lewis represented the American social scene. To a large extent, Lewis's brilliant acceptance speech, delivered on December 12, 1930, in Stockholm, addressed that critique. The speech and the cultural response to it illustrate the tension between concern and freedom that informed the nation during the 1920s, so much so that it should be analyzed as an important representative anecdote.

Lewis framed his address as a literary declaration of in/dependence, turning the tables on Van Dyke and the AAAL and asserting allegiance to the American myth of concern. Although it presses the bounds of common sense to claim that the speech was as aesthetically important as some of the other works analyzed earlier, it did demonstrate that Lewis was aware of the cultural conflict then raging over his achievement. It also brilliantly illustrated a breaking away from oppressive enslavement through the regenerative experience of America metanoia.

The speech, entitled "The American Fear of Literature," foregrounds from its outset the climate of cultural conflict that surrounded Lewis's selection as Nobel laureate. To be completely frank about the state of literary affairs in America, he stated, "it will be necessary for me to be a little impolite regarding certain institutions and persons of my own greatly beloved land."[36] For example, Lewis explained that at times he had been "somewhat warmly denounced," and he associated such criticisms with men of religious affiliations: "There was one good pastor in California who upon reading my *Elmer Gantry* desired to lead a mob and lynch me, while another holy man in the State of Maine wondered if there was no respectable and righteous way of putting me in jail" (4). There was also one "learned and most amiable old gentleman who has been a pastor, a university professor, and . . . a member of the American Academy of Arts and Letters" who claimed publicly that the "Nobel Committee and the Swedish Academy had insulted America" (5).

Lewis was taking the unnamed Van Dyke to task for his earlier charges.[37] Perhaps, he surmised, Van Dyke intended "to have an international incident made of" the award and demand that the American government "land Marines in Stockholm to protect American literary rights." The problem with critics such as Van Dyke, Lewis claimed, is that they are "shocked by a writer whose most anarchistic assertion has been that America, with all her wealth and power, has not yet produced a civilization good enough to satisfy the deepest wants of human creatures." Such critics, and most readers, "are still afraid of any literature which is not a glorification of everything American." Readers and critics alike prefer writers who in a hearty and edifying chorus chant that the America of a hundred and twenty million population is still as simple, as pastoral, as it was when it had forty million . . . that America has gone through the revolutionary change from rustic colony to world-empire without having in the least altered the bucolic and Puritanic simplicity of Uncle Sam."[38]

Lewis then leveled an attack at several culprits who held in common old-fashioned and romantic views of literature. According to Lewis, the most powerful contemporary culprits were the typically staid academics who were members of "that curious institution" the AAAL, which had "[cut itself] off from so much of what is living and vigorous and original in American letters. . . . It does not represent literary America of today—it represents Henry Wadsworth Longfellow" (11). The AAAL was the preeminent example of "the divorce in America of intellectual life from all authentic standards of importance and reality" (12). Professors of literature in America, argued Lewis, consider literature to be "something dead; it is something magically produced by superhuman beings. . . . Our American professors like their literature clear and cold and pure and very dead" (13).

Lewis also attacked the historical culpability of the genteel tradition's longstanding influence in American letters, particularly as represented by William Dean Howells, "one of the gentlest, sweetest, and most honest of men [who] had the code of a pious old maid whose greatest delight was to have tea at the vicarage. . . . He was actually able to tame Mark

Twain, perhaps the greatest of our writers, and to put that fiery old savage into an intellectual frock coat and top hat" (15). Hamlin Garland, originally a "harsh and magnificent realist," became "cultured and Howellized," a lamentable transformation that changed him into a "genial and insignificant lecturer" (15, 16). Garland, claimed Lewis, would be "annoyed" to realize that his influential early novels "made it possible for me to write of America as I see it, and not as Mr. William Dean Howells so sunnily saw it . . . it is a completely revelatory American tragedy, that in our land of freedom, men like Garland, who first blast the roads to freedom, become themselves the most bound" (16).

The speech, despite being composed primarily of critiques of various institutional weaknesses, ended in an invocation of a characteristic American assurance: "I want to close this dirge with a very lively sound of optimism. I have, for the future of American literature, every hope and every eager belief. We are coming out, I believe, of the stuffiness of safe, sane, and incredibly dull provincialism" (17).

It is important that Lewis ended his declaration emphatically with an act of benediction and an appeal to optimism. Throughout the speech he had described with critical acuity the achievements of a number of gifted, mainly young American authors. His praise fell on Theodore Dreiser, who, "marching alone . . . has cleared the trail from Victorian and Howellsian timidity and gentility" (7). Lewis, in a panoramic survey of contemporary American literature, also paid tribute to Willa Cather, Ernest Hemingway, James Branch Cabell, and Eugene O'Neill, along with dozens of other writers. As Malcolm Cowley claimed in 1936, "It seemed to Sinclair Lewis that all these writers were united into one crusading army by their revolt against the genteel tradition."[39]

Response to Lewis's speech, similar to the announcement of his victory more than a month earlier, was mixed. A writer for the *New York Times* characterized the address by its tone of dismay and spitefulness: "There was bitterness in Mr. Lewis's address tonight—bitterness because American literature, in his opinion, is still suffering from the gentility and 'stuffy domesticity' of earlier generations."[40] The *Chicago Daily News* found the Stockholm celebration and Lewis's speech in "singularly poor taste and a curious lack of fitness." The *Buffalo Courier-Express* took great exception to Lewis's claim that America was a crude nation: "America never proved its crudeness so stupidly as when it made Sinclair Lewis a celebrity." According to the *New York Herald Tribune*, "the propagandist grew at the expense of the novelist. . . . and Mr. Lewis . . . could not resist the temptation to use the opportunity, the most conspicuous of his life, to sell his stuff. As he had damned Main Street, so now he proceeded to damn his country. . . . So far from rejecting their Main Streets, as Mr. Lewis urged, most Americans have become rather proud of them, much prouder, we are bound to say, than they can feel of Mr. Lewis in his hour of nakedness at Stockholm."[41] Such remarks constitute a defense of the American village against the insurgent charges of "propagandists" such as Lewis. Worth noting is the questionable premise that Lewis had "urged" Americans to "reject" their small towns as a result of his searing "damnation" of them.

Even those who supported Lewis were taken aback by the severe chastisements of the speech. In a letter of congratulation written two months after the award ceremony, Edith Wharton expressed dismay over Lewis's criticism of W. D. Howells: "The only quarrel I have with it—or you—is that you should have made it the occasion of saying anything depreciatory of Howells. In spite of his limitations (which wd. probably have been ours, at that date, & in a country reeking with sentimentality and shuddering with prudery) he gave the first honestly realistic picture of the American mediocracy, & 'A Modern Instance' . . . [helped] pave the way for 'Main Street.'"[42]

As Ellen Phillips Dupree notes, Wharton's defense may seem at first surprising because she had rarely mentioned Howells's influence elsewhere. Yet she indicated respect for Howells's accomplishment and his role as a mentor for her realistic fiction along with the works of other modernists such as Lewis. She likely was criticizing him for ignoring Howells's (and, implicitly, her own) contribution to his work. Wharton had read Lewis's speech and was aware that he had failed to mention her as a writer who represented emerging American literature. She may have thought that his reference to Howells as being old-fashioned and genteel was meant for her; "bitterness at the younger generation's treatment of her is apparent in her autobiography."[43] In one passage from *A Backward Glance*, for example, Wharton seethes over the trend of younger radicals to list her with the Victorian and the genteel and belittle her contribution to the emergence of the modern style: "The amusing thing about this turn of the wheel is that we who fought the good fight are now jeered at as the prigs and prudes who barred the way to complete expression."[44]

According to William Lyon Phelps, professor of English at Yale University, the address was "very inspiring" and Lewis "fully deserved" the Nobel Prize, but the attack on the AAAL was overstated and a "mistake."[45] Phelps, despite his criticism of Lewis's attack on the AAAL, recognized the features of the acceptance speech that marked it as a major literary event. "I can think of no speech on literature in my lifetime that had such an audience or stirred up such a rumpus as the acceptance speech of Lewis. Never had a literary man had such an opportunity. The

Nobel Committee must have been delighted by the international excitement."[46] Phelps interpreted the speech as a strong indication that Lewis was the representative American idealist and evangelist. Most important was that the address had been highly successful and created a major cultural episode centering on the status of literature and the arts in American society and their sponsorship by the AAAL: "[Lewis] says the wrong people are in the Academy and others say the wrong man got the prize. This is beneficial. I like to see Americans excited on questions of art and literature."[47]

Phelps's interest was founded on a keen recognition that the episode represented a conflict that far surpassed the temporal chain of events that dramatized it. In fact, the "international excitement" constituted a representative anecdote signifying central cultural tensions within American society. As Phelps recognized in 1930, the controversy regarding Sinclair Lewis's Nobel Prize triumph and the subsequent clamor about his speech can be understood as one of the many cultural disputes that are battles in the "comprehensive and momentous struggle to define the meaning of America."[48]

The address was an inspirational, patriotic reframing of American literature that can be, and often has been, described as a literary declaration of in/dependence. Some contemporary commentators invoked Jefferson's Declaration in referring to Lewis's speech. Harry Hansen of the *New York World*, for example, felt that the episode demonstrated "that evolving America is a suitable theme for the novelist, and . . . Sinclair Lewis is representative. . . . It is as much a victory for the point of view of H. L. Mencken as for that of Sinclair Lewis. . . . the gains of the liberating movement of the last fifteen years are being added up. . . . the Nobel Prize, by placing emphasis on a novelist who considers emerging America satirically, supports the movement of independence from smothering paternalism preached in Harvard and Princeton."[49]

Hansen was cognizant of an underlying cultural conflict: Mencken and Lewis pitted against the academics of the Ivy League, the "liberating movement" of young literati versus the "smothering paternalism" of the genteel establishment. His analysis also indicated awareness that Lewis's and Mencken's side was on the verge of winning and that the academy's choice of Lewis was a recognition of that victory. Finally, Hansen recognized that Lewis's award constituted the full support of the "liberating movement"—the "movement of independence." That association of Lewis's speech with the original Declaration of Independence was echoed in various other periodicals. One article in *Literary Digest*, for example, was entitled "Lewis Declares Independence." And, in questioning Lewis's apparent desire to sever American literature from the

British tradition, the *London Morning Post* characterized the remarks as a "new declaration of independence."[50]

Thus, Phelps's and Hansen's comments suggest how Lewis's speech came to be identified as a critical articulation of an underlying cultural conflict marking an entire era, a view Lewis anticipated. In his peroration he asserted his most cherished and patriotic ideas, all of which were to be features of a new literature that would emerge victorious from the culture war:

> I have, for the future of American literature, every hope and every eager belief. We are coming out, I believe, of the stuffiness of safe, sane, and incredibly dull provincialism. . . . I salute [the emerging generation of writers], with a joy in being not yet too far removed from their determination to give to the America that has mountains and endless prairies, enormous cities and lost farm cabins, billions of money and tons of faith, to an America that is as strange as Russia and as complex as China, a literature worthy of her vastness.[51]

That Whitmanesque ending contains a number of traditionally mythic elements that include the "mountains and endless prairies," the "cabins," and "faith." As in Whitman's "Song of Myself" and elsewhere, Lewis called for literature to open fully to the multitudes of voices, settings, and ethnicities within the teeming borders of America. The nation's literature, above all, must respond to and become worthy of America's "vastness." Thus, in a sense, Lewis's speech advanced dramatically the cultural regionalism undertaken by Mark Twain in his speech at the Whittier birthday dinner. In so doing, Lewis also posited what I previously called an "oppositional elsewhere." "We are coming out," he asserted. His speech was a declaration of the full independence of a new American author from the "provincialism" and "stuffiness" of the stultified national traditions and myths symbolized by Henry Van Dyke and the AAAL.

Oddly enough, and despite that bold assertion, Lewis's artistic output in the end upheld many of the central components of the American myth of concern, including the characteristically paradoxical stance of the American metanoia and its concomitant declaration of in/dependence. The Nobel speech, despite being the bitter feelings of a man under attack, portrays a man consumed by the same idealistic tendencies and weighty hopes of many of America's great artists. Such a divided stance is depicted in his fiction as well.

Main Street (1920) and *Babbitt* (1922) are likely Lewis's most enduring creations.[52] In general, both are now read as massive critiques of rural towns and mid-sized cities. Both also succeed, however, in creating characters who are memorable well after the novels have been read. Carol

Kennicott and George Babbitt resonate as archetypes representing both the negative and the positive aspects of the American character. Both characters illustrate a strong pull away from concern and toward a more freedom-oriented view of American life. They rise to the level of mythic archetypes not merely because they represent one side of the paradox pitting concern versus freedom but because of their ambivalent relationship toward concern and freedom. *The Man Who Knew Coolidge: Being the Soul of Lowell Schmaltz, Constructive and Nordic Citizen* (1928), in contrast, is much less successful at producing such a mythic resonance because it focuses almost entirely on one side of the equation and illustrates conformity and bad faith yet ignores the paradox of freedom and rebellion. Conversely, *Main Street* and *Babbitt* reveal a thinker who remains firmly attached to the romantic ideals informing American life and literature yet often appears deeply hostile to a variety of social phenomena and ultimately rebels against them.

But it is not just the marquee characters who exhibit such a strained ambivalence as they lurch back and forth, suspended between these two sides of a paradox. In the midst of his numerous severe attacks upon America's declining pioneer spirit, to take one example, Lewis exhibited through a sympathetic evocation of characters such as Dr. Will Kennicott his deep respect for the gritty, realistic trials and often heroic perseverance required of such rural people. Generally, to be sure, Kennicott is the cartoonish caricature of an average small-town denizen caught in the web of conformity. He offers, for example, opinions on literature after Vida Sherwin has read passionately from the works of Yeats: "That's great stuff. . . . I like poetry fine—James Whitcomb Riley and some of Longfellow—this 'Hiawatha.' Gosh, I wish I could appreciate that highbrow art stuff. But I guess I'm too old a dog to learn new tricks."[53]

Sometimes, however, Lewis characterizes the doctor's courage and compassion in highly romantic terms. One example concerns Will (whose name points to power and dedication) going through storms and blizzards to treat the sick or injured: "He went out, hungry, chilling, unprotesting: and [Carol], before she fell asleep again, loved him for his sturdiness, and saw the drama of his riding by night to the frightened household on the distant farm; pictured children standing at a window, waiting for him. He suddenly had in her eyes the heroism of a wireless operator on a ship in a collision; of an explorer, fever-clawed, deserted by his bearers, but going on—jungle—going———" (174).

On one occasion, after Carol has accompanied the doctor on an emergency call in the midst of a howling winter storm, she compliments him: "You're so strong and yet so skillful and not afraid of blood or storm or———." "Used to it," he replies. "Only thing that's bothered me was the chance the ether fumes might explode, last night." Carol is dumbfounded to learn that they both might have been killed because an assistant had mistakenly sent inflammable ether instead of chloroform and the surgical procedure had been lighted by burning lamps. "You knew all the time that—Both you and I might have been blown up?" she implores. "You knew it while you were operating?" Will, who "had to operate, of course," responds nonchalantly: "Sure. Didn't you? Why, what's the matter?" (190–91). In effect, Carol, the vicarious observer, emphatically affirms the near-mythic valor of her doctor husband. Far from being just a cardboard village dolt, he is revealed to be a heroic pioneer spirit animating frontier society.

Glen A. Love points out that during the 1920s numerous critics of the pioneer village, exemplified by Harold Stearns's anthology *Civilization in the United States* (1922), were much more pessimistic than Lewis. For Stearns, "American society was hostile to art and intellect, and there was little hope for improvement in that regard." Compared with Stearns's dark indictment, however:

> Lewis had a much more positive conception of American pioneering, born out of his sense of his own western heritage. Lewis's work reflects values that are largely frontier and pioneer inspired, with a heroic view of the past and an essentially hopeful and progressive conception of the future. Out of the awareness of the swift conversion of his own upper-Midwest country from agrarian frontier to machine civilization arises Lewis's sense of the myriad possibilities for individual human lives.[54]

Thus, in Lewis, who claimed to be a "fanatic American" and was, despite the tone of his Nobel address, profoundly patriotic throughout the Nobel ceremonies period, "we see shared strains of two characteristic American voices: the Jeremiad scourging of our national failings and the optimistic celebration of our potentialities."[55] Despite being branded by various critics as a sinister leader of the revolt from the village movement, Lewis wrote of, and discussed in the Nobel address, a highly ambivalent strain of "optimistic celebration" that darker and more cynical critics such as Stearns would have found embarrassing.

In focusing almost exclusively on Lewis's brilliant eye for social detail and occasionally relentless and tiresome acidity, critics have overlooked the fundamentally patriotic and optimistic aspect of his achievements. His reputation has suffered from reductionist versions of him as a devilish provocateur and even as someone who hated America, a caricature that grew slowly throughout the 1920s from the success of *Main*

Street to the culminating effect of the Nobel Prize. That aspect of Lewis is altogether too well known, but perhaps it should not be all that surprising. As James Hunter has argued, ongoing cultural dialogues regarding any emotional subject, such as the debates about the literary representation of America in which Lewis found himself entangled throughout the 1920s, produce highly polarized versions of the dispute. The effect of such polarization is the "eclipse of the middle," by which the moderate position on any issue or controversy becomes concealed.[56] The eclipse of the ambivalent middle ground on which Lewis stood obscures and simplifies the complexity of Lewis's character and artistic creations.

The contemporary critical conception of Lewis also overlooks his affinities with the transcendental strains he seemed at times to denounce. Daniel Aaron argues that "the key to the blurred thesis of *Main Street*" lies in the work of Henry David Thoreau, who Lewis "repeatedly named" as the "pervasive influence on all of his work."[57] Aaron's assertion suggests that a full conception of Lewis's achievement must come to terms with his romantic yearnings and thereby focus anew on the deeply divided nature of his relation to the almost hegemonic middle-class myth of concern as it manifested itself in America after World War I. As Lewis revealed to Perry Miller, "I love America . . . I love it, but I don't like it."[58]

Of course, Lewis severely mocked and satirized America's beloved ideological apparatus, particularly in *Main Street* and *Babbitt*. He did so, however, only when those ideologies had become empty and useless apologies for mediocrity and no longer embodied the spirit upon which the American dream might be built. The enigma of Lewis as an artist and person was reflected in his best novels and the Nobel speech; all betray "a persistent conflict of values that clashed no less within him."[59] Perhaps the most amazing example of Lewis's conservatism and deeply divided loyalties was his decision to accept an invitation to join the National Institute of Arts and Letters in 1935 and be admitted as a full member of the American Academy of Arts and Letters in 1938.[60]

Instead of rehearsing Lewis's familiar iconoclasm, I would like to foreground his other, less well-represented side—his function as a faithful progeny of Endicott's ghost who maintained a solid dedication to the transcendent American idea. In contrast to charges that Lewis entertained a vitriolic hatred for everyday Americans, his solid embrace of the fictional inhabitants of Zenith and Main Street are apparent in the following anecdote: "William Rose Benet tells of how he and Sinclair Lewis once met a traveling salesman, and of how Lewis entered into a long conversation with the man, while Benet remained disapprovingly aloof. '"That's the trouble with you, Bill,' said Lewis afterwards, 'you regard him as hoi polloi, he doesn't even represent the cause of labor or anything dramatic—but I understand that man—by God, I love him.'"[61]

Even in 1930, a number of critics noted the reverence for humanity in Lewis's work. William Lyon Phelps, for example, observed that "Lewis loves the people he attacks; he roars with mirth at Babbitt, but loves to hear him talk."[62] And Robert E. Sherwood wrote, "His portrait of George F. Babbitt was not prompted by scorn or hatred; it was the natural result of an immense relish for its subject, and a profound and unalterable sympathy for it."[63] Lewis's love and respect for many if not most of his characters was sincere, even if he appeared to ridicule and satirize them. He was a faithful proponent of the jeremiad mode and should therefore be included among those writers who both criticize the originating ideologies of American social life and create new manifestations of America's dominant myth of concern by which the failures of the past might be transcended. The Nobel speech articulates both impulses. It is, on the one hand, a declaration of independence from the "stuffy domesticity" of the past. On the other hand, and perhaps less well understood, the speech, like Lewis's best novels, was simultaneously a declaration of dependence—a strong, yearning, at times even Thoreauvian belief in America's future—and a call to cultural coherence and consensus in working to create a literature in America "worthy of her vastness."

The simultaneity of these seemingly opposite impulses marks Lewis's speech as a classic enactment of the American metanoia. Numerous observers understood that almost from the day of its publication. More than any of the fiction he created, it is possible that Lewis's declaration of in/dependence at the moment of his greatest public triumph, and the cultural conflict of which it was the exemplary expression and in which he was a central player, have sealed his legacy and ensured his long-term status as a classic American author.

8 Trilling's Frost versus Kennedy's Frost

Competing Poles of a Paradox within America's Regnant Myth

On March 26, 1959, at Robert Frost's eighty-fifth birthday celebration, Lionel Trilling's speech honoring the poet featured an interpretation at odds with the generally accepted version of Frost and his work, sending shock waves through much of America's cultural community. Trilling asserted that the public conception of Frost was faulty and that the poet's best work represented the ambivalent, often "terrifying" musings of a man wracked with pain, doubt, and misgivings about the frightening world that engulfed him. The commonplace notion of Frost, by contrast, was as pastoral farmer-poet, a rugged individual typifying the Emersonian self-reliance by which the nation had been carved out of the wilderness. That version romantically praised nature's beauty and grandeur and featured a poet of encouragement, edification, and good cheer.

Trilling was careful to develop full accounts of both versions in his speech. For example, he recognized the popular idea of Frost: "We all of us know that we celebrate something that lies beyond even Mr. Frost's achievement as a poet. . . . We do not need to wait upon the archaeologists of the future to understand that Robert Frost exists not only in a human way but also in a mythical way. We know him, and have known him so for many years, as nothing less than a national fact. We have come to think of him as virtually a symbol for America, as something not unlike an articulate, an actually poetic, Bald Eagle."[1]

167

It was clear from the outset of the speech that Trilling recognized the weight of what he called the "mythical" Frost. The established stature of the poet involved grand themes: Frost was "nothing less than a national fact," he was "virtually a symbol for America," and he was associated with the majestic beauty of one of the nation's most revered images, the bald eagle (capitalized by Trilling in the published version). Trilling and his listeners recognized "something that lies beyond" Frost's work as poet. In that regard, he compared Frost favorably with Sophocles: "Like [Frost], Sophocles lived to a great age, writing well; and like [Frost], Sophocles was the poet his people loved the most. Surely they loved him in some part because he praised their common country. But I think that they loved him chiefly because he made plain to them the terrible things of human life: they felt, perhaps, that only a poet who could make plain the terrible things could possibly give them comfort."[2]

Two aspects of Sophocles (and, by inference, of Frost) are presented in that passage. One is of the poet who "praised their common country," and the other "a poet who could make plain the terrible things." The first description, invoking patriotism, consensus, and sentimentality, results in Frost being embraced as a poet "loved the most" by the people. Generally, Trilling did not openly criticize the popular version but rather did so subtly. The words "but I think," for example, are suggestive qualifiers.

The mythical version of Frost, invoked as expected by the keynote speaker at a birthday commemoration, was treated throughout the speech with some condescension. In the passage regarding Sophocles, for example, Trilling claimed that Frost was somehow "comforting" to Americans because "he made plain to them the terrible things of human life." Trilling was privileging what he termed a more "human" conception of Frost, which he described in detail and with greater approval. He also noted the contradictory "dark" aspect inherent in Frost's work, citing specifically "Design" and then "Neither Out Far Nor In Deep," which he claimed might be "the most perfect poem of our time."[3]

Trilling celebrated Frost's ambiguities, tensions, anxieties, and alienation, features attesting to the poet as a keeper of the high modernist mode and therefore inaccessible to general readers. He dubbed that version of the poet "my Frost," which he initially defined through a series of negatives:

> I have to say that my Frost—*my Frost*: what airs we give ourselves when once we believe that we have come into possession of a poet!—I have to say that my Frost is not the Frost I seem to perceive existing in the minds of so many of his admirers. He is not the Frost who confounds the characteristically modern practice of poetry by his notable democratic sim-

plicity of utterance: on the contrary. He is not the Frost who controverts the bitter modern astonishment at the nature of human life: the opposite is so. He is not the Frost who reassures us by his affirmation of old virtues, simplicities, pieties, and ways of feeling: anything but. I will not go so far as to say that my Frost is not essentially an American poet at all: I believe that he is quite as American as everyone thinks he is, but not in the way that everyone thinks he is.[4]

What are notable are the three sentences that begin with "he is not," foregrounding opposition to the popular notion of the poet. There is trivialization, even condescension, in the words "the Frost I seem to perceive existing in the minds of so many of his admirers."

Thus, Trilling's speech constitutes a sustained attack upon the popular, "mythical" version of the poet.[5] He juxtaposed two versions of Frost the man and Frost the poet and identified what is now apparent to many: Frost had a dual nature, seemed to foster it, and took delight in it.[6] Trilling appeared prescient about whether interest in this "cultural episode" would endure: "I have no doubt that the episode will yield cultural conclusions to whoever wants to draw them."[7]

Not surprisingly, Trilling's remarks affected numerous observers, including the poet. Stanley Burnshaw depicted Frost just after the speech as a man deeply disturbed by the "penetrating" analysis Trilling offered, muttering over and over, "But *am* I terrifying? . . . Do I terrify *you?*" Later he anxiously worried about whether Trilling's depiction of his dark side would make a "lasting difference" in his reputation.[8] Remarks such as these suggest that Frost was keenly aware of his public persona, that he worked to foster it, and that he was tormented by whether his reputation would endure, and what it would be for future critics and readers.

Representative of the popular press's critical response to Trilling was an article in *Newsweek* entitled "How Terrifying a Poet?" in which the debate had become a "holy war" between highbrow and middlebrow. The accompanying photographs featured the two men. Trilling's large, luminous eyes glare at the reader, his head is set deeply into shadows, and the "eminent professor" takes on a sinister, even demonic quality. Frost is well-lit and smiling sheepishly.[9] Both Frost and *Newsweek* seized upon the same haunting word: "terrifying." The photographs, conversely, indicate *Newsweek*'s stance that it is Trilling and not the poet who was most disturbing.

The most widely read response to the event was likely that of J. Donald Adams, a columnist for the *New York Times Book Review* and in attendance at the birthday dinner. In his review, Adams energetically asserted that Trilling represented a "literary snobbery" unable to grasp "the meaning of the American experience" or understand writers such as Frost who are "indubitably American." His reliance on D. H. Lawrence and Freud to interpret Frost was a mistake of profound proportions: "If he had re-read, or read, Emerson instead, he might have lost his Frost and discovered the one he turned his back on." And it is insulting to think of Frost as "terrifying": "Holy Mackerel! Frost simply sees the universe as it is and accepts it . . . and, as I said before, he got it from Emerson."[10]

Leaving aside the strange idea that there is nothing problematic or frightening about Emerson (perhaps Adams should also have gone back to "Experience" or the journals) as well as the odd notion that Frost "simply sees the universe" (whatever that might mean), it appears that much of the emotion of Adams's response depended upon an association of the popularized Frost with a mythologized concept of America. He viewed an attack on Frost as an attack on a conservative and consensual idea of the American experience. A nationalistic final paragraph made that point explicit:

> All this country needs is to recapture its earlier vision. One of the silliest remarks ever made about the American experience came from one of the editors of [Trilling's] favorite magazine, the *Partisan Review.* Mr. William Phillips solemnly observed that American literature has played hide-and-seek with American experience for lack of "an image, or cluster of images, of the national experience available to literature." No such lack exists, and both [Trilling and Phillips] should re-read one of the great American poems. It is by Robert Frost, and it is called "The Gift Outright."[11]

Adams was no longer concerned with Frost's reputation, and his invective rose to new heights. His jeremiadic motivation is evident when he whines, "all this country needs is to recapture its earlier vision." It was a plea for a generalized, greatly reductionist American experience and conflated the idea of Frost with the idea of America into one myth, rendered faithfully in "The Gift Outright." The numerous, often irate responses to the speech demonstrate that this popular conception of Frost had by the end of the 1950s become well established as a conservative icon of considerable strength. In contrast, Trilling associated Frost with the "ultimate radicalism" that he argued characterizes all great American artists. According to Trilling, that theory of radicalism, which he attributed to D. H. Lawrence, consists of "a disintegration and sloughing off of the old consciousness . . . and the forming of a new consciousness underneath." Frost did not enforce but rather undermined the traditional values and social forms as envisioned by Adams: "He is not the Frost who reassures us by his affirmation of old virtues, simplicities, pieties, and ways of feeling: anything but."[12]

By favoring his radical version of the poet, however, Trilling was guilty of the narrowmindedness he was attacking when he discounted any interpretation but his own. In addition, he committed some of the mistakes Russell J. Reising has identified in *The Unusable Past.* In contrast to Trilling's resistance to and dismissal of the mythical Frost, Reising argues that critics might benefit by posing questions that could form the basis for an emerging cutting edge in the study of myth and ideology:

> [defining] America exclusively in symbolic terms and then granting those terms a primacy in literature and culture as a whole draw our attention away from the production and reproduction of the very ideology which mythicizes the meaning of America to begin with. For instance, how and why did such a conception of America gain such strength? Does it have 'radical' as well as 'conservative' implications? How have its various manifestations reflected different tensions in American culture? And, most important for literary studies, how have writers treated the myth of America and American selfhood?[13]

In short, Trilling failed to consider, in a slight alteration of Reising's words, How and why did such a [popular] conception of Frost gain such strength? Does Frost have "radical" as well as "conservative" implications? And how do these two "manifestations" of Frost reflect "different tensions in American culture?"

To respond to the second question, the two versions of Frost foregrounded by Trilling's speech represent radical and conservative manifestations of Frost and his work. The representations can be usefully associated with the myths of concern (conservatism) and freedom (radicalism). Both impulses can be detected in Frost's writings throughout his career. The Trilling episode, however, engendered one of the most explicit public dialogues concerning Frost's achievements and the meanings of his work.

The two views of the poet reflect tensions that began to surface during the final few years of Frost's life (1959–63), when the conservative Eisenhower administration gave way to Kennedy's highly charged vision of the New Frontier.[14] The Trilling episode provided a representative anecdote that signaled the underlying tensions of a transitional moment in American cultural history. Moreover, Trilling's brazen representation of the radical emphasis of Frost's poetry on an occasion set apart to memorialize and honor his conservative achievement was seemingly an attempt to declare independence from the ingrained and ossified perspectives of the cold war era. It was yet another manifestation of the American metanoia.

To begin, Frost's own political views leave much to speculation and are of little value in the context of this argument. He wrote sparingly, sometimes glibly, on political issues, and disdained categories. In "Ten

Mills," for example, he remarks, "I never dared be radical when young /
For fear it would make me conservative when old." Elsewhere, Frost jibed
"liberals" who are "so altruistically moral / [they] never take [their] own
side in a quarrel."15

Despite such whimsy, it is clear from Frost's letters that he viewed
political systems and institutions with the same profound sense of an
impending tragic fall evident in much of his best-known poetry. He held
little or no faith in the ability of political systems to assuage the suffering of other humans or erase the deep-seated guilt, sorrow, and grief that
he believed were the bases of life. Politics, he considered, is powerless to
change the tragic essence of daily existence, a cynical outlook depicted
especially well in epistolary exchanges with Louis Untermeyer. Untermeyer, Frost's good friend, a well-known poet in his own right, and an
avowed Marxist, later collected, edited and published a volume of those
letters. An example of the candid remarks made throughout this volume
is the following: "I consider politics settled . . . no change of system could
possibly make me a bit better or abler, the only two things of importance
to me personally."16

Despite such cynicisms, Frost's letters to Untemeyer show that he
held a high view of democracy as the best form of government and of
individual freedom as its most valuable political virtue. He also maintained a lifelong loyalty to the Democratic Party, even when he perceived
it to be departing from its traditional doctrines under the influence of
Franklin Delano Roosevelt and other New Deal politicians.

Frost did not mention the topic of politics in the majority of his poems, and what he did say has seldom been invoked. Some poems, to be
sure, do directly or indirectly take up government as their topic or theme.
"A Case for Jefferson," for example, betrays a sneering disdain for a particular Marxist ideologue: "He's Freudian Viennese by night / By day he's
Marxian Muscovite."17 The lengthy "Build Soil," subtitled "A Political
Pastoral," remarks on topics such as socialism and argues for an individ-
ualized ethical system of politics. It ends with the memorable lines, "You
see the beauty of my proposal is / It needn't wait on general revolution.
/ I bid you to a one-man revolution— / The only revolution that is coming" (324). Those lines are echoed in a later poem: "I advocate a semi-
revolution" (363). "To a Thinker" can be understood as a criticism of New
Dealism, particularly of Roosevelt. Frost charges that his doctrines are
"leaning on dictatorship" (326). Much of *A Masque of Mercy* also concerns issues of political import; the poem includes a character called
"Keeper" who may be read as a thinly veiled New Dealer (again, perhaps
as Roosevelt himself). Despite his frequently voiced animosity toward

socialistic practices, in "An Equalizer" Frost discussed the problems caused by class difference: "when we get too far apart in wealth, / 'Twas his idea that for the public health, / So that the poor won't have to steal by stealth, / We now and then should take an equalizer" (363). Another poem is entitled "On Taking from the Top to Broaden the Base" (298). "The Vanishing Red" considers the historic abuse of Native Americans even as it foregrounds Frost's characteristic ambivalence, and its poetic sophistication makes it one of Frost's strongest political efforts. Overall, however, none of these poems intone the jingoistic mythos that conservatives such as Adams associated with "The Gift Outright." Conversely, they do not support the more socialistic, left-leaning agenda that might be associated with critics like Trilling or Untermeyer.

Rather than search for Frost's political views, however, my interest lies in what he had come to represent at the important cultural and political moment of John F. Kennedy's inauguration.[18] It seems clear that Trilling's remarks were not only perceived as an attack on the individual poet but also as an attack on mythic concern. Frost had been associated with American myth for most of his public life and so representative of a ruling consensus. Thus, Trilling's comments, by attacking such a symbol or casting doubt upon the veracity of the mythical qualities represented by the aging poet, were interpreted by people such as Adams as a subversive attack on the conservative ideologies of the Eisenhower era.

"The Gift Outright" is associated with Frost's eighty-fifth birthday in another way that would have a major impact on his remaining years. During an interview in conjunction with the birthday celebration a journalist had asked whether New England had lost its vitality. Frost answered a resounding no and then predicted that the next president would be from Boston: "Pressed for the name, Frost shrugged. 'He's a Puritan named Kennedy. The only Puritans left these days are the Roman Catholics. There! I guess I wear my politics on my sleeve.'"[19]

That remark gained widespread attention, and headlines throughout the country proclaimed Frost's endorsement of John F. Kennedy.[20] Kennedy acknowledged the apparent support with some satisfaction in a note dated April 11, 1959, and later met briefly with Frost at the Library of Congress. According to Frost's friend Stewart Udall, a member of Congress from Arizona, the men hit it off well at that meeting. As the 1960 campaign progressed, "Kennedy [often] used [a] familiar Frost quotation as a late evening farewell to his followers": "But I have promises to keep / And miles to go before I sleep / And miles to go before I sleep." By constantly using some of Frost's most resonant verses Kennedy enlisted him as one of his "quiet collaborators in the 1960 campaign." It was a collaboration of which Frost apparently approved.[21]

After Kennedy's election Frost wired congratulations: "Great Days for Boston, democracy, the Puritans and the Irish." The same undated telegram responds to the news of December 1, 1960, that Kennedy had chosen Udall to join his cabinet: "Your appointment of Stewart Udall of an old Vermont religion reconciles me once for all to the party I was born into."[22] It was Udall's suggestion that the poet be invited to participate in Kennedy's inauguration, but Kennedy initially feared being upstaged. [23] Nevertheless, he came to like the idea and asked Udall to contact Frost and determine whether he was interested. When Frost accepted the invitation, Kennedy himself chose the poem for the poet to read—"The Gift Outright."[24]

Udall's version of the event differs from Frost's official biographers only in claiming that it was Frost who suggested "The Gift Outright," which he called his "most national" poem. Thomas G. Smith has found evidence suggesting that Frost's long-time assistant Kay Morrison recommended that specific verse, which, she said, "is top Frost and a great American poem."[25] In any event, the politician and the poet came to a consensus. "The Gift Outright" is unique in American history—the first poem to be recited in full at a presidential inauguration.

The fact that "a pastoral poet, Robert Frost, was accorded a place of honor on [the] occasion (of Kennedy's inaugural) is worth thinking about," observed Leo Marx. He describes the "inherently ambiguous relationship" between artists and those in political power, because artists are "likely to be affiliated with, and in some measure beholden to, those in power; yet at the same time they also are prone to a feeling of estrangement."[26] In at least a limited sense, Frost, by accepting Kennedy's invitation, affiliated himself with the political regime and tacitly consented "in some measure" to the national ideology represented by such an occasion. Yet he was simultaneously unsettled by some amount of estrangement.

"American myth," according to Sacvan Bercovitch, "reflects and affects particular social needs . . . it persists through its capacity to influence people in history" and is made concrete through "a series of rituals designed to keep the system going."[27] Any presidential inauguration, and certainly that of Kennedy at the outset of what many anticipated would be one of America's most idealistic administrations, is among those rituals which foster and confirm American ideology. In that context, what precisely was Frost aligning himself with by this appearance? What idea of America did he "[seek] to justify and perpetuate" through his participation in one of the nation's most sacred civil rituals? Although Frost was well into his eighties and the prestige of participating in the event cannot be discounted, it is more logical to focus on the phenomenon of his appearance culturally rather than on his motives. Why, for example, did the politicians consider the poet's appearance to be an asset, and why did Kennedy request that specific poem? To address these questions, it is helpful to consider the text of the poem that J. Donald Adams praised so highly.

"The Gift Outright" was written more than twenty years before the inauguration, at the end of the 1930s, when, "through the dark pain of depression, Americans came into a new consciousness of American history, of their country's worth . . . a consciousness [which] deepened when democracy was threatened by the scourge of dictatorship from Hitler."[28] Frost's first public reading of the poem occurred just two days before the attack on Pearl Harbor, on December 5, 1941, before the Phi Beta Kappa Society at William and Mary College. The poem resonates with patriotic fervor and is composed of a brief yet stirring historical treatment of the founding and settlement of America. As Michael Kammen has pointed out, "In the United States, more often than not, memory has served as a bulwark for social and political stability—a means of valorizing resistance to change."[29] "The Gift Outright" has been called "one of the best patriotic poems ever written in our country" by as eminent a critic as Randall Jarrell and has been ranked as "one of Frost's best shorter poems."[30]

The poem presents certain tensions and ambiguities that reflect Frost's seemingly oppositional aspects. It begins with one of the more memorable lines in all of Frost—"the land was ours before we were the land's"—immediately foregrounding a key theme, that of possession.[31] How can "we" be possessed by a "land"? Furthermore, who exactly is this "we"? And yet through that statement the narrator immediately incorporates the reader into some sort of social grouping or identity. The paradoxical nature of that co-optation recalls the simple opening of the U.S. Constitution: "We the people." The immediate assumption must be that "we" represents all true Americans, past, present, and future, and from the beginning of the poem a consensus is posited. The act of positing that collective group, or naming that "we," is a speaking into existence, such as God did at the Creation: "Let there be light." There is also a timeless quality inherent in such a naming because of the implication that "we" includes all Americans at all times, perhaps even those not yet born. Whether minorities such as African Americans and Native Americans are included is doubtful. For example, later, in claiming that "we were England's," the narrator ignores other heritages and strategically omits other nations such as France and Spain that had territorial claims in North America. The majority of what is now called America was not England's.

The immediate image is of the land, which is consistent with the frontier myth of America as outlined by numerous critics, notably Henry Nash Smith. The initial claim is one of ownership. Smith's classic *Virgin Land* demonstrates clearly the ideological strategy of using Manifest Destiny to further the expansion of nineteenth-century America.[32] Even older than the notion of Manifest Destiny, however, is the Puritan dogma, rooted in a more general Reformation worldview that has been called the "dominion mandate." Based on God's first commission, humanity is to go forth and take dominion of the earth as stewards: "Let us make man in our image, after our likeness; and let them have dominion. . . . And God blessed them, and God said unto them, 'Be fruitful, and multiply, and replenish the earth, and subdue it'" (Genesis 1:26, 28).

Frost's narrator invokes both positions, claiming that America "was our land more than a hundred years / Before we were her people."[33] The ownership of the North American continent predates the Declaration of the new nation in 1776 by a century and legitimizes its expansion to the Pacific. "She was our land," the poet states, emphasizing the feminine aspect of the country. As Annette Kolodny has argued, mythic constructs in America have long identified the land as a woman awaiting male ownership.[34] Thus, even in these opening lines, Frost draws on several well-known mythic traditions.

The confusing, even paradoxical, nature of possession is explored in the next lines: "But we were England's, still colonials, / Possessing what we were still unpossessed by, / Possessed by what we now no more possessed."[35] Here, true patriotism, or perhaps national consensus, involves two aspects. One must fully possess and be possessed by the land, something described as the poem progresses:

> Something we were withholding made us weak
> Until we found out that it was ourselves
> We were withholding from our land of living,
> And forthwith found salvation in surrender.
> Such as we were we gave ourselves outright.[36]

In order to be fully possessed by the land, one must "surrender." "Salvation," equated with being fully possessed, is accomplished by no longer "withholding" but rather giving ourselves "outright." In that way it is possible to enter into "our land of living." The lines resound with religious words and phrases suggesting Christian repentance to such an extent that the act of becoming "possessed" by the land constitutes religious self-surrender and a Kierkegaardian leap of faith into some idea represented by the land. The phrase, "our land of living," echoes a phrase used frequently in the Old Testament:

> I had fainted, unless I had believed to see the goodness of the Lord
> In the land of the living. (Psalms 27:13)

> I will walk before the Lord in the land of the living. (Psalms 116:9)

There are two senses to the notion of the "land of the living." It describes the earth, and it implies a spiritual life derived from the special relationship of Christian believers with God. The pilgrimage in America, therefore, can be abundant and full, a type of everlasting life. That key passage associates the true American experience with the giving of oneself patriotically, a view that led one critic to interpret the poem as a "poetic definition of the American state of mind."[37] Furthermore, the dedication is to be done with the uncompromising commitment of a religious zealot. Subscribing to a national consensus of the American idea and vision is equated with being born anew.

If, in the Christian faith, believers give themselves to God, to what is the giver to "give" himself or herself "outright" in Frost's poem? The suggestion seems to be that we give ourselves to the myth of America by way of one of the nation's most enduring symbols, the land:

> we gave ourselves outright
> (The deed of gift was many deeds of war)
> To the land vaguely realizing westward,
> But still unstoried, artless, unenhanced,
> Such as she was, such as she would become.[38]

The fact that we "gave ourselves outright" to the land can be understood in several ways. First, people give themselves by immigrating and becoming workers, cultivators, builders, and shapers of a new and open frontier. Second, countless settlers literally gave their lives in the wars inspired by the cause of nationhood. On another level, immigrants must commit themselves to the idea of the land, a key aspect of the myth of America. Finally, the sacrifice must be completed "outright"—utterly and without reservation. In order to attain fully the salvation described in the poem, one must give oneself unswervingly to the consensual idea of America, most significantly associated with the symbol of the virgin land.

Just as important is the description offered of the land. It is "vaguely realizing westward, / But still unstoried, artless, unenhanced." Using a form of the word *vague* to describe the land creates an image of ambivalence, uncertainty, and perhaps a fear of the unknown. The notion of "the land vaguely realizing" cloaks the vision of American progress in ambiguity. The force of realizing, meaning to comprehend fully or to make real, is countered by "vaguely," that is, with a lack of clarity. The word *still,* despite not being followed by a comma, retains a triple meaning and suggests the adverbial "until this moment [of discovery or settlement]" and "beyond this moment to the present" as well as the adjective "quiet." Finally, the past tense of *gave* presents a difficulty: Is it a subtle suggestion that this type of commitment is a thing of the past?

The movement in the poem is emphatically westward, a reminder of the historical progression of rugged pioneers, a standard ingredient in the nation's collective myth:

> One of the most persistent generalizations concerning American life and character is the notion that our society has been shaped by the pull of a vacant continent drawing population westward through the passes of the Alleghenies, across the Mississippi Valley, over the high plains and mountains of the Far West to the Pacific coast. This axiom . . . comes to us bearing the personal imprint of a Wisconsin historian, Frederick Jackson Turner. . . . Despite a growing tendency of scholars to react against the Turner doctrine, it is still by far the most familiar interpretation of the American past.[39]

The statement regarding the Turner doctrine, the so-called frontier hypothesis, being "still by far the most familiar interpretation of the American past" should be considered in light of the fact that Henry Nash Smith wrote it at the end of the 1940s, the heyday of critical consensus in America. The poem endorses a historical claim that has since come under critical attack as the preeminent ideological justification for numerous egregious social injustices.[40] In that sense Frost's mythical reconstruction can be associated with the more conservative and less historically based treatments of the cold war era.

Perhaps most significant, however, is the poem's insistence that the land was found to be "unstoried, artless, unenhanced." Historically, of course, that is not true. The continent was peopled by millions of Native Americans who would later be violently oppressed by invading Europeans. It is a common aspect of the American mythic pattern, however, that the unfortunate existence of the Indian nations and their subsequent mistreatment should be ignored. The image is reminiscent of the Puritan notion of the dominion mandate of the first chapter of Genesis, where God instructs humanity to "fill and subdue" and "cultivate." As James O. Robertson explains:

> Discovery and exploration of worlds no one ever knew existed were part of the magic attraction across the Ocean Sea. But there was a contradic-

tion in that magic. It was hidden and easy to ignore: if the lands being discovered were peopled, then they weren't really being discovered: people knew about them. But not the right people. The theme of "discovery" required a contrast with an Old World . . . . The image of discovery remains valid, however, if the people who lived in the "discovered" lands are made nonexistent by the power of the myth.[41]

If Native Americans are acknowledged, they can still be "subdued" because they are not "the right people," apparently meaning the people of God. Even Henry Nash Smith, one of the critics most influential in the study and advancement of the concept of American myth, made trenchant comments concerning its appropriation and abuse in one of his final published critical works:

> My own attitudes were influenced by the basic myth or ideology of America to a greater extent than I had realized. This conditioning was the perhaps inevitable result of the intellectual climate of the academic community within which I had received my formal training. . . . An even more important failure on my part to comprehend fully the assumptions underlying Turner's view of American history concerned the celebrated declaration that "the existence of an area of free land, its continuous recession, and the advance of American settlement westward explain American development." The term "free land" is integral to Turner's definition of the frontier. . . . Thus I took over from Turner the attitude . . . characteristic of American culture, a refusal to acknowledge the guilt intrinsic to the national errand into the wilderness.[42]

Just as Smith admitted that perhaps his assumptions and misrepresentations could be attributed to "the intellectual climate of the academic community," the fact that Frost bolstered the image of an empty continent may simply be a "characteristic of American culture."

The final line of the poem has been the source of some confusion: "Such as she was, such as she would become." The syntax of the long concluding sentence is intricate. Clearly, the first part of the line, "such as she was," refers to the land's being "unstoried, artless, unenhanced." As one critic has explained, readers are "startled" by the words "such as she would become" because a parallel construction "makes Frost seem to predict America's future would also be 'unstoried, artless, unenhanced.'"[43] But that is not what Frost meant. He claims that "we gave ourselves" completely to the land, both as it was ("artless") and as it "would become" (not artless).[44] The line can also be read as pitting historical fact ("such as she was") against an idealized, millennial vision ("such as she would become"). The ending provides tension between the reality of America so far attained and the remaining prophetic fulfillment.

President-elect Kennedy's one request for the reading of "The Gift

Outright" involved that line. He asked Frost to change the final verb from *would* to *will* in order to emphasize the inevitable fulfillment of the prophecy: "such as she will become." That minor change also alleviates the tension in the original line between the real and the ideal. As it turned out, when the poet completed his reading he expanded Kennedy's emendation even more: "Such as she *would* become, *has* become, and—and for this occasion let me change that to—what she *will* become."[45]

Despite the seemingly straightforward jingoism that appealed to conservative critics such as Adams, the poem presents serious interpretive problems. The final line, for example, can be read as revealing disappointment in how the dream of America had turned out in reality: "Such as she was, such as she would become" suggests chagrin over the nation's vast unfulfillment. The reference to "many deeds of war" provides a grim reminder of the thousands of deaths, some of which were undoubtedly heroic but some of which were perhaps random and vain. Word choices such as "gave," "still," and the notion of "the land vaguely realizing" are problematic and suggest Frost's deep-seated ambivalence.

"The Gift Outright" is so filled with references to various possessions and deeds that one critic has called it "an expanded pun on 'possession.'"[46] Frost admitted as much when commenting on the poem:

> All there is is belonging and belongings; belonging and having belongings. You belong and I belong. The sincerity of their belonging is all I have to measure people by. I hate to take great names in vain, but I am tempted to call some men quislings that perhaps some of you would not like to hear me call quislings. Men in great places. I can't quite take them. My namesake anyway, Robert Lee, never came up to Washington to curry favor with those that had licked him. He sawed wood. That was the only thing for him to do when beaten.
>   You have to ask yourself in the end, how far will you go when it comes to changing your allegiance.[47]

On the surface, that seems straightforward. An odd tension is evoked, however, in the form of what might be termed sincere and insincere belonging. Some of the nation's leaders who appear to be the most committed to the American vision may in fact be "quislings" or puppets and traitors manipulated by unseen sinister forces.

Frost demonstrates a readiness to draw on myth by invoking his "namesake" Lee, who "never came up to Washington to curry favor." That compliment loses some of its flavor, given that Frost might be accused of doing exactly what he condemns through participating in the inaugural. Instead of compromising, Lee (and, by implication, Frost) showed that he remained wedded to the American frontier myth: "He sawed wood." Thus, he belonged to a certain idea of America by refusing to belong to a corrupted version. Brower argues that the poem's focus on possession emphasizes the contradictions inherent to the "American state of mind," and Frost's comments on the poem support that recognition of tension.[48] "The Gift Outright," although appearing to represent patriotism at its best, hints at another darker version of the American myth that Frost made explicit in several other poems.

"The Gift Outright" also holds the distinction of being the only Frost poem to be published in more than one of his single volumes. That is because Frost chose to reprint it in his final volume *In the Clearing*, issued in March of 1962, some fourteen months after the inaugural. The reinsertion is of more than passing interest for two reasons. First, it is preceded in the text by "For John F. Kennedy: His Inaugural," a long poem written especially for the occasion. Second, and more important, several poems that lead up to these two in the volume, especially "Pod of the Milkweed," "Away!" "A Cabin in the Clearing," and "America Is Hard to See," deal explicitly with the issue of the meaning and myth of America. When read as a sequence, the opening poems, followed abruptly by the two concerning the inaugural, create a tension typical of much of Frost's greatest work and assert his paradoxical sense of America's regnant myth.

The title *In the Clearing* invokes the clearing of a wilderness in the New World. In "Pod of the Milkweed," the opening poem of the collection, the pod itself is a metaphor for the idea or myth of America.[49] "Calling all brethren of every race / From source unknown but from no special place" (411) contrasts sharply with the clear sense of England as origin as depicted in "The Gift Outright." The special relationship with England has deteriorated, and immigrants arrive from other locales as well. The pod also invokes a "theme of wanton waste in peace and war" and a "thirst on hunger to the point of lust" characterizes the butterflies feeding on it (411). The narrator admits that the pod "flows / With milk and honey" (411), a clichéd figure derived from the Israelites' dream in the Book of Exodus. Here, however, it is "bitter milk" that "tastes as if it might be opiate" (411), an image that faintly echoes the Marxist indictment of middle-class idealism as being an opiate for the masses. "The distilled honey is so sweet / It makes the butterflies intemperate" (411) is a confusing line that seems to admit to the value of the honey, and yet it is "distilled," perhaps altered, and certainly intoxicating. That it affords "no slumber" (411) echoes far-off Frostian favorites such as "After Apple Picking" or "Stopping by Woods." There is no real comfort or surcease, only an "inheritance of restless dream" (412). The poem ends with a grim statement that might be a more forthright restatement of the veiled ending to "The Gift Outright": "He seems to say the reason why so much / Should come to nothing must be fairly faced" (412). The assertion that the grandiose idea of America "should come to nothing," a line reminiscent of "such as she would become," can be understood as a poignant reminder of the nation's failure to meet its promise, a failure that "must be fairly faced."

The vision itself may be part of the problem. Frost suggests in these poems that the notion of consensus with regard to the mission, role, or meaning of America is dubious. Another poem, "A Cabin in the Clearing," takes the form of a dialogue between two features of the wilderness that the pioneers must subdue: the "Mist" and the "Smoke" (413–15). Ironically, both elements undermine visual accuracy. The Mist laments, "And still I doubt if they know where they are. / And I begin to fear they never will." Later, when the Smoke asks, "Why don't they ask the Red Man where they are?" the Mist responds with an account of the American obsession with "where they are":

> They often do, and none the wiser for it.
> So do they also ask philosophers
> Who come to look in on them from the pulpit.
> They will ask anyone there is to ask—
> In the fond faith accumulated fact
> Will of itself take fire and light the world up.
> Learning has been a part of their religion. (414)

The passage depicts a strange conflation of Native American lore, philosophy, learning, and religion into the generic "accumulated fact" that Americans hope might "take fire and light the world up," invoking the nation's mythical world mission. Calling that hope America's "fond faith" seems dismissive and condescending, and Americans, despite attempts at self-knowledge, remain "none the wiser for it."

The irony of these opening poems of the volume is advanced in what may be Frost's most skeptical poem concerning American myth: "America Is Hard to See" (416–19). The poem describes the voyages of Columbus to "the race's future trial place, / A fresh start for the human race." Instead of fulfilling such promises of a "more than Moses' exodus," however, the narrator laments that Columbus's discoveries merely "spread the room / Of our enacting out the doom" of human society. Again, a key problem is seeing America for what it truly is:

> America is hard to see.
> Less partial witnesses than he

> In book on book have testified
> They could not see it from outside—
> Or inside either for that matter.
> We know the literary chatter.

America cannot be faithfully discerned from inside or out, so the vast numbers of written accounts, for all intents and purposes, are meaningless. Instead of holding to testimonial reports concerning the nation's meaning as depicted in "book on book," it is better to recognize them as nothing more than "literary chatter."

Thus, the opening section of *In the Clearing* juxtaposes ironic analyses of America's myths, mission, and meaning as depicted in the first seven poems with the more conservative versions presented in the eighth and ninth (the Kennedy inaugural poem and "The Gift Outright"). It is odd to read a condemnation of "literary chatter" and then a few pages later encounter the following:

> Our venture in revolution and outlawry
> Has justified itself in freedom's story
> Right down to now in glory upon glory . . .
> A democratic form of right divine
> To rule first answerable to high design . . .
> It makes the prophet in us all presage
> The glory of a next Augustan age. (423–24)

Are we to understand the meaning of America to be merely another form of communal doom covered by "literary chatter" or a heroic "venture" repeatedly "justified" in "glory upon glory"? However one might conclude, any critic attempting to pigeonhole Frost's concept of America and its myths of origin and purpose must somehow reckon with the mixed signals of the opening pages of *In the Clearing.* The rich texture of the tension in these poems reflects the "different tensions in American culture" and therefore justifies interest.[50] In the space of only nine poems Frost provides conservative as well as radical views of American mythical constructs. He is at once Trilling's Frost and Adams's (or Kennedy's) Frost.

Despite Trilling's unwillingness to accept the public persona fostered by Frost and celebrated by his "true American" admirers like Adams, there is no doubt that the poet embraced his newly enhanced public life after the inauguration.[51] He mentioned to Untermeyer that it had been the first time a poet had read at an American inauguration, and Untermeyer later explained that Frost hesitated to have his letters published near the end of his life because he "was reluctant to destroy the image his countrymen had formed of him when he read 'The Gift Outright' before the leaders of the nation."[52] *Time* magazine was close to the truth in asserting, "Frost relishes his role as a kind of foxy grandpa of letters" and was "plainly delighted with his new role among men since he recited his 'The Gift Outright' at the inauguration. [Frost stated,] 'Kennedy gave me a kind of status that nobody ever had before . . . It's been a new world for me.'"[53] Because he was interested in "the image his countrymen had formed of him," perhaps his decision to affiliate himself with the ruling powers should not be criticized.

Trilling and Adams were only able to embrace incomplete Robert Frosts, and thus they misjudged his mythic resonance. That mistake will always be symptomatic of attempts to co-opt an artist as complex as Frost as being solely affiliated with any political agenda. A balanced approach must concede that both the conservative and the radical versions of the poet hold cultural legitimacy and that neither can rightfully be privileged. Instead of arguing for either view, a cultural critique of the representative anecdote would indicate that competing views underline the inherent ambivalence of the era and the symbiotic nature of America's myth of concern throughout its history. A full understanding and admiration of Robert Frost (and of American myth) can best be attained by not only accepting but also embracing both views as characteristic expressions. Readers must accept both aspects as "two poles of a paradox." The highly ambivalent character of the poet, his poetical work, and his culture's representation of him are manifestations of the underlying tensions and conflicts that mark an entire social myth. Frost was aware of that understanding and perhaps viewed it as essential: "The point I tried to make was that I was a very hard person to make out if I am any judge of human nature. I might easily be most deceiving when most bent on telling the truth."[54]

The resonance of Frost, along with that of Emerson, Twain, and Lewis (and, for that matter, Hawthorne, Douglass, Truth, Stowe, Lincoln, and many others), can be attributed to their inherent liminalities. Frost was aware of his proclivities toward dependence and independence and his overwhelming urge toward the individual and the communal, the romantic and the realistic, and the conservative and the liberatory. According to the theory advanced by Robert Bellah and his associates, the heart of American individualism is its "intrinsic ambivalence/ambiguity," an idea brought to America's attention long ago by Alexis de Tocqueville and others.[55]

If that concept is accurate, a dialectic pitting autonomy and self-reliance versus a desire for community and tradition, for example, may get at the heart of America—and perhaps at the heart of Frost. Thus, both versions of Frost—Adams's popular, concern-oriented, mythical Frost and the darker, more frightening, and yet more freedom-oriented version espoused by Trilling—comport with the dialectical mode of viewing American culture that I have attempted to develop. Frost appears to have endorsed such a perspective. He occasionally made pithy, aphoristic statements regarding the apparent paradoxical and contradictory nature of his artistic achievement and of himself and American culture: "All truth is a dialogue," "all of a man's art is a bursting unity of opposites," and "everything in life contains a varying blend of order and riot."[56]

In the end, the same might be said for the nation's highly complex yet always dynamic regnant myth. American cultural history is often generated from relatively minor moments that somehow touch a collective nerve and so are mythologized into representative anecdotes. Numerous other events have also been taken up and thoroughly examined by a culture still bent on self-discovery and self-definition. For example, the 1960s, that most turbulent of decades, provides a plethora of personalities and public moments that drew upon the tropes of the Declaration and Christian repentance, received critical response, and thus engendered thorough and heated debates about the American ideal. Other more recent moments, including Bill Clinton's selection of Maya Angelou as inaugural poet in 1993, revive and sustain the historical American conversation about central values, myths, and ideologies. As Clinton put it in the memorable first line he spoke as president, "Today we celebrate the mystery of American renewal." As always, the renewal and the conversation continue. Perhaps they are one and the same.

Notes

Introduction

1. The critical and historical materials approaching American literature and culture from this perspective are rich and extensive. Typical of the critical assumptions of the era after World War II are the opening remarks in *Literary History of the United States*, 3d ed., ed. Robert E. Spiller et al. (1948, repr. New York: Macmillan, 1973), xvii. For a modern reconsideration of the thematics of American "newness," see Terence Martin, *Parables of Possibility: The American Need for Beginnings* (New York: Columbia University Press, 1995).

2. The quotation is from Myra Jehlen, *American Incarnation: The Individual, the Nation, and the Continent* (Cambridge: Harvard University Press, 1986), 25. Throughout this volume, I will use the term *ideology* loosely, preferring a concise definition such as that supplied by Sacvan Bercovitch in "The Problem of Ideology in American Literary History," *Critical Inquiry* 12 (Summer 1986): 631–53: "the ground and texture of consensus . . . the web of rhetoric, ritual, and assumption through which society coerces, persuades, and coheres" (635). Thus, ideology consists of the beliefs, values, philosophies, and religions by which individuals and societies conduct their lives and construct their worldviews. I will avoid lengthy philosophical considerations of the many uses and streams of thought to which the word *ideology* has become indebted, including Marxism, Freudian and Lacanian psychoanalysis, and cultural anthropology. For a partial yet lengthy listing of the ways the term is employed, see Terry Eagleton, *Ideology: An Introduction* (London: Verso, 1991).

3. On entelechy, see Jehlen, *American Incarnation*, 1–42. America's "originating ideas were neither original nor exceptional," as Jehlen points out (3). They were powerfully shaped by the cultural conversations spawned during the Reformation and the Enlightenment. But Jehlen is correct in arguing that these political ideas became fused with the natural landscape available in America. The "concept of New World could not occur as pure abstraction; it had to interpret some actual territory, a real place" (9–10). That fusion was a unique manifestation of the emergent modern spirit, which "completed its genesis by becoming flesh in the body

of the American continent" (4). Leo Marx also foregrounds the conflation of the American continent with such political ideas as destiny and mission. See *The Pilot and the Passenger* (New York: Oxford University Press, 1988), 315–36. Edmundo O'Gorman has described the European "invention" of the New World in *The Invention of America: An Inquiry into the Historical Nature of the New World and the Meaning of its History* (Bloomington: Indiana University Press, 1961).

4. Quotations from Wigglesworth and Edwards in Conrad Cherry, *God's New Israel* (Englewood Cliffs: Prentice-Hall, 1971), 45, 59; quotation from Dwight in Henry Nash Smith, *Virgin Land: The American West as Symbol and Myth* (Cambridge: Harvard University Press, 1950), 11.

5. Jehlen, *American Incarnation,* 25.

6. Emory Elliott, *Revolutionary Writers: Literature and Authority in the New Republic, 1725–1810* (New York: Oxford University Press, 1986), 11.

7. Myths are stories and narratives by which humans make sense of their lives, their relationships, and their worlds. The term *mythos* (myth) should never be associated with a sense of denigration or repudiation of what some consider to be historical fact or religious certainty. Through their ability to inspire, encourage, educate, and exhort, myths include some of the most resonant and consistently powerful stories of communal history when measured in terms of their effects in the lives of humans and human communities. As Richard Slotkin observes, "Myth does not argue its ideology; it exemplifies it. It projects models of good or heroic behavior that reinforce the values of ideology." See "Myth and the Production of History," in *Ideology and Classic American Literature,* ed. Sacvan Bercovitch and Myra Jehlen (New York: Cambridge University Press, 1986), 84.

To balance such a strong endorsement of the functions and office of mythos, myths can conversely be used to deceive, oppress, or mislead their hearers, as numerous Marxist, feminist, and New Historicist critics have argued. *Myth,* like a knife that can be used both for the preparation of dinner and the murder of the cook, is a term brimming with both positive and negative connotations. Myths can be conceived as ethical vehicles awaiting readers and responders. As I use it, the term should not be interpreted as pejorative of the veracity, the historicity, or, ultimately, the reality of the mythic events themselves.

8. All Scripture quotations in this book will come from the translation that Americans, particularly of the nineteenth century, have commonly used, especially for literary and political purposes: the King James Version.

9. W. E. Vine, *An Expository Dictionary of New Testament Words* (Old Tappan: Fleming H. Revell, 1966), 279–80; see also 69 for analysis of the word *nous.*

10. The classic articulation of the jeremiad mode in American culture is Sacvan Bercovitch, *American Jeremiad* (Madison: University of Wisconsin Press, 1979); the quotation is from xi. Bercovitch's formulation is both indebted to and in conversation with that of his mentor Perry Miller, who describes the jeremiad tradition most fully in *Errand into the Wilderness* (Cambridge: Harvard University Press, 1956) and *Nature's Nation* (Cambridge: Harvard University Press, 1967).

11. Miller, *Nature's Nation,* 23; in particular, see the chapter entitled "Declension in a Bible Commonwealth," 14–49.

12. Charles Colson, *Against the Night: Living in the New Dark Ages* (Ann Arbor: Vine, 1989), 140.

13. Colson, *Against the Night,* 140. I draw upon the written work of Charles Colson because I believe that he has a hand on the pulse of middle-class, evan-

gelical America of the 1980s and 1990s. He enjoys great popularity among evangelicals, and his life exemplifies the seemingly miraculous "change of heart" from being a power-mongering political lackey of Richard Nixon to a soul-winning, prison-ministering evangelist. Thus, his definition of repentance holds much sway among contemporary Evangelicals. For an extended account of his act of repentance, see Charles Colson, *Born Again* (Old Tappan: Chosen, 1976).

14. For many believers, "knowledge of the specific time, day, and place in which this experience occurs is accorded preeminence, as though such knowledge was itself a central aspect of the salvation process." James Davison Hunter, *American Evangelicalism: Conservative Religion and the Quandary of Modernity* (New Brunswick: Rutgers University Press, 1983), 65.

15. Northrop Frye, *The Secular Scripture: A Study of the Structure of Romance* (Cambridge: Harvard University Press, 1976), 170–71.

16. This theme has been treated to some extent in various influential volumes written by the generation of cold war critics. For example, R. W. B. Lewis offers a typically mythic description of a recently arrived settler: "an individual emancipated from history, happily bereft of ancestry, untouched and undefiled by the usual inheritances of family and race; an individual standing alone, self-reliant and self-propelling . . . in his very newness he was fundamentally innocent." See Lewis, *The American Adam: Innocence, Tragedy and Tradition in the Nineteenth Century* (Chicago: University of Chicago Press, 1955), 5.

17. Marx, *The Pilot and the Passenger*, xi. Although claims such as Marx's appear to be on the cutting edge, his is not a recent revelation. In the early 1930s, for example, Bernard DeVoto argued that "a theory that is capable of calling the America of 1700–1860 homogeneous racially, intellectually, emotionally, philosophically, economically, or aesthetically, is powerless to describe America." See DeVoto, *Mark Twain's America* (Cambridge: Harvard University Press, 1932), 226.

18. Kenneth Burke, *The Philosophy of Literary Form*, 3d ed. (Berkeley: University of California Press, 1974), 110–11; compare Lionel Trilling, "Reality in America," in *The Liberal Imagination* (New York: Viking, 1950). Trilling's original concept of culture, which characterized American culture as dialectical and conversational in nature, continues to influence some of the more interesting work of contemporary Americanists. Such a conception of American culture, based on a dialectical opposition, has marked numerous studies of American critics, from D. H. Lawrence's groundbreaking *Classic American Literature* (1923, reprt. New York: Penguin, 1977), through many of the cold war critics, to Robert Bellah et al., *Habits of the Heart: Individualism and Commitment in American Life* (Berkeley: University of California Press, 1985); James Davison Hunter, *Culture Wars: The Struggle to Define America* (New York: Basic Books, 1991); Sam Girgus, *Desire and the Political Unconscious in American Literature: Eros and Ideology* (New York: St. Martin's Press, 1990); and Alessandro Portelli, *The Text and the Voice: Writing, Speaking, and Democracy in American Literature* (New York: Columbia University Press, 1994). For a brief discussion of this tendency, see Harold K. Bush, Jr., "Structural America: The Persistence of Oppositional Paradigms in American Literary Theory," *College Literature* 9 (June 1996): 181–89.

19. Mailloux's method is explained and demonstrated in *Rhetorical Power* (Ithaca: Cornell University Press, 1989), see esp. 3–18, quotations from 15.

20. Northrop Frye, *The Critical Path: An Essay on the Social Context of Literary Criticism* (Bloomington: Indiana University Press, 1971), 37, 44–45.

21. Miller, *Nature's Nation,* 163; in particular see the chapter entitled "Emersonian Genius and the American Democracy," 163–74.

22. Frye, *The Critical Path,* 55.

23. Hunter, *Culture Wars,* 42, 42–43, 51. Hunter analyzes how Americans, representing a wide array of ethnic, social, sexual, and geographical backgrounds, are able to discuss and ponder, as a society, such metaphysical issues as the true representation and significance of the historical past of the United States or the real meaning of America. Hunter's analysis begins with the assumption that the public sphere is the central location for cultural dialogue concerning primary social belief. It is in the public realm of discourse that "cultural dialogues" may be carried out. As Hunter argues, however, such dialogues may be better understood as cultural conflict, even, as his title suggests, as culture wars.

24. My focus on such moments has been influenced by Kenneth Burke's notion of the "representative anecdote," an idea used with great insight by Leo Marx and renamed the "representative event." See Burke, *A Grammar of Motives and a Rhetoric of Motives* (New York: Meridian Books, 1962), 59; and Marx, *The Machine in the Garden: Technology and the Pastoral Idea in America* (New York: Oxford University Press, 1964), 37.

25. Jefferson is thought of as the single writer of the Declaration, but of course it was "authored" by a committee, including John Adams, and "authorized" by the entire Congress. Various phrases and even whole sentences were contributed by others, such as Benjamin Franklin and Richard Henry Lee. For simplicity, however, I will treat Jefferson as singular author. The fact that the document is traditionally attributed to Jefferson is a mythologized conception worth more consideration. An account of the genesis of the document and an astute discussion of Jefferson's efforts to mythologize his participation in the creation of the Declaration can be found in Pauline Maier, *American Scripture: Making the Declaration of Independence* (New York: Knopf, 1997).

26. Thomas Jefferson, *Writings,* ed. Merrill D. Peterson (New York: Library of America, 1984), 1501.

27. Edward Gittleman, "Jefferson's Slave Narrative: The Declaration of Independence as a Literary Text," *Early American Literature* 8 (1974): 239–56, esp. 246–47. All references to the text of the Declaration come from Jefferson, *Writings,* 19–24.

28. Miller, *Nature's Nation,* 94.

29. For examples of the most influential scholarship on the rhetoric of the Declaration, see Carl Becker, *The Declaration of Independence: A Study in the History of Political Ideas* (New York: Vintage, 1958); Stephen E. Lucas, "Justifying America: The Declaration of Independence as a Rhetorical Document," in *American Rhetoric: Context and Criticism,* ed. Thomas W. Benson (Carbondale: Southern Illinois University Press, 1989): 67–103; and Garry Wills, *Inventing America: Jefferson's Declaration of Independence* (Garden City: Doubleday, 1978). Valuable commentary on the Declaration is also found throughout Thomas Gustafson, *Representative Words: Politics, Literature, and the American Language, 1776–1865* (New York: Cambridge University Press, 1992), esp. 252–66.

30. Jay Fliegelman, *Declaring Independence: Jefferson, Natural Language, and the Culture of Performance* (Stanford: Stanford University Press, 1993), 24–25, 4.

31. See Patricia Caldwell, *The Puritan Conversion Narrative: The Beginnings of American Expression* (New York: Cambridge University Press, 1983).

32. Roger Lundin, *The Culture of Interpretation: Christian Faith and the Post-modern World* (Grand Rapids: Eerdmans, 1993), 139. The quotation from Miller is found in Kenneth Murdock, "Introduction," in Miller, *Nature's Nation*, xiv.

33. Frye, *The Critical Path*, 48.

34. Garry Wills, *Lincoln at Gettysburg: The Words That Remade America* (New York: Simon and Schuster, 1992). Maier argues persuasively that Wills's focus on Lincoln is exaggerated and reductionist, see *American Scripture*, xix–xx.

35. Among major antebellum figures, perhaps George Lippard, Walt Whitman, Henry Thoreau, Margaret Fuller, Herman Melville, or John Brown would be worthy topics for this approach.

36. Studies that have given much attention to the cultural work performed specifically by the Declaration in antebellum America are: Martin, *Parables of Possibility*; Wills, *Lincoln at Gettysburg*; Fliegelman, *Declaring Independence*; Gustafson, *Representative Words*; Maier, *American Scripture*; Paul Goetsch and Gerd Hurm, eds., *The Fourth of July: Political Oratory and Literary Reactions, 1776–1876* (Tubingen: Gunter Narr Verlag, 1992); Philip Foner, ed., *We the Other People: Alternative Declarations of Independence by Labor Groups, Farmers, Woman's Rights Advocates, Socialists, and Blacks, 1829–1975* (Urbana: University of Illinois Press, 1976); Philip F. Detweiler, "The Changing Reputation of the Declaration of Independence: The First Fifty Years," *William and Mary Quarterly* 19 (1972): 557–74; Barbara Bardes and Suzanne Gossett, *Declarations of Independence: Women and Political Power* (New Brunswick: Rutgers University Press, 1990); and Len Travers, *Celebrating the Fourth: Independence Day and the Rites of Nationalism in the Early Republic* (Amherst: University of Massachusetts Press, 1997). Some mention is made of the Declaration in various more specialized studies, for example, Eric Sundquist in *To Wake the Nations: Race and the Making of American Literature* (Cambridge: Harvard University Press, 1993), provides useful analysis of how African Americans used the revolutionary motif and the Declaration's idealism within their own rhetorical projects. A thorough analysis of the Declaration myth and its pervasive presence throughout American literature and culture remains to be done.

Chapter 1: Reinventing the Puritans

1. Frye, *The Critical Path*, 49.

2. As early as 1935, Austin Warren argued in "Hawthorne's Reading," *New England Quarterly* 8 (1935): 480–97, for the view of Hawthorne as highly adept historian. Among more recent critics holding a similar position, see Neal Frank Doubleday, *Hawthorne's Early Tales: A Critical Study* (Durham: Duke University Press, 1972); Michael Davitt Bell, *Hawthorne and the Historical Romance of New England* (Princeton: Princeton University Press, 1971); Michael Colacurcio, *The Province of Piety: Moral History in Hawthorne's Early Tales* (Cambridge: Harvard University Press, 1984); Michael Colacurcio, "Introduction," in Nathaniel Hawthorne, *Selected Tales and Sketches* (New York: Penguin, 1987); and Frederick Newberry, *Hawthorne's Divided Loyalties: England and America in His Works* (Rutherford: Fairleigh Dickinson University Press, 1987). It is widely known that Hawthorne held a nearly obsessive personal interest in Puritan history due to the participation of his ancestors in such notorious acts as the Salem witch trials. In addition, Hawthorne's sister-in-law, who owned a Boston book-

store, frequently gave him books, especially those by transcendentalists including Bancroft and Parker; see Jean Normand, *Nathaniel Hawthorne: An Approach
to an Analysis of Artistic Creation* (Cleveland: Case Western Reserve University Press, 1970), 90. Colacurcio has characterized Hawthorne's principal interest
as revealed by the Atheneum record as "something we might almost risk calling
by the name of 'American Studies'" ("Introduction," xv), elsewhere claiming that
"Hawthorne is indeed, among other things, our first significant intellectual historian" (*Province of Piety*, 3).

3. See Marion L. Kesselring, *Hawthorne's Reading, 1828–1850: A Transcription
and Identification of Titles Recorded in the Charge-Books of the Salem Atheneum* (New York: New York Public Library, 1949).

4. Colacurcio, *Province of Piety*, 3.

5. Historically, the name is spelled "Endecott." For some reason, Hawthorne
saw fit to change the spelling to include an *i* for the second *e*. To be consistent, I
will use Hawthorne's refashioned spelling throughout this chapter. All quotations
from "Endicott and the Red Cross" and "The May-Pole of Merry Mount" will be
taken from *The Centenary Edition of Nathaniel Hawthorne*, vol. 9: *Twice-told
Tales* (1837, repr. Columbus: Ohio State University Press, 1974); subsequent page
references will appear in the text.

6. Hunter, *Culture Wars*, 51.

7. Allen Guttman, *The Conservative Tradition in America* (New York: Oxford
University Press, 1967), 20.

8. My depictions of historians here and throughout the chapter are all general-
izations needing some qualification. Even Hutchinson, for example, cannot always be labeled merely as a Tory; his historical achievement includes many
moments that conflict with such a reductive view. In addition, many historians,
notably Hannah Adams and Jedediah Morse, drew heavily from Hutchinson's
insights, admired his analysis, and thoroughly respected his accomplishment;
Webster was not in 1820 the thoroughgoing conservative that he would become
by 1850; and Bancroft was not always so consistently romantic as my general
discussion might suggest.

9. See Paul D. Erickson, "Daniel Webster's Myth of the Pilgrims," *New England
Quarterly* 57 (1984): 44–64, who observes (49), "Webster uses the terms Pilgrim
and Puritan interchangably." The sense that there was little or no difference between these two groups has been fairly widespread throughout U.S. history. In
*Mystic Chords of Memory: The Transformation of Tradition in American Cul-
ture* (New York: Alfred A. Knopf, 1991), 64, Michael Kammen notes that "there
has long been a tendency . . . to blend the two groups [Puritans and Pilgrims]." Of
course, New England had historically looked to the Bible and the New England
forebears for vision and example. Standard texts that established the scholarly
tradition investigating these phenomena include Miller, *Errand into the Wilderness*; Wesley Frank Craven, *The Legend of the Founding Fathers* (New York: New
York University Press, 1956); Ernest Tuveson, *Redeemer Nation: The Idea of
America's Millennial Role* (Chicago: University of Chicago Press, 1968); and Sacvan Bercovitch, *The Puritan Origins of the American Self* (New Haven: Yale
University Press, 1975).

10. As Irving described popular sovereignty, "I have seen, in short, that awful
despot, the People, in the moment of unlimited power . . . like some lunatic re-

lieved from the restraints of his strait waistcoat." See Washington Irving, *The Works of Washington Irving*, vol. 7: *Salmagundi* (1807, repr. New York: Putnam, 1867), 210–11. Discussion of the mob in literature of the nineteenth century can be found in Larzer Ziff, *The Declaration of Literary Independence in America* (New York: Penguin, 1982), and Portelli, *The Text and the Voice*.

11. Daniel Webster, *Works of Daniel Webster*, 18 vols. (Boston: Little, Brown, 1856), 1:181–82, 186–87.

12. Erickson, "Daniel Webster's Myth," 44.

13. Moise Ostrogorski, *Democracy and the Organization of Political Parties* (New York: Macmillan, 1902), 2:26–27.

14. Erickson, "Daniel Webster's Myth," 53.

15. Kammen, *Mystic Chords of Memory*, 63–64.

16. Doubleday, *Hawthorne's Early Tales*, 92–93.

17. Fred Somkin, *Unquiet Eagle: Memory and Desire in the Idea of American Freedom, 1815–1860* (Ithaca: Cornell University Press, 1967), 185–86.

18. Discussion regarding typology is found in Bell, *Hawthorne and the Historical Romance of New England*, esp. 8–14. Typology is also well covered in numerous works by Bercovitch, particularly *American Jeremiad* and *The Puritan Origins of the American Self*.

19. George Bancroft, *The History of the United States* (1834, repr. Boston: Little, Brown, 1856), 1:340–41. Bancroft consistently spelled Endicott with one *t*.

20. Guttman, *Conservative Tradition*, 20.

21. Bancroft, *History*, 1:371–72.

22. A discussion of Theodore Parker's (and, to a lesser extent, George Bancroft's) transcendental view of American history, including his powerful influence upon Abraham Lincoln, is found in Wills, *Lincoln at Gettysburg*, 90–120. Additional analysis of Lincoln's affinity with transcendental thought can be found in James M. McPherson, *Abraham Lincoln and the Second American Revolution* (New York: Oxford University Press, 1990).

23. Jan Dawson, *The Unusable Past: America's Puritan Tradition, 1830 to 1930* (Chico: Scholar's Press, 1984), 27.

24. Colacurcio, *Province of Piety*, 207.

25. Colacurcio, "Introduction," xv–xvi.

26. Kesselring, *Hawthorne's Reading*, 39.

27. Colacurcio, "Introduction," xvi.

28. Sacvan Bercovitch, "Endicott's Breastplate: Symbolism and Typology in 'Endicott and the Red Cross,'" *Studies in Short Fiction* 4, no. 4 (1967): 289.

29. Russell J. Reising, *The Unusable Past: Theory and the Study of American Literature* (New York: Methuen, 1986), 83.

30. Bercovitch, "Endicott's Breastplate," 296, 295.

31. Bell, *Hawthorne and the Historical Romance of New England*, 54.

32. J. C. Furnas, *The Americans: A Social History of the United States, 1587–1914* (New York: Putnam, 1969), 64.

33. Bercovitch, *American Jeremiad*, 133.

34. Newberry, *Hawthorne's Divided Loyalties*.

35. Bercovitch, *American Jeremiad*, xi–xiv.

36. Reising, *The Unusable Past*, 83.

37. Slotkin, "Myth and the Production of History," 81.

38. Bancroft, *History*, 1:372.

39. Newberry, *Hawthorne's Divided Loyalties*, 18.

40. Bell, *Hawthorne and the Historical Romance of New England*, 57.

41. Colacurcio, *Province of Piety*, 226.

42. Mark A. Noll, *A History of Christianity in the United States and Canada* (Grand Rapids: Eerdmans, 1992), 60.

43. Noll, *A History of Christianity*, 58–60.

44. Colacurcio, *Province of Piety*, 230.

45. Thomas Pribek, "The Conquest of Canaan: Suppression of Merry Mount," *Nineteenth-Century Literature* 40 (Dec. 1985): 345–47.

46. Bell, *Hawthorne and the Historical Romance of New England*, 129.

47. Colacurcio, *Province of Piety*, 254.

48. Bell, *Hawthorne and the Historical Romance of New England*, 57, 60.

49. John McWilliams, *Hawthorne, Melville, and the American Character: A Looking-Glass Business* (New York: Cambridge University Press, 1984), 47.

50. For discussion of this process in the 1820s and 1830s, see Travers, *Celebrating the Fourth*, 191–227, and Maier, *American Scripture*, 154–208.

Chapter 2: Revolutionary Enactment

1. For a sweeping analysis of republicanism as found in early national sermons and pamphlets, including extensive, otherwise difficult-to-find primary quotations, see Nathan Hatch, *Sacred Cause of Liberty: Republican Thought and the Millennium in Revolutionary New England* (New Haven: Yale University Press, 1977). Other relevent documentation and analysis of the association of American political ideology and Christian idealism are found in Cherry, *God's New Israel*. For the surprising "lateness" of interest in the Declaration, see Detweiler, "The Changing Reputation of the Declaration of Independence."

2. A thorough study of the construction of equality throughout American rhetorical history is in Celeste Michelle Condit and John Louis Lucaites, *Crafting Equality: America's Anglo-African Word* (Chicago: University of Chicago Press, 1993). I am indebted to their study of African American antebellum rhetoric for numerous insights incorporated into this chapter. Langston Hughes, "Freedom's Plow," in *The Selected Poems of Langston Hughes* (New York: Knopf, 1959).

3. Gustafson, *Representative Words*, passim.

4. Rush Welter, *The Mind of America, 1820–1860* (New York: Columbia University Press, 1975), 396.

5. Donald Mathews, "The Second Great Awakening as an Organizing Process," *American Quarterly* 21 (1969): 23–43. Charles Finney's profound influence, rarely discussed in critical works centered on American literary history, will be elaborated in chapter 3 and the introduction to part 2.

6. William G. McLoughlin, *Revivals, Awakenings, and Reform: An Essay on Religion and Social Change in America, 1607–1977* (Chicago: University of Chicago Press, 1978), 103, 104. McLoughlin's concept of religion owes a debt to Clifford Geertz, who defined religion as "(1) a system of symbols which acts to (2) establish powerful, pervasive, and long-lasting moods and motivations in men by (3) formulating conceptions of a general order of existence and (4) clothing those concepts with such an aura of factuality that (5) the moods and motivations seem uniquely

real." See *The Interpretation of Cultures: Selected Essays* (New York: Basic Books, 1973), 90. Thus Geertz, by describing "a system of symbols which acts," is closely aligning the work of religion with the rhetorical process of "enactment" as defined by Karlyn Kohrs Campbell. Geertz's full conception of a "system of symbols" can be associated with Frye's notion of a myth of concern, and some of the most telling examples of "enactment" or "practical action," all steeped in the "power of enactment," can be seen as individual declarations of in/dependence.

7. Geertz, *Interpretation of Cultures*, 90.

8. Numerous studies have focused on millennialism in American culture: see especially Hatch, *Sacred Cause of Liberty*; Tuveson, *Redeemer Nation*; and Ruth Bloch, *Visionary Republic: Millennial Themes in American Thought, 1756–1800* (New York: Cambridge University Press, 1985).

9. Fliegelman, *Declaring Independence*, 24–25, 4.

10. An impressive and thorough study of the annual performance of the Declaration, as well as the surrounding events as carried out in Boston, Philadelphia, and Charleston, S.C., is in Travers, *Celebrating the Fourth*.

11. Condit and Lucaites, *Crafting Equality*, 69–70. On the contributions of African American rhetors, see 69–100. Another historical overview is found in "Introduction to the American Series: Black Abolitionists in the United States, 1830–1865," in *The Black Abolitionist Papers*, ed. C. Peter Ripley et al. (Chapel Hill: University of North Carolina Press, 1991), 3:3–69.

12. Frederick Douglass, *Frederick Douglass' Paper*, Sept. 29, 1854.

13. See Condit and Lucaites, *Crafting Equality*, esp. 77. For information on the contributions of African American women to this emerging national voice, see Carla L. Peterson, *"Doers of the Word": African-American Women Speakers and Writers in the North (1830–1880)* (New York: Oxford University Press, 1995).

14. John M. Werner, *Reaping the Bloody Harvest: Race Riots in the United States during the Age of Jackson, 1824–1849* (New York: Garland, 1986), esp. 298.

15. Werner, *Reaping the Bloody Harvest*, 18.

16. Ripley et al., "Introduction," 19.

17. David Walker, *Appeal, in Four Articles; Together with a Preamble, to the Coloured Citizens of the World, but in Particular, and Very Expressly, to Those of the United States of America* (1829, repr. New York: Hill and Wang, 1965), 2, 12.

18. Walker, *Appeal*, 14, 21.

19. Sundquist, *To Wake the Nations*, 32.

20. Ibid., 36, 47; see also Edmund S. Morgan, *The Challenge of the American Revolution* (New York: W. W. Norton, 1976), esp. 139–73.

21. Eugene Genovese, *From Rebellion to Revolution: Afro-American Slave Revolts in the Making of the New World* (New York: Random House, 1979), 49.

22. See the "Confessions of Nat Turner" taken from *The Southhampton Slave Revolt of 1831: A Compilation of Source Material*, ed. Henry Irving Tragle (Amherst: University of Massachusetts Press, 1971), 306ff, quotations on 306–7. I agree in principle with Sundquist's view of Turner's controversial authorship of that text. Turner, to an unknowable extent, did assert some authority over the transcribed text published by Thomas Gray, and the text he helped create must be considered to some degree a highly ingenious rhetorical performance with certain political ends in mind.

23. "Confessions of Nat Turner," 309, 310.

24. My suggestion that Douglass's stories can be read as declarations has much in common with the theory of slave narratives as proposed by William Andrews: "In the slave narrative the quest is toward freedom from physical bondage and the enlightenment that literacy can offer. . . . perhaps the most important [motive] is the need of an other to *declare* himself through various linguistic acts, thereby reifying his abstract unreality, his invisibility in the eyes of his readers, so that he can be recognized as someone to be reckoned with. Such declarative acts . . . include . . . the appropriating of empowering myths and models of the self from any available resource." William L. Andrews, *To Tell a Free Story: The First Century of Afro-American Autobiography, 1760–1865* (Urbana: University of Illinois Press, 1986), 7.

25. Andrews, *To Tell a Free Story*, 217.

26. Ibid.

27. William L. Andrews, "Introduction to the 1987 Edition," in Frederick Douglass, *My Bondage and My Freedom*, ed. William L. Andrews (Urbana: University of Illinois Press, 1987), xv; William L. Andrews, "African-American Autobiography Criticism: Retrospect and Prospect," in *American Autobiography: Retrospect and Prospect*, ed. John Paul Eakin (Madison: University of Wisconsin Press, 1991), 207.

28. Houston A. Baker, *The Journey Back: Issues in Black Literature and Criticism* (Chicago: University of Chicago Press, 1980), 39. Baker appears to view Douglass as a poor former slave co-opted and stripped of all cultural power and individual moral responsibility by the white patriarchy. For Baker, it is darkly ironic that Douglass "adopted cherished values from the white world that held him in bondage" and demonstrated an "uncritical acceptance of the perspective made available by literacy in the *Narrative* itself" (38).

29. Waldo E. Martin, Jr., *The Mind of Frederick Douglass* (Chapel Hill: University of North Carolina Press, 1984), 27, 275, 277.

30. The texts that I will use are *Narrative of the Life of Frederick Douglass, an American Slave*, ed. and with an introduction by Houston A. Baker, Jr. (New York: Penguin, 1986); and *My Bondage and My Freedom*, ed. and with an introduction by William L. Andrews (Urbana: University of Illinois, 1987). Page comparisons are approximations because the number of lines and words per line vary in these editions; subsequent page references will appear in the text.

31. Donald B. Gibson, "Faith, Doubt, and Apostasy: Evidence of Things Unseen in Frederick Douglass's *Narrative*," in *Frederick Douglass: New Literary and Historical Essays*, ed. Eric J. Sundquist (New York: Cambridge University Press, 1991), 89.

32. Condit and Lucaites, *Crafting Equality*, 80.

33. Lewis, *The American Adam*, 5.

34. Andrews, *To Tell a Free Story*, 217.

35. These texts are found in Douglass, *The Life and Writings of Frederick Douglass*, ed. Philip Foner (New York: International, 1950–75), 2:220, 244, 255.

36. See Aileen S. Kraditor, *Means and Ends in American Abolitionism: Garrison and His Critics on Strategy and Tactics, 1834–1850* (New York: Pantheon, 1969) for a discussion of the issues concerning the Constitution, the Garrisonians, and Douglass's relationship with them. A more recent treatment of similar issues

is in T. Gregory Garvey, "Frederick Douglass's Change of Opinion on the U.S. Constitution: Abolitionism and the 'Elements of Moral Power,'" *ATQ: Nineteenth-Century American Literature and Culture* 9 (Sept. 1995): 229–43.

37. David Blight, *Frederick Douglass's Civil War: Keeping Faith in Jubilee* (Baton Rouge: Louisiana State University Press, 1989), 33.

38. Douglass, *The Life and Writings*, 189, 192.

39. Ibid., 181–88.

40. Ibid., 188.

41. Andrews, "Introduction," xv.

42. John Louis Lucaites, "The Irony of 'Equality' in Black Abolitionist Discourse: The Case of Frederick Douglass's 'What to the Slave Is the Fourth of July,'" presented at the Third Biannual Public Address Conference, University of Minnesota, Sept. 11–13, 1992, 5. Free blacks began to solidify a national consciousness as early as the 1830s, but a great majority of slaves, especially those who were illiterate, were not included in this emerging social unity. In that way Douglass's project entailed a missionary outreach.

43. A reference to Psalms 68:31.

44. McLoughlin, *Revivals*, 105.

45. Sundquist, *To Wake the Nations*, 36.

Chapter 3: Holiness and the Sanctification Gap

1. McLoughlin, *Revivals*, 113; the quotation from Jackson is on 139.

2. Timothy L. Smith, "Righteousness and Hope: Christian Holiness and the Millennial Vision of America, 1800–1900," *American Quarterly* 31 (Spring 1979): 44; see also William G. McLoughlin, *Revivals*; Perry Miller, *The Life of the Mind in America: From the Revolution to the Civil War* (New York: Harcourt Brace, 1965), 49–58, 64–84; and Robert Handy, *A Christian America: Protestant Hopes and Historical Realities* (New York: Oxford University Press, 1971).

3. McLoughlin, *Revivals*, 123, 125.

4. Cited in Melvin Easterday Dieter, *The Holiness Revival of the Nineteenth Century* (Metuchen: Scarecrow Press, 1980), 4; for general introductions to Wesleyan and subsequent Holiness theology see 1–156. See also Vinson Synan, *The Holiness-Pentecostal Movement in the United States* (Grand Rapids: Eerdmans, 1971), 13–76; Timothy L. Smith, *Revivalism and Social Reform in Mid-Nineteenth Century America* (New York: Abingdon, 1957); and Charles Edward White, *The Beauty of Holiness: Phoebe Palmer as Theologian, Revivalist, Feminist, and Humanitarian* (Grand Rapids: Asbury, 1986).

5. Synan, *The Holiness-Pentecostal Movement*, 28.

6. White, *The Beauty of Holiness*, 178.

7. Richard F. Lovelace, *Dynamics of Spiritual Life: An Evangelical Theology of Renewal* (Downers Grove: InterVarsity, 1979), 232–35.

8. McLoughlin, *Revivals*, 147–48.

9. Henry Wadsworth Longfellow, "A Psalm of Life" (1838), in *The Norton Anthology of American Literature*, 2d ed., ed. Nina Baym et al. (New York: W. W. Norton, 1985), 1319–20.

10. Karlyn Kohrs Campbell, "Style and Content in the Rhetoric of Early Afro-American Feminists," *Quarterly Journal of Speech* 72 (Nov. 1986): 435, 444.

11. Dorothy Sterling, *We Are Your Sisters: Black Women in the Nineteenth Century* (New York: W. W. Norton, 1983), 105. See also Nancy Cott, *The Bonds of Womanhood: "Women's Sphere" in New England, 1780–1835* (New Haven: Yale University Press, 1977).

12. Peterson, *"Doers of the Word,"* 3.

13. Jean Fagan Yellin, *Women and Sisters: The Anti-Slavery Feminists in American Culture* (New Haven: Yale University Press, 1989), xiv–xv.

14. I do not disagree with feminist analyses such as Yellin's, which demonstrate that the rhetoric of these women firmly opposed the prevailing patriarchal hegemony of the time. But such an opposition to reigning myths and political practice is a key element in the American metanoia. In addition, a focus on gender issues alone displaces attention from the powerful voice of consensus in the American myth of concern, a voice that these women so often employed.

15. Alma Lutz, *Created Equal: A Biography of Elizabeth Cady Stanton, 1815–1902* (New York: John Day, 1940), 44–45.

16. Mary D. Pellauer, *Toward a Tradition of Feminist Theology: The Religious Social Thought of Elizabeth Cady Stanton, Susan B. Anthony, and Anna Howard Shaw* (Brooklyn: Carlson, 1991), 71.

17. Stanton subscribed to a view of natural rights and natural law that underlies the Declaration; see Pellauer, *Toward a Tradition of Feminist Theology,* 321, 12. Further, Stanton's central point in her overall "theology" was that a "fourfold bondage presented systemic obstacles to the development of women as individuals" (16). As with "the abolitionists, [Stanton] applied eighteenth-century natural rights doctrine to nineteenth-century sexual inequality." Elisabeth Griffith, *In Her Own Right: The Life of Elizabeth Cady Stanton* (New York: Oxford University Press, 1984), 54. In light of Stanton's close association of democratic politics and religion, Pellauer labels her an "exponent of a 'civil religion'": "the American idea of individual rights [is] more sacred than any civil or ecclesiastical organizations" (17).

18. Wills, *Inventing America,* xiv.

19. Yellin, *Women and Sisters,* 42–43.

20. Ibid., 35, 39, emphasis in the original.

21. Angelina Grimké and Sarah Grimké, *The Public Years of Sarah and Angelina Grimké: Selected Writings, 1835–1839,* ed. Larry Ceplair (New York: Columbia University Press, 1989), 38, 54–55, emphasis in the original.

22. Bardes and Gossett, *Declarations of Independence,* 10–11.

23. Sarah Grimké, *Letters on the Equality of the Sexes and the Condition of Women, Addressed to Mary S. Parker* (1838, repr. Temucala, Calif.: Reprint Services, 1991), 45.

24. Lutz, *Created Equal,* 63–65.

25. Yellin, *Women and Sisters,* 45, 46, 48.

26. Ibid., 52.

27. Sue E. Houchins, "Introduction," in *Spiritual Narratives: Jarena Lee; Zilipha Elaw; Virginia Broughton; Sara Mix; Julia Foote; Maria Stewart; and Rebecca Stewart,* ed. Sue E. Houchins (New York: Oxford University Press, 1988), xxix. The volume includes Maria W. Stewart, *Productions of Mrs. Maria W. Stewart* (1835), and Jarena Lee, *Religious Experience and Journal of Mrs. Jarena Lee, Giving an Account of Her Call to Preach the Gospel* (1836 version). All references to these texts will be to this volume, and subsequent page references will appear in the text.

28. Peterson, *"Doers of the Word,"* 66.

29. Campbell, "Style and Content," 435, 444.

30. Some scholars working on Sojourner Truth have questioned the historicity of some of the most traditionally accepted "legendary" events of Truth's prominent public years, such as the rebuke of Frederick Douglass and the exact words of the "A'rn't I a Woman?" speech. See Carleton Mabee, *Sojourner Truth: Slave, Prophet, Legend* (New York: New York University Press, 1993) and Nell Irvin Painter, *Sojourner Truth: A Life, a Symbol* (New York: Norton, 1996). My analysis will treat these events as historic yet possibly "enlarged" over the years by well-meaning admirers—not an unusual phenomenon among American mythographers.

31. Sojourner Truth, *Narrative of Sojourner Truth; A Bondswoman of Olden Time, with a History of Her Labors and Correspondence Drawn from Her "Book of Life,"* ed. Jeffrey C. Stewart (New York: Oxford University Press [the Schomburgh Library edition], 1991), 168 (subsequent page references will appear in the text). Truth's "autobiography" presents certain textual difficulties, the chief of which may be the fact that she dictated her tale to Olive Gilbert, a white abolitionist whose asides remain a remarkable feature of the published volume. Yellin goes so far as to consider the *Narrative* as a "secondary source" (*Women and Sisters* 198n3). It was first published in 1850, but the assorted writings "by" and about Truth were assembled and published as her "Book of Life," together with the *Narrative,* in 1878.

32. Harriet Beecher Stowe, "Sojourner Truth: A Libyan Sibyl," *The Atlantic,* April 1863, reprinted in Truth, *"Book of Life,"* 150 (quotation), 73.

33. Esther Terry, "Sojourner Truth: The Person behind the Libyan Sibyl," *Massachusetts Review* 26 (Summer–Autumn 1985): 428.

34. Stowe, "Sojourner Truth," 150.

35. Yellin, *Women and Sisters,* 81–82.

36. For a summary of Stowe's theories and beliefs on the topic of race, see Thomas Gossett, Uncle Tom's Cabin *and American Culture* (Dallas: Southern Methodist University Press, 1985), 64–86, 299–303, 391–95.

37. Yellin, *Women and Sisters,* 81–82.

38. Campbell, "Style and Content," 444.

39. For information on this group, see William L. Stone, *Matthias and His Impostures* (New York: Harper and Brothers, 1835), and Paul E. Johnson and Sean Wilenz, *The Kingdom of Matthias* (New York: Oxford University Press, 1994).

40. See Bardes and Gossett, *Declarations of Independence,* 58–59.

41. Peterson, *"Doers of the Word,"* 22.

42. Yellin, *Women and Sisters,* 80; Campbell, "Style and Content," 435.

43. Much of the speech as delivered has been lost; what remains has been taken from the Schomburgh Library edition, xxxiii.

44. Kenneth Cmiel, *Democratic Eloquence: The Fight over Popular Speech in Nineteenth-Century America* (New York: William Morrow, 1990), passim.

45. Campbell, "Style and Content," 435.

46. Elizabeth Ammons, "Stowe's Dream of the Mother-Savior: Uncle Tom's Cabin and American Women Writers before the 1920s," in *New Essays on* Uncle Tom's Cabin, ed. Eric J. Sundquist (New York: Cambridge University Press, 1986).

47. James R. Andrews, *The Practice of Rhetorical Criticism,* 2d ed. (New York: Longman, 1990), 55.

48. Andrews, *Practice of Rhetorical Criticism,* 55.

Chapter 4: Closing the Sanctification Gap

1. Richard Yarborough, "Strategies of Black Characterization in *Uncle Tom's Cabin* and the Early Afro-American Novel," in *New Essays on* Uncle Tom's Cabin, ed. Eric J. Sundquist (New York: Cambridge University Press, 1986), 53.

2. Yarborough, "Strategies"; Jane Tompkins, *Sensational Designs: The Cultural Work of Fiction, 1790–1860* (New York: Oxford University Press, 1985); Ann Douglas, *The Feminization of American Culture* (New York: Knopf, 1977).

3. Tompkins, *Sensational Designs*, 139. Tompkins's focus on gender is hardly the exception to Stowe criticism. Yarborough, among others, agrees with such a reading: "Stowe's fiercest critique [in *Uncle Tom's Cabin*] was not directed at the patriarchal slave system at all, but rather at male domination in American society generally." "Strategies of Black Chracterization," 65.

4. Bardes and Gossett, *Declarations of Independence*, 58.

5. John L. Thomas, "Romantic Reform in America, 1815–1865," *American Quarterly* 17 (Winter 1965): 659.

6. Theodore R. Hovet, "Christian Revolution: Harriet Beecher Stowe's Response to Slavery and the Civil War," *New England Quarterly* 47 (1974): 538. Stowe's essay, "The Interior or Hidden Life," appeared in the *New York Evangelist* on April 17, 1845. Hovet has also discussed other influences on Stowe's conception of mystical religious experience, including Thomas Upham, Horace Bushnell, and James B. Walker. See Theodore R. Hovet, "Modernization and the American Fall into Slavery in *Uncle Tom's Cabin*," *New England Quarterly* 54 (Dec. 1981): 499–518.

7. Harriet Beecher Stowe, *The Key to* "Uncle Tom's Cabin" (Boston: Jewett, 1853), in Uncle Tom's Cabin: *A Norton Critical Edition*, ed. Elizabeth Ammons (New York: W. W. Norton, 1994), 421.

8. Stowe, *The Key to* "Uncle Tom's Cabin," 419.

9. See, for example, Charles H. Foster, *The Rungless Ladder: Harriet Beecher Stowe and New England Puritanism* (Durham: Duke University Press, 1954); Lawrence Buell, "Calvinism Romanticized: Harriet Beecher Stowe, Samuel Hopkins, and *The Minister's Wooing*," *ESQ: A Journal of the American Renaissance* 24, no. 3 (1978): 119–32; and Christopher Felker, *Reinventing Cotton Mather in the American Renaissance: Magnalia Christ, Americana in Hawthorne, Stowe, and Stoddard* (Boston: Northeastern University Press, 1993), 119–60.

10. Peterson, *"Doers of the Word,"* 3.

11. Eric Sundquist, "Slavery, Revolution, and the American Renaissance," in *The American Renaissance Reconsidered*, ed. Walter Benn Michaels and Donald Pease (Baltimore: Johns Hopkins University Press, 1985), 6.

12. McLoughlin, *Revivals*, 104.

13. Smith, "Righteousness and Hope," 44.

14. Harriet Beecher Stowe, Uncle Tom's Cabin: *A Norton Critical Edition*, ed. Elizabeth Ammons (New York: W. W. Norton, 1994), 13 (subsequent page references will appear in the text).

15. Douglass, *The Life and Writings*, 2:192. It is not clear who may have been influencing whom in this particular case. Douglass's 1852 speech came after Stowe wrote this scene, but he regularly used the second person mode before her book's publication as well. For more information about the strategies of antebellum

African American rhetoric with specific reference to the Declaration, see Condit and Lucaites, *Crafting Equality*. For an analysis of slave reaction to Fourth of July celebrations in Charleston, S.C., see Travers, *Celebrating the Fourth*, 145–54.

16. Welter, *The Mind of America*, 396. On Fourth of July celebrations and orations, see also Martin, *Parables of Possibility*, particularly 35–43; and Travers, *Celebrating the Fourth*.

17. Douglass, *Narrative*, 6.

18. Stowe, *Uncle Tom's Cabin*, 97 (subsequent page references will appear in the text).

19. Sundquist, *To Wake the Nations*, 36.

20. For a detailed analysis of the depiction of "Mother-Savior," see Ammons, "Stowe's Dream of the Mother-Savior."

21. Jane Tompkins, "Sentimental Power: *Uncle Tom's Cabin* and the Politics of Literary History," in Uncle Tom's Cabin: *A Norton Critical Edition*, ed. Elizabeth Ammons (New York: W. W. Norton, 1994), 519.

22. Stowe, *Uncle Tom's Cabin*, 122 (subsequent page references will appear in the text).

23. For historical background on Kinmont and on romantic racialism, see George M. Frederickson, "Uncle Tom and the Anglo-Saxons: Romantic Racialism in the North," in Uncle Tom's Cabin: *A Norton Critical Edition*, ed. Elizabeth Ammons (New York: W. W. Norton, 1994), 429–38.

24. According to personal correspondence with Joan Hedrick, Stowe "was familiar with Kinmont," who lectured while she lived in Cincinnati; Stowe "remarks on his death" in a letter she wrote in December 1838. See also Joan Hedrick, *Harriet Beecher Stowe: A Life* (New York: Oxford University Press, 1994), 437n31.

25. Stowe, *The Key to* "Uncle Tom's Cabin," 420–21; for analysis of Stowe's general views on race, see Gossett, Uncle Tom's Cabin *and American Culture*, 64–86, 299–303, 391–95.

26. See, for example, James Baldwin's classic "Everybody's Protest Novel," in Uncle Tom's Cabin: *The Norton Critical Edition*, ed. Elizabeth Ammons (New York: W. W. Norton, 1994), 495–500; see also Yarborough, "Strategies of Black Characterization."

27. Catharine E. O'Connell, "'The Magic of the Real Presence of Distress': Sentimentality and Competing Rhetorics of Authority," in *The Stowe Debate: Rhetorical Strategies in* Uncle Tom's Cabin, ed. Mason I. Lowance et al. (Amherst: University of Massachusetts Press, 1994), 26.

28. Tompkins, "Sentimental Power," 517.

29. Quoted in Hovet, "Christian Revolution," 536, 543.

30. Gerd Hurm, "'A Noisy Carnival': Parodies and Burlesques of Fourth of July Rhetoric," in *The Fourth of July: Political Oratory and Literary Reactions, 1777–1876*, ed. Paul Goetsch and Gerd Hurm (Tubingen: Gunter Narr Verlag, 1992), 244. Additional coverage of these phenomena is found in Walter Blair, "Burlesques of Nineteenth-Century American Humor," *American Literature* 2 (1930–31): 236–47; Barnet Baskerville, "Nineteenth-Century Burlesque of Oratory," *American Quarterly* 20 (1968): 726–43; and Michael Kammen, *A Season of Youth: The American Revolution and the Historical Imagination* (New York: Oxford University Press, 1978), 260–69.

31. Hurm, "'A Noisy Carnival,'" 244.

32. Stowe, *Uncle Tom's Cabin*, 64 (subsequent page references will appear in the text).

33. Baldwin, "Everybody's Protest Novel," 578–85.

34. John H. Wigger, "Taking Heaven by Storm: Enthusiasm and Early American Methodism, 1770–1820," *Journal of the Early Republic* 14 (Summer 1994): 167–68, 170, 172–73.

35. Ann Douglas, "Introduction: The Art of Controversy," in Harriet Beecher Stowe, *Uncle Tom's Cabin* (1852, repr. New York: Penguin, 1981), 23, 27.

36. Stowe, *Uncle Tom's Cabin*, 357 (subsequent page references will appear in the text); see also Luke 23:46.

37. See, for example, Christina Zwarg, "Fathering and Blackface in *Uncle Tom's Cabin*," in Uncle Tom's Cabin: *The Norton Critical Edition*, ed. Elizabeth Ammons (New York: W. W. Norton, 1994), 568–84; the discussion of the portrait of Washington is concentrated on 572–74.

Chapter 5: Abraham Lincoln as America's Revivalist

1. Mississippi seceded on January 9, Florida on January 10, Alabama on January 11, Georgia on January 19, Louisiana on January 26, and, finally, Texas on February 1. See James McPherson, *Battle Cry of Freedom: The Civil War Era* (New York: Oxford University Press, 1988), 235, 262.

2. The major sites, including Indianapolis, Cincinnati, Columbus, Cleveland, Syracuse, Trenton, New York City, and Philadelphia, represented the most important industrial and political centers of the North. The inclusion of small towns, such as Lafayette and Lawrenceburg in Indiana, Milford and Xenia in Ohio, and Little Falls, New York, demonstrated Lincoln's ties with grass-roots rural voters.

3. McPherson, *Battle Cry of Freedom*, 261; Stephen Oates, *With Malice Toward None: The Life of Abraham Lincoln* (New York: New American Library, 1977), 223, 225.

4. The key exception is the speech delivered at Indianapolis to Gov. Oliver P. Morton and a rousing crowd of nearly five thousand Hoosiers. That address was characterized by blatant humor directed toward the enemy as well as Lincoln's boldest insinuations of the trip concerning a strong governmental response to any outlawry committed by the South. It seems likely that he was afterward advised by confidantes to tone down such rhetoric for the remainder of the trip, and no further such episodes ensued until the Inauguration.

5. Wills, *Inventing America*, xiv. Wills reaffirms and develops this point in *Lincoln at Gettysburg*, which focuses primarily on the importance and cultural context of the Gettysburg Address. These constitute somewhat reductionist claims, for which Pauline Maier has taken Wills to task; see Maier, *American Scripture*, xix–xx. Although fully aware of the myriad contributors to the building of an American mythos, I am in accord with Wills's focus on the centrality of Lincoln's key speeches. That focus will be expanded to include a discussion of these train-journey speeches as antecedents of Lincoln's rhetorical masterpieces: his two inaugural addresses (1861, 1865) and the Gettysburg Address (1863). As Maier correctly argues, however, the antebellum culture constituted a pervasive form of antecedent as well.

6. Waldo Braden, *Abraham Lincoln: Public Speaker* (Baton Rouge: Louisiana State University Press, 1988), 44.

7. Bercovitch, "The Problem of Ideology," 635.

8. Abraham Lincoln, *Speeches and Writings, 1859–1865*, ed. Don E. Fehrenbacher (New York: Library of America, 1988), 206. The definitive edition of Lincoln's work remains Roy P. Basler, ed., *The Collected Works of Abraham Lincoln*, Marion Deloris Pratt and Lloyd A. Dunlap, asst. eds., 9 vols. (New Brunswick: Rutgers University Press, 1953–55).

9. Burke, *A Grammar of Motives*, 567.

10. Lincoln, *Speeches and Writings*, 200, 203, 205.

11. Wills, *Inventing America*, xix.

12. Travers, *Celebrating the Fourth*, 6.

13. McPherson, *Abraham Lincoln and the Second American Revolution*, 113–14.

14. Lincoln, *Speeches and Writings*, 213, emphasis added (subsequent page references will appear in the text).

15. Wills, *Inventing America*, xxi.

16. Foner, ed., *We the Other People*.

17. Robert Bellah, "Civil Religion in America," *Daedalus* 96 (1967): 1–21.

18. Bellah, "Civil Religion," 13.

19. Lincoln, *Speeches and Writings*, 199–200 (subsequent page references will appear in the text).

20. Robert G. Gunderson, "Lincoln and the Policy of Eloquent Silence: November, 1860, to March, 1861," *Quarterly Journal of Speech* 47 (Feb. 1961): 4.

21. Braden, *Abraham Lincoln*, 75.

22. Lincoln, *Speeches and Writings*, 224.

23. Braden, *Abraham Lincoln*, 44.

24. Kammen, *Mystic Chords of Memory*, 59.

25. Sarah Josepha Hale, from *Women's Record* (1855), quoted in Douglas, *The Feminization of American Culture*, 108.

26. Douglas, *The Feminization of American Culture*, 108, 103, 102.

27. McLoughlin, *Revivals*, 103.

28. Harold Holzer, Gabor S. Boritt, and Mark E. Neely, Jr., *The Lincoln Image: Abraham Lincoln and the Popular Print* (New York: Scribner's, 1984), 149.

29. See David T. Valentine, ed., *Obsequies of Abraham Lincoln in the City of New York. . . .* (New York: Edmund Jones, 1866).

30. Waldo Braden, ed., *Building the Myth: Selected Speeches Memorializing Abraham Lincoln* (Urbana: University of Illinois Press, 1990), 25–26.

31. Charles J. Stewart, "The Pulpit and the Assassination of Lincoln," *Quarterly Journal of Speech* 50 (Oct. 1964): 299–300.

32. Stewart, "The Pulpit," 302.

33. Ibid.

34. The speeches by Emerson, Beecher, and Brooks are reprinted in *Building the Myth*, ed. Braden, quotations on 34, 37–38, 49, 52, and 60.

35. Roy P. Basler, *The Lincoln Legend: A Study in Changing Conceptions* (Boston: Houghton Mifflin, 1935), 164.

36. Harold Holzer, "Columbia's Noblest Sons: Washington and Lincoln in Popular Prints," *Journal of the Abraham Lincoln Association* 15 (Winter 1994): 24–69.

37. Holzer, Boritt, and Neely, *The Lincoln Image*, 164.

Part 2: Introduction

1. For a reading of Emerson as heroic leader of a revolutionary war against patriarchy and champion of antinomianism, see Joel Porte, *Representative Man: Ralph Waldo Emerson in His Time* (New York: Oxford University Press, 1979). In *Emerson's Fall: A New Interpretation of the Major Essays* (New York: Continuum, 1982), Barbara Packer emphasizes his essays as contending with the stultifying fears and intellectual tyrannies that plagued antebellum American culture, especially in light of such idealistic statements as the Declaration and the Bill of Rights. General information about this critical period of Emerson's life is found in Ralph L. Rusk, *The Life of Ralph Waldo Emerson* (New York: Columbia University Press, 1949), 249–74; Gay Wilson Allen, *Waldo Emerson: A Biography* (New York: Viking, 1981), 268–318; John McAleer, *Ralph Waldo Emerson: Days of Encounter* (Boston: Little, Brown, 1984), 234–70; and Maurice Gonnaud, *An Uneasy Solitude: Individual and Society in the Works of Ralph Waldo Emerson* (Princeton: Princeton University Press, 1987), 236–47.

2. Porte, *Representative Man*, 91.

3. Oliver Wendell Holmes, *Ralph Waldo Emerson* (Boston: Houghton, 1885), 115.

4. Ernest Erwin Leisy, *American Literature: An Interpretive Survey* (New York: Crowell, 1929), 82.

5. Ludwig Lewisohn, *Expression in America* (New York: Harper and Brothers, 1932), 122.

6. James D. Hart, *The Oxford Companion to American Literature* (New York: Oxford University Press, 1948), 27.

7. Arthur Hobson Quinn, ed., *The Literature of the American People* (New York: Appleton-Century-Crofts, 1951), 284.

8. Theodore L. Gross, *The Heroic Ideal in American Literature* (New York: Free Press, 1971), 13.

9. Larzer Ziff, *Literary Democracy: The Declaration of Cultural Independence in America* (New York: Penguin, 1981), 18.

10. William Peterfield Trent et al., eds., *The Cambridge History of American Literature* (New York: Macmillan, 1943), 1:328, 262.

11. Vernon L. Parrington, *The Romantic Revolution in America, 1800–1860* (New York: Harcourt Brace, 1927), 390.

12. Fred Lewis Pattee, *The First Century of American Literature, 1770–1870* (New York: D. Appleton-Century, 1935), 457–58. Pattee seemed aware of the mythologized nature of his account. He mentions prominently his view that Emerson's speech contained "nothing new" (457).

13. Frederic I. Carpenter, *American Literature and the Dream* (New York: Philosophical Library, 1955), 5.

14. See Edward W. Said, *Beginnings: Intention and Method* (New York: Basic, 1975), 49. See also Mircea Eliade, *The Myth of the Eternal Return; or, Cosmos and History*, trans. Willard R. Trask (1954, repr. Princeton: Princeton University Press, 1971), esp. 51–62, for a discussion of secular society's need to reenact important and often sacred past events.

15. A good selection of material related to the cultural conflict surrounding not just Emerson's speeches but also the lengthy feud between Norton and Brown-

son, Ripley, and the others, along with brief but helpful explanatory headnotes, is found in Perry Miller, *The Transcendentalists: An Anthology* (Cambridge: Harvard University Press, 1967), 157–246; the quotation from Norton is on 210. See also McAleer, *Ralph Waldo Emerson:* "To do Norton justice, he was speaking from provocation and his remarks were not addressed to Emerson alone" (263).

16. In foregrounding literary or cultural history over religious history, even "The American Scholar" becomes more the end of a long process rather than a beginning. William Ellery Channing's "On National Literature" (1830), for example, could just as easily be considered such a starting point, as could similar written works by James Kirke Paulding or speeches by Edward Everett. Gulian Verplanck's "American Scholar" (similar in spirit and identical in title) was published a full year earlier in 1836. For a full development of this idea, see Robert Spiller, *The American Literary Revolution: 1783–1837* (Garden City: Anchor, 1967), which brings together a wealth of documents supporting such a view. Spiller also argues that Emerson's pronouncements should be regarded as the end rather than the beginning of a lengthy historical revolution. Manfred Putz expands Spiller's arguments in "Dissenting Voices of Consent: Margaret Fuller and Ralph Waldo Emerson on the Fourth of July," in *The Fourth of July: Political Oratory and Literary Reactions, 1776–1876*, ed. Paul Goetsch and Gerd Hurm (Tubingen: Gunter Narr Verlag, 1992), 167–84.

17. David Simpson, ed., *German Aesthetic and Literary Criticism: Kant, Fichte, Schelling, Schopenhauer, Hegel* (New York: Cambridge University Press, 1984), 161; see also 80: "The general tendency observable in the history of philosophy between Kant and Hegel or Schopenhauer [is] roughly speaking a movement from an emphasis on knowledge to an emphasis on will."

18. Emerson mentions Finney's preaching abilities in a brief journal entry of January 30, 1832, only months after the sermon: William H. Gilman and Alfred R. Ferguson, ed., *The Journals and Miscellaneous Notebooks of Ralph Waldo Emerson*, vol. 3: *1826–1832* (Cambridge: Harvard University Press, 1963), 324. The entry suggests that Emerson may have on some occasion heard Finney preach.

19. See Iain H. Murray, *Revival and Revivalism: The Making and Marring of American Evangelicalism, 1750–1858* (Carlisle, Pa.: Banner of Truth, 1994), esp. 161–298; and Sidney Earl Mead, *Nathaniel William Taylor, 1786–1858: A Connecticut Liberal* (Chicago: Archon, 1967).

20. Nathan O. Hatch, *The Democratization of American Christianity* (New Haven: Yale University Press, 1989), 22.

21. Cmiel, *Democratic Eloquence.*

22. Hatch, *The Democratization of American Christianity*, 36, 69–70, 71.

23. Martin, *Parables of Possibility*, esp. 3–80.

24. Robert Spiller, "The American Literary Declaration of Independence," in *Literatur und Sprache der Vereinigten Staaten*, ed. Hans Helmcke et al. (Heidelberg: Carl Winter, 1969), 62–73.

25. See Harold K. Bush, Jr., "Emerson, John Brown, and 'Doing the Word': The Enactment of Political Religion at Harpers Ferry, 1859," in *The Emerson Dilemma: Ralph Waldo Emerson and Social Activism*, ed. T. Gregory Garvey (in press).

26. On this mistake, in part based on Brown's studied art of deception, see Gilbert Ostrander, "Emerson, Thoreau, and John Brown," *Mississippi Valley Historical Review* 39 (1953): 722, and Oswald Garrison Villard, *John Brown, 1800–1859: A Biography Fifty Years Later* (Boston: Houghton Mifflin, 1910), 10.

27. John J. McDonald, "Emerson and John Brown," *New England Quarterly* 44 (1971): 382.

28. Ralph Waldo Emerson, "Speech at a Meeting to Aid John Brown's Family," in *Emerson's Antislavery Writings*, ed. Len Gougeon and Joel Myerson (New Haven: Yale University Press, 1995), 118, 117.

29. On Emerson's use of the jeremiadic mode in the sermons, see Wesley T. Mott, *"The Strains of Eloquence": Emerson and His Sermons* (University Park: Pennsylvania State University Press, 1989), esp. 127–29 and 151–55.

30. Emerson, "Address to the Citizens of Concord," in *Emerson's Antislavery Writings*, ed. Len Gougeon and Joel Myerson (New Haven: Yale University Press, 1995), 56 (subsequent page references will appear in the text).

31. Mott, *"The Strains of Eloquence,"* 155.

32. Emerson, "Speech at a Meeting to Aid John Brown's Family," 118, 119; Bertram Wyatt-Brown, "'A Volcano beneath a Mountain of Snow': John Brown and the Problem of Interpretation," in *His Soul Goes Marching On: Responses to John Brown and the Harpers Ferry Raid*, ed. Paul Finkelman (Charlottesville: University of Virginia Press, 1995), 22.

33. Emerson, "Speech at a Meeting to Aid John Brown's Family," 120.

34. Ralph Waldo Emerson, *The Complete Sermons of Ralph Waldo Emerson*, ed. Albert J. von Frank (Columbia: University of Missouri Press, 1989), 1:312.

35. Ralph Waldo Emerson, "The Fugitive Slave Law," in *Emerson's Antislavery Writings*, ed. Len Gougeon and Joel Myerson (New Haven: Yale University Press, 1995), 83.

36. Frederick Douglass, *Frederick Douglass' Paper*, Sept. 29, 1854.

37. Bertram Wyatt-Brown, *Yankee Saints and Southern Sinners* (Baton Rouge: Lousiana State University Press, 1985), 125.

38. Robert E. McGlone, "Forgotten Surrender: John Brown's Raid and the Cult of Martial Virtues," *Civil War History* 60, no. 3 (1994): 189, 192.

39. McGlone, "Forgotten Surrender," 187.

40. Paul Finkelman, "Manufacturing Martyrdom: The Antislavery Response to John Brown's Raid," in *His Soul Goes Marching On: Responses to John Brown and the Harpers Ferry Raid*, ed. Paul Finkelman (Charlottesville: University of Virginia Press, 1995), 61, 60.

41. Mott, *"The Strains of Eloquence,"* 32.

42. A brief recapitulation of this controversy is provided in McDonald, "Emerson and John Brown," 386–87, esp. notes 27–29. Len Gougeon also remarks on this controversy in "Historical Background," in *Emerson's Antislavery Writings*, xlvii.

43. McDonald, "Emerson and John Brown," 387.

44. Gougeon, "Historical Background," xlvii. See also David Mead, *Yankee Eloquence in the Middle West: The Ohio Lyceum, 1850–1870* (East Lansing: Michigan State University Press, 1951), 48–49.

45. Mead, *Yankee Eloquence*, 49.

46. *Lafayette Daily Journal*, Feb. 4, 1860.

47. Emerson, "Speech at a Meeting to Aid John Brown's Family," 119, and Emerson, "John Brown," in *Emerson's Antislavery Writings*, ed. Len Gougeon and Joel Myerson (New Haven: Yale University Press, 1995), 123.

48. Emerson, "Speech at a Meeting to Aid John Brown's Family," 118.

49. Wyatt-Brown, "Volcano," 23.

50. Emerson, "Speech at a Meeting to Aid John Brown's Family" and "John Brown," 118, 117, 121, 122.

51. Bellah et al., *Habits of the Heart*, 150–51.

52. A summary and analysis of attempts to "de-transcendentalize" Emerson is in Michael Lopez, "De-Transcendentalizing Emerson," *ESQ: A Journal of the American Renaissance* 34, nos. 1–2 (1988): 77–139. A much briefer discussion of the trend is in Lawrence Buell, "The Emerson Industry in the 1980's: A Survey of Trends and Achievements," *ESQ: A Journal of the American Renaissance* 30, no. 2 (1984): 123–29.

53. John Carlos Rowe, *At Emerson's Tomb: The Politics of Classic American Literature* (New York: Columbia University Press, 1997), 21, 24, 22.

54. Edmund S. Morgan, *The Puritan Dilemma: The Story of John Winthrop* (Boston: Little, Brown, 1958). Mott refers to Morgan's version of Winthrop in *"The Strains of Eloquence,"* 114.

55. Mott, *"The Strains of Eloquence,"* 143.

56. Leo Marx, "Pastoralism in America," in *Ideology and Classic American Literature*, ed. Sacvan Bercovitch and Myra Jehlen (New York: Cambridge University Press, 1986), 36–69, quotation on 43–44.

57. Marx, "Pastoralism in America," 43–44. Other authors (and their public actions) also provide sites for the types of cultural excavations I am undertaking, for example, Walt Whitman, Ernest Hemingway, Gertrude Stein, William Faulkner, Ralph Ellison, Toni Morrison, James Baldwin, and Norman Mailer.

58. Twain's speech at the Whittier dinner has been described as both the "locus classicus" and the "primal scene" of Twain studies in Richard S. Lowry, *"Littery Man": Mark Twain and Modern Authorship* (New York: Oxford University Press, 1996), 14, 24.

Chapter 6: The Myth of the Oppositional West

1. Philip Fisher, "Introduction," in *The New American Studies: Essays from Representations*, ed. Philip Fisher (Berkeley: University of California Press, 1991), xiii.

2. Richard Brodhead, "Literature and Culture," in *The Columbia Literary History of the United States*, ed. Emory Elliott (New York: Columbia University Press, 1988), 472–73. The quotation from Whitman is from "Specimen Days," in *The Portable Walt Whitman*, ed. Mark Van Doren (New York: Viking Penguin, 1977), 423.

3. John Greenleaf Whittier, "Snow-Bound," in *The Norton Anthology of American Literature*, 2d ed., ed. Nina Baym et al. (New York: W. W. Norton, 1985), 1343–44.

4. See William Dean Howells, "My First Visit to New England" (1894), first collected in *Literary Friends and Acquaintances* (New York: Harper, 1900). The definitive edition of Howells's work is *A Selected Edition of William Dean Howells*, vol. 32, ed. David F. Hiatt and Edwin H. Cady (Bloomington: Indiana University Press, 1968); the quotations come from 26, 14, 16, 38, and 39.

5. Rebecca Harding Davis, *Bits of Gossip* (Boston: Houghton Mifflin, 1904), 42–43.

6. For accounts of the event, see Henry Nash Smith, "That Hideous Mistake of Poor Clemens," *Harvard Library Bulletin* 9 (1955): 145–80; Ellen Ballou, *The Building of the House: Houghton Mifflin's Formative Years* (Boston: Houghton Mifflin, 1970), 217–23; and Arthur Gilman, "Atlantic Dinners and Diners," *Atlantic Monthly* 100, no. 5 (1907): 646–57.

7. Quoted in "Honor to a Poet," *New York Herald*, Dec. 18, 1877, 17.

8. Published in the *Boston Evening Transcript*, Dec. 18 , 1877, 3, quoted in Smith, "That Hideous Mistake of Poor Clemens," 170.

9. Samuel Clemens will be referred to throughout this volume by his chosen pseudonym. In light of the event's purpose, it may seem strange that a renowned jokester such as Twain was even asked to speak. It was common in such instances, however, to invite at least one speaker who could add humor to the gathering. As Henry Nash Smith put it, "When he was invited to speak . . . he was expected to provide comic relief in a program that was certain to be long and laden with sentiment" ("That Hideous Mistake of Poor Clemens," 149). Furthermore, Twain, a regularly featured contributor to *The Atlantic*, also represented one more star in that periodical's impressive firmament of leading American authors.

10. Lowry, *"Littery Man,"* 14, 24.

11. There is irony in the fact that by the time of this event in 1877, Emerson, the mythic embodiment of radical independence, could be lumped together with the other poets as representatives of a conservative cultural hegemony centered in Boston.

12. Although he was forty-two at the time, a mythologized although mistaken tradition consistently depicts Twain as a young man when he spoke before the elder statesmen of Boston letters.

13. Grant C. Knight, *American Literature and Culture* (New York: Long and Smith, 1932), 269.

14. Alexander Cowie, *The Rise of the American Novel* (New York: American Book, 1948), 643.

15. Smith provides additional evidence supporting a view that the speech was a great success. See "That Hideous Mistake of Poor Clemens," 146–49, quotations on 147. See also Henry Nash Smith, *Mark Twain: The Development of a Writer* (Cambridge: Harvard University Press, 1962), 92–112.

16. "Honor to a Poet," *New York Herald*, Dec. 18, 1877, 17.

17. Kenneth E. Eble, *Old Clemens and W.D.H.: The Story of a Remarkable Friendship* (Baton Rouge: Louisiana State University Press, 1985), 95.

18. "The Pow-wow against Mark Twain's Dinner Speech: The General Conclusion," *Chicago Tribune*, Dec. 30, 1877, 1.

19. Smith, "That Hideous Mistake of Poor Clemens," 159–60.

20. Edwards Roberts, "Literary Boston," *San Francisco Chronicle*, June 14, 1885, 5–6.

21. John Lauber, *The Inventions of Mark Twain* (New York: Hill and Wang, 1990), 44; Louis J. Budd, "A 'Talent for Posturing': The Achievement of Mark Twain's Public Personality," in *The Mythologizing of Mark Twain*, ed. Sara de-Saussure Davis and Phillip D. Beidler (University: University of Alabama Press, 1984), 84.

22. Frederick Anderson et al., eds., *Selected Mark Twain–Howells Letters, 1872–1910* (Cambridge: Harvard University Press, 1967), 102–3.

23. Anderson et al., eds., *Selected Mark Twain–Howells Letters,* 103.

24. William Dean Howells, *Selected Letters 1873–1881,* ed. George Arms and Christoph K. Lohmann (Boston: Twayne, 1979), 182. John Seelye has argued that Howells's widely read novel of 1885, *The Rise of Silas Lapham,* was a direct response to the indecorous speech by Twain in 1877 at the Whittier dinner. Seelye suggests direct links between the paint entrepreneur Lapham and Twain. Both the fictional character and the author embarrassed themselves at stylish Boston social events and after doing so suffered powerful self-abasement. See Seelye, "The Hole in Howells: The Lapse in *Silas Lapham,*" in *New Essays on* The Rise of Silas Lapham, ed. Donald E. Pease (New York: Cambridge University Press, 1991), 47–66.

25. Howells, *Selected Mark Twain–Howells Letters,* 104.

26. Ibid., 105.

27. Those accounts were Twain's rendition published first in the *North American Review* in December 1907 and then collected as part of *Mark Twain's Autobiography* (New York: Harper, 1924), Albert Paine's massive *Mark Twain: A Biography* (New York: Harper, 1912), and Howells's memoir, *My Mark Twain* (New York: Harper, 1910).

28. Susan Gillman, *Dark Twins: Imposture and Identity in Mark Twain's America* (Chicago: University of Chicago Press, 1989), 21.

29. Susan K. Harris, *The Courtship of Olivia Langdon and Mark Twain* (New York: Cambridge University Press, 1996), esp. 70–105.

30. The interview with Shaw appeared in *Harper's Weekly,* July 20, 1907. The remarks are quoted in Justin Kaplan, *Mr. Clemens and Mark Twain: A Biography* (New York: Touchstone, 1966), 382.

31. Howells, *Literary Friends and Acquaintances,* 264.

32. Lauber, *The Inventions of Mark Twain,* 44.

33. Alice Cary, *Clovernook; or, Recollections of Our Neighborhood in the West,* in *Clovernook Sketches and Other Stories,* ed. Judith Fetterley (1852, repr. New Brunswick: Rutgers University Press, 1987), 7.

34. Edward Eggleston, *The Hoosier School-Master* (1871, repr. Bloomington: Indiana University Press, 1984), 5.

35. Robert E. Spiller, *The Cycle of American Literature* (New York: Macmillan, 1955), 111–12.

36. For background information on the cultures of performance associated with the West, see Randall Knoper, *Acting Naturally: Mark Twain in the Culture of Performance* (Berkeley: University of California Press, 1995); and Eric Lott, *Love and Theft: Blackface Minstrelsy and the American Working Class* (New York: Oxford University Press, 1993).

37. See Lowry, *"Littery Man,"* 35: "But to figure Twain solely as a crasher at the gates of Culture . . . both obscures the shape of Twain's authorial career and overly simplifies the complex and changing world he had entered as an author."

38. For a discussion of the divisions within Howells's literary sensibility, see Edwin Cady, *The Road to Realism: The Early Years, 1883–1885, of William Dean Howells* (Syracuse: Syracuse University Press, 1956).

39. Kenneth S. Lynn, *William Dean Howells: An American Life* (New York: Harcourt Brace Jovanovich, 1971), 217.

40. See the discussion of this controversy in Jonathan Thomas and David J. Nordloh, "Introduction," in William Dean Howells, *A Chance Acquaintance*

(1873, repr. Bloomington: Indiana University Press, 1971), xxv–xxvii (subsequent page references will appear in the text). Most controversial was Howells's flaccid and drearily lifeless representative of the effete East, Miles Arbuton.

41. Mark Twain, *The Innocents Abroad* (1869, repr. New York: New American Library, 1966), 136. Another irony of Twain's staunch iconoclasm is that he is surely the nation's most certifiably iconic literary star; see, for example, Budd, "A 'Talent for Posturing,'" as well as Louis J. Budd, *Our Mark Twain: The Making of His Public Personality* (Philadelphia: University of Pennsylvania Press, 1983); and Louis J. Budd, "Mark Twain as an American Icon," in *The Cambridge Companion to Mark Twain,* ed. Forrest G. Robinson (New York: Cambridge University Press, 1995), 1–26. See also Shelley Fisher Fishkin, *Lighting Out for the Territory: Reflections on Mark Twain and American Culture* (New York: Oxford University Press, 1996), esp. 127–81.

42. The text of the speech is available in several sources. All references to the speech in this chapter are from Mark Twain, *Mark Twain's Own Autobiography,* ed. Michael Kiskis (Madison: University of Wisconsin Press, 1990), 230–33 (subsequent page references will appear in the text). On the tall tale as an oppositional form, see Henry Wonham, *Mark Twain and the Art of the Tall Tale* (New York: Oxford University Press, 1993).

43. Knoper, *Acting Naturally,* 25.

44. Twain, *Mark Twain's Own Autobiography,* 231.

45. The quotation is an excerpt from Emerson's "Mithridates."

46. Twain, *Mark Twain's Own Autobiography,* 231 (subsequent page references will appear in the text).

47. The quotation is an excerpt from Holmes's "Mare Rubrum 1858."

48. The quotation is an excerpt from Emerson's "Monadnoc."

49. The quotation is an excerpt from Longfellow, "A Psalm of Life."

50. On a "literary system of distinction" see Lowry, *"Littery Man,"* 28–33; in employing this concept, Lowry draws upon Pierre Bourdieu, *Distinction: A Social Critique of the Judgement of Taste,* trans. Richard Nice (Cambridge: Harvard University Press, 1984).

51. Twain, *Mark Twain's Own Autobiography,* 233.

52. Lowry, *"Littery Man,"* 29.

53. Evidence from newspaper sources indicates that some readers of the speech were horrified with offense.

54. Forrest G. Robinson, *In Bad Faith: The Dynamics of Deception in Mark Twain's America* (Cambridge: Harvard University Press, 1986).

55. Smith, "That Hideous Mistake of Poor Clemens," 167. Longfellow claimed that nobody was "much hurt." Perhaps more striking is that Longfellow, writing some three weeks after the dinner, indicates that there had been some sort of disreputable "report . . . in the morning papers" that had apparently gained some credibility and had begun to engender scandalous gossip. The source to which Longfellow alludes remains uncertain.

56. Burke, *A Grammar of Motives,* 59.

57. Howells, *Literary Friends and Acquaintances,* 170.

58. William Simonds, *A Student's History of American Literature* (Boston: Houghton Mifflin, 1909), 307.

59. John Nichol, *American Literature: An Historical Sketch, 1620–1880* (Edinburgh: Adam and Charles Black, 1882), 426.

60. Barrett Wendell, *A Literary History of America* (New York: Scribner's, 1900), 513.

61. See Guy Cardwell, "Mark Twain: The Metaphoric Hero as Battleground," *ESQ: A Journal of the American Renaissance* 23, no. 1 (1977): 52–66, for a summary of the Brooks–DeVoto debate regarding Mark Twain.

62. Vernon Louis Parrington, *The Beginnings of Critical Realism in America, 1860–1920* (New York: Harcourt Brace, 1930), 86–87.

63. Fishkin, *Lighting Out for the Territory*, 7 (subsequent page references will appear in the text).

64. This concept is derived from Harold Bloom, *The Anxiety of Influence: A Theory of Poetry* (New York: Oxford University Press, 1973).

65. Hunter, *Culture Wars*, 51.

66. Kaplan, *Mr. Clemens and Mark Twain*, 322. The quotation about Nook Farm is on 140–41, the amount of $250,000 is given on 317, and the quotation about Rogers is on 321.

67. Ibid., 93; see also Harris, *Courtship*, 102.

68. Harris, *Courtship*, esp. 93–105, quotations on 95, 100, and 101.

69. Kaplan, *Mr. Clemens and Mark Twain*, 225–26.

70. Mark Twain, *Collected Tales, Sketches, Speeches, and Essays: 1852–1890*, ed. Louis J. Budd (New York: Library of America, 1992), 728–29.

71. Twain, *Collected Tales, Sketches, Speeches, and Essays*, 940. The letter appeared originally in *Camden's Compliment to Walt Whitman*, ed. Horace Traubel (Philadelphia: David McKay, 1889), 64–65.

72. Kaplan, *Mr. Clemens and Mark Twain*, 96.

73. Twain, *Collected Tales, Sketches, Speeches, and Essays*, 782.

74. Examples of this trend are Knoper, *Acting Naturally*; Wonham, *Mark Twain and the Art of the Tall Tale*; Lowry, *"Littery Man"*; Gillman, *Dark Twins*; and Shelley Fisher Fishkin, *Was Huck Black? Mark Twain and African American Voices* (New York: Oxford University Press, 1993). Further discussion can be found in Harold K. Bush, Jr., "Acting Like Mark Twain: Performance in Nineteenth-Century American Culture," *American Quarterly* 49 (June 1997): 429–37.

Chapter 7: Cultural Conflict Makes the Man

1. John Tipple, ed., *Crisis of the American Dream: A History of American Social Thought, 1920–1940* (New York: Pegasus, 1968), 35–36.

2. George M. Marsden, *Fundamentalism and American Culture: The Shaping of Twentieth-Century Evangelicalism, 1870–1925* (New York: Oxford University Press, 1980), 153.

3. Garry Wills, *Under God: Religion and American Politics* (New York: Simon and Schuster, 1990), 68.

4. Tipple, ed., *Crisis of the American Dream*, 41, 39. An account of the Red Scare can be found in Robert K. Murray, *Red Scare: A Study of National Hysteria, 1919–1920* (Minneapolis: University of Minnesota Press, 1955).

5. George E. Mowry, ed., *The Twenties: Fords, Flappers, and Fanatics* (Englewood Cliffs: Prentice-Hall, 1963), 147, 146–47.

6. Tipple, *Crisis of the American Dream*, 49.

7. Warren Harding, "Inaugural Address" (1921), reprinted in *Crisis of the American Dream: A History of American Social Thought, 1920–1940*, ed. John Tipple (New York: Pegasus, 1968), 97–98.

8. Walter Lippmann, *Men of Destiny* (New York: Macmillan, 1927), 28.

9. See Frederick J. Hoffman, *The Twenties: American Writing in the Postwar Decade* (New York: Viking, 1955); and Lewis Atherton, *Main Street on the Middle Border* (Chicago: University of Chicago Press, 1966). Atherton develops his thesis with an abundance of evidence from the McGuffey readers; see *Main Street on the Middle Border*, 65ff (quotation on 65).

10. Charles Fenton, "The American Academy of Arts and Letters vs. All Comers: Literary Rags and Riches in the 1920's," *South Atlantic Quarterly* 58 (1959): 572–73, 575, 574.

11. See Hoffman, *The Twenties*, esp. 344–408.

12. Carl Van Doren, "Contemporary American Novelists: The Revolt from the Village, 1920," *The Nation*, Oct. 12, 1920, 407. Later critics, and common-sense understanding of American literary history, locate the beginnings of such a "revolt" well before Van Doren's emphasis on Masters, something Van Doren suggests by invoking several earlier writers. For example, William Dean Howells and Mark Twain critiqued small towns in a variety of books during the 1870s and 1880s, and Harold Frederic's *The Damnation of Theron Ware* (1894) constitutes a searing indictment of small town conformity and rotten-to-the-core Christianity. E. W. Howe, Mary Wilkins Freeman, Hamlin Garland, and Sarah Orne Jewett also made notable contributions to the turning away from the village myth. See Anthony Channell Hilfer, *The Revolt from the Village, 1915–1930* (Chapel Hill: University of North Carolina Press, 1969). Lewis read and liked, for instance, both Frederic, whose novel Carol Kennicott reads in *Main Street* (New York: Signet, 1980), 68–69, and Garland. See Harry E. Maule and Melville H. Cane, eds., *The Man from Main Street: Selected Essays and Other Writing, 1904–1950* (New York: Random House, 1963), 15–16.

13. Hilfer, *The Revolt from the Village*, 27–34. The quoted phrase is a reference to the content and tone of Matthew Arnold's "The Buried Life."

14. "Brent Raps 'Main Street,'" *New York Times*, July 14, 1921, 17.

15. Meredith Nicholson, *The Man in the Street: Papers on American Topics* (New York: Scribner's, 1921), 11, 17, 18, 25.

16. Fenton, "The American Academy of Arts and Letters," 576, 576–77.

17. Edward Weeks, "The Meaning of Literary Prizes," *The Atlantic* 156 (Oct. 1935): 472.

18. Mark Schorer, *Sinclair Lewis: An American Life* (New York: Delta, 1961), 549.

19. Fenton, "The American Academy of Arts and Letters," 583.

20. Information describing the committee's decision process can be found in Schorer, *Sinclair Lewis*, 543–49; and W. A. Swanberg, *Dreiser* (New York: Bantam, 1967), 443–44.

21. Swanberg, *Dreiser*, 443.

22. David D. Anderson, "Sinclair Lewis and the Nobel Prize," *Midamerica* 8 (1981): 10.

23. Lewis Mumford, "The America of Sinclair Lewis," *Current History* 33 (Jan. 1931): 533.

24. "Skoal for Red Lewis," *Literary Digest*, Nov. 22, 1930, 17.

25. "Babbitt Abroad," *Commonweal*, Nov. 19, 1930, 61.

26. Ibid.

27. Sheldon Grebstein, "Sinclair Lewis and the Nobel Prize," *Western Humanities Review* 13 (1959): 167.

28. R. H. Palmer, "The Nobel Prize Jury Judges America," *Christian Century*, Nov. 26, 1930, 1448.

29. "Sinclair Lewis," *The Nation*, Nov. 19, 1930, 544.

30. "Do We Love Shaw's Abuse?" *Literary Digest*, Jan. 3, 1931, 17.

31. Robert E. Sherwood, "Literary Sign-Posts: Is the Nobel Prize an Insult?" *Scribner's Magazine*, Jan. 1931, 11.

32. Sherwood, "Literary Sign-Posts," 11–12.

33. H. L. Mencken, "Sinclair Lewis," *Vanity Fair* 35 (Jan. 1931): 48.

34. Lewis Mumford, "The America of Sinclair Lewis," *Current History* 33 (Jan. 1931): 532.

35. Fenton, "The American Academy of Arts and Letters," 578.

36. Sinclair Lewis, "The American Fear of Literature," in *The Man from Main Street: Selected Essays and Other Writing, 1904–1950*, ed. Harry E. Maule and Melville H. Cane (New York: Random House, 1963), 4 (subsequent page references will appear in the text).

37. Although Lewis never directly named Van Dyke, most commentators understood him to be the target of Lewis's anger. Numerous complaints were made that Lewis had been too hard on Van Dyke even though Lewis never mentioned the name explicitly, a fact that provides further evidence of the widespread nature of the scandal engendered by Van Dyke's charges. See, as a representative example, William Lyon Phelps, "As I Like It," *Scribner's Magazine*, March 1931, 32: "I think [Lewis] should have omitted personalities. His attack on Henry van Dyke was not worthy of the speaker or of the occasion."

38. Lewis, "The American Fear of Literature," 6–7 (subsequent page references will appear in the text).

39. Malcolm Cowley, "Foreword: The Revolt against Gentility," in *After the Genteel Tradition: American Writers since 1910* (New York: W. W. Norton, 1937), 17. Other writers singled out as worthy of honor were Henry L. Mencken, Sherwood Anderson, Upton Sinclair, Joseph Hergesheimer, James Huneker, Thomas Wolfe, Thornton Wilder, William Faulkner, John Dos Passos, Stephen Benet, and Michael Gold. In addition, Lewis critiqued the membership of the AAAL, first by noting the writers who were members (Edwin Arlington Robinson, Robert Frost, Edith Wharton, Hamlin Garland, Owen Wister, Brand Whitlock, and Booth Tarkington) and then by suggesting those who had been excluded—those already noted and a host of others, including, among others, Ring Lardner, Louis Bromfield, Edna Ferber, Mary Austin, Edna St. Vincent Millay, Carl Sandburg, Vachel Lindsay, Robinson Jeffers, and Edgar Lee Masters.

40. "Sinclair Lewis Hits Old School Writers, Champions the New," *New York Times*, Dec. 13, 1930, 1.

41. "Sinclair Lewis Struts His Stuff," *Literary Digest*, Dec. 27, 1930, 14, 15.

42. Ellen Phillips Dupree, "Wharton, Lewis, and the Nobel Prize Address," *American Literature* 56 (May 1984): 265, 268.

43. Dupree, "Wharton, Lewis, and the Nobel Prize Address," 268.

44. Edith Wharton, *A Backward Glance* (New York: Appleton-Century, 1934), 126–27.

45. "Dr. Phelps Praises Lewis Prize Speech," *New York Times* Dec. 15, 1930, 14.

46. Phelps, "As I Like It," 325–26.

47. Ibid., 325, 327.

48. Hunter, *Culture Wars*, 51.

49. "Sinclair Lewis Struts His Stuff," 16.

50. "Lewis Declares Independence," *Literary Digest*, May 9, 1931, 18–19.

51. Lewis, "The American Fear of Literature," 17.

52. After these novels, Lewis's most notable works were *Arrowsmith* (1925), *Elmer Gantry* (1927), *The Man Who Knew Coolidge* (1928), and *Dodsworth* (1929). Only one of Lewis's post-Nobel works has garnered much close attention—*It Can't Happen Here* (1936).

53. Lewis, *Main Street*, 120 (subsequent page references will appear in the text).

54. Glen A. Love, *Babbitt: An American Life* (New York: Twayne, 1993), 9, 11.

55. Love, *Babbitt*, 86.

56. Hunter, *Culture Wars*, 159–70.

57. Daniel Aaron, "Sinclair Lewis: *Main Street*," in *The American Novel: From James Fenimore Cooper to William Faulkner*, ed. Wallace Stegner (New York: Basic Books, 1965), 171.

58. Perry Miller, "The Incorruptible Sinclair Lewis," *The Atlantic* 187 (April 1951): 34.

59. Schorer, *Sinclair Lewis*, 4.

60. Grebstein, "Sinclair Lewis and the Nobel Prize," 170.

61. D. J. Dooley, *The Art of Sinclair Lewis* (Lincoln: University of Nebraska Press, 1967), 241.

62. Phelps, "As I Like It," 326.

63. Sherwood, "Literary Sign-Posts," 11.

Chapter 8: Trilling's Frost versus Kennedy's Frost

1. Lionel Trilling, "A Speech on Robert Frost: A Cultural Episode," *Partisan Review* 26 (Summer 1959): 447–48.

2. Trilling, "A Speech on Robert Frost," 452.

3. Ibid., 451.

4. Ibid., 450, emphasis in the original.

5. Trilling could have been much more critical of Frost; he had serious reservations about him as an artist that perhaps were betrayed by his ironic tone during the speech. As Daniel T. O'Hara has shown in *Lionel Trilling: The Work of Imagination* (Madison: University of Wisconsin Press, 1988), Trilling reserved his most caustic criticisms of Frost to the privacy of his journal, where he denounced Frost's "play of public mask and private sensibility" (143). This brief excerpt suggests Trilling's awareness of the tension ("play") between the popular Frost ("public mask") and the terrifying poet ("private sensibility").

6. Trilling's portrayal of Frost's darker side was not news to literary critics in 1959. Randall Jarrell had given that reading of Frost's poetry eloquent and thorough expression in *Poetry and the Age* (New York: Knopf, 1953): see "The Other Frost" (28–36) and "To the Laodiceans" (37–69).

7. Trilling, "A Speech on Robert Frost," 457.

8. Stanley Burnshaw, *Robert Frost Himself* (New York: Braziller, 1986), 105–6, 120–21.

9. "How Terrifying a Poet?" *Newsweek*, July 27, 1959, 89.

10. J. Donald Adams, "Speaking of Books," *New York Times Book Review*, April 12, 1959, 48.

11. Adams, "Speaking of Books," 48.

12. Trilling, "A Speech on Robert Frost," 451, 450. Lawrence's theory of American radicalism is from *Studies in Classic American Literature.*

13. Reising, *The Unusable Past*, 78–79.

14. For examples of cultural analyses emphasizing the clash between conservatism and radicalism during these years, see Morris Dickstein, *Gates of Eden: American Culture in the Sixties* (New York: Basic Books, 1977); Todd Gitlin, *The Sixties: Years of Hope, Days of Rage* (New York: Bantam Books, 1987); John Hellman, *American Myth and the Legacy of Vietnam* (Columbus: Ohio State University Press, 1986); Diane Ravitch, *The Troubled Crusade: American Education 1945–1980* (New York: Basic Books, 1983); and Irwin Unger, *The Movement: A History of the American New Left, 1959–1972* (New York: Dodd, Mead, 1974). Whether or not this moment was actually a key transitional moment is not the point of my argument. Numerous historians might dispute the assertion that Kennedy brought a radical policy with him to Washington. That Kennedy, as political practitioner, occupied a middle ground in many respects is suggested, for example, by his conduct regarding Cuba and his halting policy on race. It is enough to claim that many Americans understood the election of Kennedy to be a major transitional moment, especially in retrospect. He and Frost make an ideal pair precisely because both were, in the early 1960s, highly ambivalent, transitory figures—liminal figures.

15. Robert Frost, *The Poetry of Robert Frost*, ed. Edward Connery Lathem (New York: Holt, Rinehart and Winston, 1969), 309, 354.

16. Robert Frost, *The Letters of Robert Frost to Louis Untermeyer*, ed. Louis Untermeyer (New York: Holt, Rinehart and Winston, 1963), 243. Untermeyer's collection provides the best source of Frost's philosophical views concerning politics and human governments; it also contains some caustic criticisms of contemporary New Dealers, including Roosevelt.

17. Frost, *The Poetry of Robert Frost*, 393 (subsequent page references will appear in the text).

18. More detailed discussion of the explicitly political philosophy of Frost as demonstrated in his poetry, essays, and letters is in Peter J. Stanlis, "Robert Frost: Politics in Theory and Practice," in *Frost: Centennial Essays II*, ed. Jac Tharpe (Jackson: University of Mississippi Press, 1976), 48–82.

18. Burnshaw, *Robert Frost Himself*, 102.

19. Ibid., 103; Stewart L. Udall, "Robert Frost, Kennedy and Khrushchev: A Memoir of Poetry and Power," *Shenandoah* 26 (Fall 1974): 53.

20. Udall, "Robert Frost, Kennedy and Khrushchev," 53–54.

21. Ibid., 54.

22. Thomas G. Smith, "Robert Frost, Stewart Udall, and the 'Last Go-Down,'" *New England Quarterly* 70 (March 1997): 3–32; the telegram is quoted on 5. Frost's remark about Udall's religion is enigmatic because Udall was a Mormon. See Smith, "Robert Frost, Stewart Udall, and the 'Last Go-Down,'" 4.

23. Ibid., 5.

24. Lawrance Thompson and R. H. Winnick, *Robert Frost: The Later Years, 1938–1963* (New York: Holt, Rinehart and Winston, 1976), 580–81, 277–78.

25. Smith, "Robert Frost, Stewart Udall, and the 'Last Go-Down,'" 6.

26. Marx, "Pastoralism in America," 62.

27. Sacvan Bercovitch, "The Rites of Assent," in *The American Self: Myth, Ideology, and Popular Culture,* ed. Sam Girgus (Albuquerque: University of New Mexico Press, 1981), 6–7.

28. Jean Gould, *Robert Frost: The Aim Was Song* (New York: Dodd, Mead, 1964), 3–4.

29. Kammen, *Mystic Chords of Memory,* 53.

30. Gould, *Robert Frost,* 4.

31. Frost, *The Poetry of Robert Frost,* 348.

32. Smith, *Virgin Land;* see also Frederick Merk, *Manifest Destiny and Mission in American History* (New York: Vintage, 1966).

33. Frost, *The Poetry of Robert Frost,* 348.

34. See Annette Kolodny, *The Lay of the Land: Metaphor as Experience and History in American Life and Letters* (Chapel Hill: University of North Carolina Press, 1975).

35. Frost, *The Poetry of Robert Frost,* 348.

36. Ibid.

37. Reuben A. Brower, *The Poetry of Robert Frost* (New York: Oxford University Press, 1963), 202.

38. Frost, *The Poetry of Robert Frost,* 348.

39. Smith, *Virgin Land,* 3–4.

40. See, for example, Richard Slotkin, *The Fatal Environment: The Myth of the Frontier in the Age of Industrialization* (New York: Atheneum, 1985), and *Regeneration through Violence: The Mythology of the American Frontier, 1600–1860* (Middletown: Wesleyan University Press, 1973); Henry Nash Smith, "Symbol and Idea in *Virgin Land,*" in *Ideology and Classic American Literature,* ed. Sacvan Bercovitch and Myra Jehlen (New York: Cambridge University Press, 1986), 21–35; James O. Robertson, *American Myth, American Reality* (New York: Hill and Wang, 1980); and Patricia Limerick, *Legacy of Conquest: The Unbroken Past of the American West* (New York: W. W. Norton, 1987).

41. Robertson, *American Myth,* 31.

42. Smith, "Symbol and Idea," 27–28.

43. Raymond D. Gozzi, "Frost's 'The Gift Outright,'" *Explicator* 41 (Spring 1983): 45.

44. Gozzi, "Frost's 'The Gift Outright,'" 45.

45. Thompson and Winnick, *Robert Frost,* 282.

46. Brower, *The Poetry of Robert Frost,* 202.

47. Robert Frost, "Speaking of Loyalty," in *Robert Frost: Poetry and Prose,* ed. Edward Connery Lathem and Lawrance Thompson (New York: Henry Holt, 1972), 411.

48. Brower, *The Poetry of Robert Frost,* 202.

49. Frost, *The Poetry of Robert Frost,* 411–12 (subsequent page references will appear in the text).

50. Reising, *The Unusable Past,* 79.

51. Trilling was by no means the only critic to underestimate Frost's interest in his own "mythical" public image, as Roy Harvey Pearce demonstrates in *The Continuity of American Poetry* (Princeton: Princeton University Press, 1961): "As

poet, he will not be a leader. The farthest thing from his mind is the desire to be a culture hero" (273).

52. Frost, *The Letters of Robert Frost to Louis Untermeyer*, 380.

53. "The Poet Laureate," *Time*, March 30, 1962, 84.

54. Lawrance Thompson, *Robert Frost: The Early Years, 1874–1915* (New York: Holt, Rinehart and Winston, 1966), xv.

55. Bellah et al., *Habits of the Heart*, 150–51.

56. All cited in Burnshaw, *Robert Frost Himself*, 289.

Index

Harold K. Bush, Jr., is an assistant professor of English at St. Louis University. He holds a Ph.D. and master's degrees from Indiana University. He has also directed the Konan-Illinois Program at Konan University, Kobe, Japan.